BOYHOODS

BOYHOODS
Rethinking Masculinities

Ken Corbett

Yale University Press   New Haven & London

Published with assistance from the foundation established in memory of
Philip Hamilton McMillan of the Class of 1894, Yale College.

Designed by James J. Johnson and set in Fairfield Medium types
by Tseng Information Systems, Inc.
Printed in the United States of America.

Library of Congress Cataloging-in-Publication Data
Corbett, Ken.
Boyhoods : rethinking masculinities / Ken Corbett.
p. cm.
Includes bibliographical references and index.
ISBN 978-0-300-14984-5 (cloth : alk. paper) 1. Boys—Psychology.
2. Masculinity—United States. 3. Sex role—United States. I. Title.
HQ775.C67 2009
155.43'2—dc22
2009001971

A catalogue record for this book is available from the British Library.

This paper meets the requirements of ANSI/NISO Z39.48-1992 (Permanence of Paper).

10 9 8 7 6 5 4 3 2 1

This book is for

Michael Cunningham

In the marrow-bones of the grown man I can, it is true, trace the outline of the child's bone, but it itself has disappeared, having lengthened and thickened until it has attained its definitive form.

SIGMUND FREUD

Give us again the ache of our boy hearts.

CARL SANDBURG

Contents

CONTENTS

Acknowledgments

This book was conceived and written over the course of many years, and there are many people I wish to thank.

I begin with a group of friends and colleagues without whom this book simply could not be, indelibly linked as it is with their hearts and minds: Judith Butler, Muriel Dimen, Virginia Goldner, and Adrienne Harris. The voice that speaks here is one, but it should be heard as something more akin to a motet, a community chorus within which I am most grateful to participate.

Others, too, have found their way into this book, teaching me and accompanying me along the way: Jessica Benjamin, Joe Boone, John Broughton, Nancy Chodorow, Marianne Goldberger, Richard Isay, James Lecesne, and Bob Vorlicky.

I had the good fortune to share this book in its final stages with a number of writers and readers to whom I am indebted for their insight and good company: Marcelle Clements, Michael Cunningham, Stacey Derasmo, Meg Giles, David

Hopson, Daniel Kaizer, Christopher Potter, Eyal Rozmarin, and Pat Towers.

While writing this book, I enjoyed being schooled in the pleasures of play, the promise of growth, and the bolt of development: Jonah Braverman Purdue, Sam Braverman Purdue, Bird Purcell, and Alex Vorlicky.

I wish to thank Elisabeth Young-Bruehl for introducing me to Ileene Smith, whom I thank, along with Dan Heaton and Alex Larson, for their lively editorial assistance. As well, I thank Meg Giles, Tom Grattan, Chris Mills, and Adrian Rosenfeld for their research and editorial assistance. I offer special adoration to Meg Giles for her personal assistance.

I gratefully acknowledge the following publications in which versions of chapters from this book first appeared: "Little Hans: Masculinity Unfolds" appeared in a different form in the *Psychoanalytic Quarterly* 78 (2009). "Nontraditional Family Reverie: Masculinity Unfolds" appeared in a different form as "Non-Traditional Family Romance" in the *Psychoanalytic Quarterly* 70 (2001). "Boyhood Femininity: Masculine Presuppositions and the Anxiety of Regulation" appeared in a different form as "Boyhood Femininity, Gender Identity Disorder, Masculine Presuppositions, and the Anxiety of Regulation" in *Psychoanalytic Dialogues* 19 (2009). "Faggot = Loser: Phallic Narcissism as Defense" appeared in a different form as "Faggot = Loser" in *Studies in Gender and Sexuality* 2 (2001).

Finally, I wish to thank my patients, with whom I learn daily, and who have so generously allowed me to share our work. I have changed their names and many of their defining details in an effort to preserve confidentiality. But I hope I have also justly preserved their unique beings, and their exquisite effort.

Introduction

THE ROOM IN WHICH I WRITE OVERLOOKS A PARK, OR rather the blocklong cement slab that passes for a park in New York City. This play space is divided in two by a chain-link fence, and further divided into two full basketball courts, three half-court basketball courts, and one miniature baseball diamond. A painted circle serves as the pitcher's mound, painted squares the bases. The sounds of the games often provide background to my writing: the ping of aluminum baseball bats (so distinct from the thwack of the wooden bats of my boyhood), the start-and-stop rhythm of dribbling, the smack of a ball hitting a mitt, the trill of a basketball hitting a metal backboard.

The park and the players are a wonderful source of distraction and reverie. I find myself at the window looking out upon the games: myself as the boy who played passable baseball wondering why the guy on first has yet to steal second; myself as the boy who grew up watching basketball in the Midwest gripped by a great shot; myself as the boy who usually observed from the sidelines, finding him once again in the middle-aged man at the window.

Multiple games can be under way at any given time, or a single game may hold court. Today: a boy with a glowing head of blond hair moves against the wind as he dribbles down-court. A few toddlers run around the bases, their caretakers drinking coffee from paper cups on the benches that line the park. Once, as though in a dream, I saw a lone hooded figure, backlit by acid-orange streetlights, shooting free throws as snow began to fall.

Skill ranges from the intense vigor of honed expertise to the dogged determination of the beginner. Hands fumble. Feet fly. Victory shouts. Dejection shouts. Occasionally, in the early morning, I see a group of elderly men and women practicing Tai Chi, their slow unified grace providing a vivid contrast to the fast practice of youth.

Skin colors vary, but run toward brown. Gender varies little. The park is populated almost exclusively by boys and young men. Girls occasionally skirt the margins, hang on the fences, jump double Dutch in the corner, but rarely enter the main game. I once relished the sight of a particularly fierce girl who hit a line drive and flipped the bird as she rounded second base.

The sights and sounds of boys at play have correlated with my efforts to capture the lives of boys, in particular the movement, the aggression, the competition, the rivalries, the friendships, and the muscular eroticism that inform boys' lives. Over time, these boys have seeped, settled, and overlapped in my mind. Even though I sometimes focus on individual players, they collect as a pattern—as Walt Whitman might have it,

"Every one disintegrated yet part of the scheme."[1] They fade and reconfigure. They disperse, only to return. The residue etches a pattern of perpetual dynamism (imagine writing—over and over again—on a chalkboard that is never fully erased).

Masculinity is a complex pattern. Boyhood is a chaotic dynamism. The terms *boyhood* and *masculinity* signify our efforts to catalogue the experience of a group of people, in this case male children from birth to full growth. *Boyhood* also strives to capture and categorize the gender pattern called masculinity, and more precisely the development of masculinity. Categorical speech, though, always fails; someone always falls out. No two boyhoods are the same. No one boy remains invariable.

Can we hold in tension the particular (the boy before us) and the general (that arises out of formalized thinking)? How might our understanding of familiar and expected gender patterns enliven, but also constrict, our understanding of masculinity? How do the presuppositions that underscore the pattern hold up? How might the particularity of any given boy offset normative expectation?

What, for instance, about the boys who are not in the park? How might we bring them into sight? What sounds do they make? How do we register their movements, their aggression, their surrender, their competition, their friendships, and their erotic embodiments? Are they kept indoors, perhaps tethered by troubled kin? Dulled by neglect? Are they collecting the collections that so often absorb boys (rocks, trading cards, dinosaurs)? Playing video games? Reading? Working on their diorama of Alaska for their social studies classes? Sugar cubes, cotton, and glue?

One neighborhood boy has often caught my eye as I have watched him grow to about the same size as his cello case. I see another boy struggle every morning under the weight of a backpack that seems about to topple him. Yet another little boy's face has finally caught up to his glasses and his ears. What are the patterns of their play? How might the consideration of their unique boyhoods deconstruct the more familiar playground boy, and the more visible patterns and performances of masculinity shouted from the basketball court? Or might these boys be playground boys as well, complicating the pattern all the more?

The challenge ahead is to capture boyhoods without dropping that -s; to tap the exclamation of masculinity and not overlook that which is cloaked in defense; to appreciate the affection of boys, while duly noting the aggression that may more often characterize their play; to recognize the femininity in masculinity; to grasp the condition known as boyhood, but at the same time recognize the contingencies (social, racial, historical, economic, religious) that qualify that condition, making it plural.

The history of psychology is replete with the dropping of the pluralizing -s. We underestimate variability and multiplicity. We relish the norm, while overlooking the productive potential to be found in variance. Even though norms capture what is most conspicuous about human development (how we are all similar), they do not capture what is perhaps most interesting about human development: the variance that is necessary for norms to exist, the fact that repetition of patterns or averages is never exact. There is always distinction.

Masculinity and Psychoanalysis

Perplexity—the humbling recognition of impending contradiction, and the expansive embrace of uncertainty—has been slow in coming to the theorization of masculinity. Paradox has yet to call itself masculine. Even within psychoanalytic theory—the psychological theory that arguably offers the most compelling epistemology for thinking about human desire and the centrality of gender in human development—masculinity remains largely undertheorized and clinically underanimated.

While it could be said that much has been written about men and masculinity throughout the history of psychoanalysis, it would be more correct to say that much has been *presumed* about masculinity through the repetition of Sigmund Freud's normative Oedipal model: a boy becomes a boy through biological expression, intertwined with desire for his mother and rivalry with his father. He grows by separating from his mother and identifying with his father, in time becoming a father himself. Masculinity in this frame is not distinguished from, and is defined through, the biology of phallic primacy (the determined interest a boy directs toward his directing penis), heterosexual desire, and the reproduction of fathering.[2]

Most early psychoanalytic theorists, through the 1930s, 1940s, and 1950s, followed upon and reiterated Freud's original male Oedipal thesis; even observations on femininity were informed by this male Oedipal frame. Boys and girls alike, according to Freud, develop in relation to the phallic organ.[3] Freud did not recognize or attribute knowledge of the vagina to the girl. The girl is depicted as growing through her response to her recognition as castrated (a claim that puts in play a phallic/castrated polarity): she wishes for a penis (penis envy), resents her mother (for her lack), and chooses her father as her object of desire (the one who can offer her the promise of a child, the symbolic equivalent of a penis). Femininity in this frame is also not distinguished from, and is defined through, phallic primacy, heterosexual desire, and the reproduction of mothering.

Virtually from the start, though, feminist interlocutors challenged this depiction of femininity. They asserted that in fact girls did have knowledge of the vagina.[4] They observed that girls' early relationships with their mothers involved more than resentment and the fraught wish for a penis.[5] They set about to distinguish feminine sexual experience beyond envy and passivity.[6] They maintained that while girls may envy the male body, so, too, boys envy the female body, and a mother's reproductive capacities in particular.[7]

Femininity was problematized. The discourse moved forward in an intricate evolution.[8] This analysis of femininity is one of the most important and lively threads in twentieth-century psychological thinking. As theory, it has lifted off the page, filtered into social space, shaped political life, created social transformations, and produced critical changes in cultural practices, including psychotherapeutic practices.[9]

The psychoanalytic discourse on masculinity has neither evolved in such a complex fashion nor had the same kind of socially transforming impact.

It was not until the mid-1960s that a significant response to Freud's theory appeared, and a second-wave theory of masculinity took shape—one that stands today as the dominant theory of masculinity. This second wave was inaugurated via Robert Stoller's analyses that shifted the focus from the problems a boy has in identifying with his father to the problems a boy has in separating from and dis-identifying with his mother.[10] A psychoanalyst well known for his theoretical considerations of gender and sexual arousal, Stoller suggested that boys become boys through their "not feminine," "not you" separation from their mothers.

Building on Stoller, and illuminating the maternal subject in these mother-son bonds, feminist scholars in the 1970s and 1980s, notably Jessica Benjamin and Nancy Chodorow, refined analyses of separation and provided new readings on the effects of maternal dis-identification.[11] Important here were considerations of how boys prematurely separate from their mothers, and in so doing split off from "not me" affect states considered to be feminine. Resultant upon this premature separation, boys are more vulnerable to depression and alienation. Boys' experiences of dejection and estrangement, it is further argued, form and inform the willful segregation from and the domination of women and girls.

In an expanding critical response to this second-wave theory, analysts at the turn of the twenty-first century began to reexamine a boy's attachment to his father.[12] These analyses spoke to a boy's need for a father of attachment versus a father of rivalry.[13] Appeals to this mentoring father of attachment have also been made to redress the routine social condition of father absence, and to garner a father's care in response to reports of boys' faltering well-being, including increased aggression, violence, depression, and learning disabilities.[14]

Resetting the Normative Masculine Narrative

Masculinity has finally become a site of inquiry: a problem, the way femininity has been regarded for nearly a century. We have come to a revised understanding of boyhood, at least in terms of boys' relations with their parents, and a somewhat more complex sociopsychological vision of masculinity.[15]

Still, the normative narrative of masculinity has yet to be reset. We have a revised story of boyhood, but the premises upon which that revision has been made remain remarkably unrevised. The narrative context continues to be set by: (1) a married, heterosexual child-rearing couple; (2) a field marked off by the guideposts of the gender binary (there can be two and only two genders, masculinity and femininity, each defined by what the other is not); (3) a centralized domestic story (mother, father, boy) versus a contextualized domestic story, one that is encased within and permeated by the cultural surround (culture [mother, father, boy] culture); and (4) the continued conflation of anatomy with gender, underplaying the intricate congress of anatomy as it is made by and with the body, mind, and culture.

It is time to reset the terms.

In my view, a key stumbling block to resetting these terms and a more comprehensive analysis of masculinity has been the way in which psychoanalysts have been slow to take into account forces of cultural order. Illustrative of this lack of attention are the ways in which psychoanalysts have not effectively attended to how culturally ordered masculine ideals corral the emotional landscape called masculinity. The fantastic underbelly of masculinity is pinched and policed. The complexity that is masculinity goes largely unrecorded; the variety that makes for complexity is only recorded as pathology. The spectrum of masculine bodies and minds is underestimated; how they evolve or how they come to matter is patrolled, and the margins are deemed pathological.

Offering a corrective illumination of this limited clinical vision, cultural theorists and feminist theorists (both inside and outside the psychoanalytic guild) have for the past twenty-five years produced any number of spectacular rereadings of psychoanalytic gender theory—readings that illustrate development, embodiment, and gendered identifications are open to a range of possibility and difference, perhaps the kinds of difference that make life worth living.[16] This body of work follows primarily on Michel Foucault's refined conception of norms: how norms not only record the expectable, but also direct social order in such a way as to *shape* the expectable, and make the intelligible human.[17] Key to analyses of how gender norms function as constructing ideals have been insights about (1) Gender's construction and constriction (boys wish, behave, express, feel in accord with a specified emotional geography); (2) the determining force of the masculine/feminine gender binary (there can be two and only two genders defined in opposition); (3) the overdrive of heterosexual gender complementarity as the privileged marker of reality and psychological coherence (the reproduction of heterosexual matrimonial relations and of heterosexual parenting as the principal markers of psychic and social well-being).

Importantly, this modern gender theorizing has largely been textual, not clinical. And when clinical attention has been paid, it has rarely been directed at boys or men. The rhetorical strategy of this book is to bridge this gap by bringing boys into clearer focus, and by offering a new psychoanalytic theory of masculinity.

This strategy reflects my own history. For the past twenty years I have written and practiced at the intersection of clinical psychoanalysis, feminism, and queer studies. I read feminist and queer theory texts in college and graduate school before I read Freud. I read Freud in tandem with Foucault. I am part of the first cohort of openly gay people to train as clinical psychoanalysts. So while the lens of this book is psychoanalytic, in the spirit of boyhood, the psychoanalysis that is spoken here is not your father's psychoanalysis.

Rethinking Masculinity

The boys who come into view within these pages are seen through a reconstituted psychological lens. Each chapter of this book tells the story of one or two boys in relation to a central premise of boyhood. It is my hope that the clinical narratives, the stories of boys told within these pages, bring life and meaning to the theory being built. The boys who emerge here reflect my belief in social transformation, including the reordering of modern culture's guiding social-symbolic order— the widening frame of marriage law, the changing definitions of family, the lessening import of traditional gender codes, the dismantling of traditional gender polarities, the expanding net of language and modes of communicative exchange, to name a few. We can no longer presume that masculinity develops within a psychically specific heteronormative domestic story: dis-identification from a mother, rivalry with a father, and identification from son to father. We cannot continue to presume that like gender produces like gender; fathers produce sons, mothers produce daughters.

Turning from these presumed domestic stories, we must now look at how masculinity is told *from* culture *through* parent to son, or put another way, how masculinity precedes parents and sons. How do norms *normalize* the family? How does the normalized family then shape the boy? How do norms move on cat's paws, silent and unthought? There they are, before we know it, in our living room, and without invitation. There they are on the playground, in the brother's voice ("Dude, don't throw like a girl"), in the nanny's nod ("That's right; defend yourself like a man").

Culture and cultural symbols, society and social orders, what we might call "backstories," build a boy. But as it turns out, over and over again, there is more than one backstory to tell, and more than one order to order. The traditional Oedipal backstory is grainy at best; we are copies of copies of copies of copies of Oedipus's children. Copies repeat. Copies degrade. Copies transform.

I do not place the traditional Oedipus complex as the major axis for human development. I do, however, look (with determination) for expressions of unconscious fantasy, for evidence of childhood wishes, and for the lingering influence of parent-child desire. As Freud would have it, there is blood in the water: the unconscious wishes of childhood "are only capable of annihilation in the same sense as the ghosts in the underworld of the *Odyssey*—ghosts which awoke to new life as soon as they tasted blood."[18]

While I may not grant as much authority to ghosts and the past as did Freud, I do value what I have come to call the "psychic envelope" of early parent-child relations. I envision this envelope as constructed through the bodied and psychic excitability of parent and child alike—a space that encapsulates the lip-smacking, drooling, kissing, biting density of early childhood sexuality; a space that promotes parent-child recognition and a child's growing capacity to think and reflect on his experience; a space that constructs childhood life, love, and sexuality through enigmatic unconscious parent-child processes—the space of blood, ghosts, and the emotional resonance of daily family fantasy/life.[19]

In my view, the appeal of Oedipal myth derives from the way in which narratives aid us in coping with blood and ghosts. I employ Oedipal theory as narrative, as a fantastic scenario (a unique and blended scene of unconscious wish and conscious imagination), not as a fixed social structure or a determining symbolic order. My clinical curiosity moves me to try to understand how children and families narrate the stories they collectively tell in order to account for their relations, and their overwhelming desires and losses. I pay close attention to how that narration unfurls and refurls in the course of treatment. I listen closely for the ways in which children and families position their stories in relation to dominant cultural narratives.

I place considerable value on the role of fantasy as it builds the boy. But I also strive, following on Judith Butler, to think about how fantasy and interiority are always-and-already constituted by cultural norms.[20] The early parent-child psychic envelope is permeable. I look toward masculinity not only as inner feeling or fantasy, but also as it is made and recognized in and through scenes of cultural narration. "*Boy*," in this frame, is built inseparably between inner feelings and states and an outer mode of social address.

How is that frame/space constructed by modes of social

address and cultural dictates? What are the guiding presuppositions of masculinity as they are enforced by the masculine/feminine gender binary? How normal (in accord with the binary) does a boy have to be to be a boy? How normal does a boy need to be in order to cohere as masculine? And what is the relationship of this so-called coherence to psychological well-being?

Taking up such questions, I turn to the ways in which feminine boys are looked upon as having stepped outside the norm, over the line, and are deemed traumatized in accord with the binary. I argue for a more perplexed and humble approach to cross-gendered fantasy and experience, one that does not mistake social consensus for well-being. Social norms are not the problem per se; they speak the collective "truth" of convention. However, convention through repetition has a way of becoming steadily more conventional; norms become more constricting.

A boy's experience of his body is often a wonderful way to measure the impact of convention, and to assess as well how cultural dictates knit with fantasy to shape the unique quality of any given boy. Children bring one toward the body: theirs as they find it; yours as they find it; yours as you find it; yours as you once found it. Conceptualizing boys' bodies is one of the cornerstones of psychoanalysis, one of Freud's inaugural moves. The phallic organ was frontmost and foremost. The penis preceded the boy.

A century hence such thinking has receded markedly. The body, the penis, and phallic strivings are given little consideration in our modern turn toward how boys relate to others (in particular their mothers), attach to others, and struggle to conceive of their and others' internal experience. We tend now to think more about how children grow through (mental) attachment versus (physical) desire.

I argue for a return to the body, and suggest that the boy's experience of his body, and the fantastic orbit that is the boy's body, must be brought back into our clinical imagination. Many (perhaps most) boys live through a kind of full-bodied muscular eroticism colored by vigorous exhibitionism and phallic narcissism. These heightened states can be employed in the service of defense, resulting in a split from the feminine. But they can also be employed toward recognition, mutual pleasure, identification, and the promise of growth. I argue for the active clinical engagement of boys' aggression and the determined interest they direct toward their bodies, often their penis in particular. I suggest that we have not managed to create much in the way of potential space to imagine phallic desire, and the fantastic penis. Without such space, we are without a means to consider that the penis and phallic states are always materializations that are dictated by fantastic readings and measurement.

Recently, I saw a five-year-old boy in consultation. Several themes began to take shape in the first hour of play, the dominant having to do with his relationship with his older brother. But what lingered most in my mind was his way of saying good-bye. We were in my waiting room. I was arranging another hour with his mother, and my back was turned to him. As I turned to say good-bye, there he stood, his shirt pulled up over his head, exquisitely comic, determinedly exhibitionistic, vulnerable and hooded. It is my hope that such moments of "boy" open in these pages, over and again.

Given the complex chaos that is boyhood, I well recognize that boys' lives overflow these pages. It is impossible to speak about masculinity in one voice, no matter how polyvocal. I speak for a category. I am claimed by a category. And I fail, as categories do. It is my hope that this study of masculinity resists the closure of categories, but I am also certain that it cannot. I speak across theoretical categories in an effort to further resist category reduction. And yet here too, the expansion I seek will and must fail. Boys are always more than the category that is masculinity. Gender is rarely, if ever, totalizing. It is rarely conscious, and only occasionally felt with much weight. Masculinity is, to paraphrase Keats, but a few steps from iron to feathers—from bodied density to fleeting fantasy.

Perhaps the best we can do is to name the various contingencies that inform how we think about boys and masculinity, and hope that readers can employ those limits as they move toward their own associations, their own thoughts that move beyond this text—beyond the boyhoods offered here. For example, as cultural theorists have been vigorously arguing for some time now, gendered identities are routinely and soundly trumped by narratives of race, class, historical epoch, and social location.[21]

Still, I believe there continues to be merit in charting the chaotic field of masculinity, or an archive of masculinity, as Foucault might have it, that illuminates how our thinking about masculinity is structured and brought to life. How a boy knows himself to be a boy, or not, continues to matter. How he comes to that knowledge in a social world continues to matter. How that social knowledge is internalized and becomes psychological continues to matter. We would, however, do well to live with the certainty that someday, even today, we will be wrong. We would do well to approach gender humbly. And reckon as well with the mystery of masculinity, the enigma of gender, and the limit of our reach as we move to consider boy hoods. In that paradox I find optimism.

PART I

Boys, Masculinity, and the Family

CHAPTER ONE

Little Hans
Masculinity Foretold

LITTLE HANS HOLDS PRIDE OF PLACE IN THE PSYCHO-
analytic canon, not only as the first psychoanalytic child but
also as the first psychoanalytic boy. Within the pages of his
Analysis of a Phobia in a Five-Year-Old Boy, Sigmund Freud in
1909 elaborated and embodied his theory of boyhood and masculinity. It is a theory that continues to stand as the canonical
psychological narrative of masculinity: we have known a boy
to be a boy through his phallic preoccupations and castration
fears, enacted alongside and through his desire for his mother
and his rivalry with his father, which in time resolve via the
boy's separation from his mother and his identification with
his father.

A return to the theory of masculinity set forth by Freud
is pivotal to the project of a new psychoanalysis for boys and
men. Hans is the Ur-boy, and through his construction and
acts of consciousness the psychoanalytic construct of masculinity is endowed with meaning. I return to this textual origin
so that we might appreciate the original terms that continue to

guide our psychoanalytic understanding of masculinity. I view this case as an illustration of how masculinity is foretold—a normative narrative that has changed little in the past one hundred years.

Still, it must also be said that the critical discourse that has followed on the textual richness of this case report can be read as a primer, illustrating evolving views on child development across the first psychoanalytic century.[1] These rereadings of Little Hans illuminate how the consideration of child development at the turn of this second psychoanalytic century is framed by thinking about early parent-child attachment, our unfolding curiosity about how children begin to contemplate (mentalize) their experience and reflect upon their relations with others, and our increased attunement to the emotional resonance of early parent-child relations.

In league with this new thinking about child development, I offer a close reading of Little Hans in order to revisit the lived dilemma of his boyhood. I focus in particular on Freud's symbolic reading of the horse that figures in Hans's phobia. I approach the horse twice, first through an explication of Freud's clinical formulation, and second through my own rereading.

My interest in rereading the horse follows on how Freud, through the dense and deconstructive discussion that follows his case history and analysis, parses and whittles the multiple interpretations he offers in the course of the treatment. This winnowing foregrounds and establishes Freud's normative Oedipal narrative. Freud also moves in his discussion to settle and regulate the unsettled conditions of masculinity that he articulates through his clinical observations of Hans. Here, in turn, we are left to question how the malleable character of masculinity, which Freud captures so well, confounds the theoretical consistency of his normative narration.

The Horse I

The clinical story narrated by Freud centers on a boy, his father, his mother, and to a lesser extent his sister. However, the principal supporting character is a horse, the object of Hans's phobic dread. We learn about the horse, about Hans's fears, and his daily life, from Hans's father, who reports his observations to Freud, who in turn guides the father in his efforts to help his young son overcome his fears. Together, the father and Freud—the shadow father—set about to reflect on the kin relations, anatomical dispositions, and hidden desires that underscore Hans's experience.

Freud's engaged and affectionate description of busy bodily boyish life resonates for any reader who has closely observed young boys. We learn about Hans's determined interest in his body, his penis in particular, or as he says, his "widdler"; his curiosity about the bodies and genitalia of others (children, adults, animals); his phallic monism as he "sees" and fantastically creates penises for everyone, including his mother and his sister ("Her widdler is quite small . . . when she grows up it'll get bigger all right"); his push toward growth; his curiosity about childbirth; his sibling rivalry; his struggle to separate from his parents, and his wish to sleep with them in their bed; his masturbatory excitement ("But it is great fun")—prompting his mother to threaten castration lest he stop his "piggish" practice, and prompting Freud to amusingly characterize "our young libertine" Hans as "a positive paragon of all the vices."[2]

We also learn about his fear of horses. Hans's father initially reports, "He is afraid *a horse will bite him in the street*, and this fear seems somehow to be connected with his having been frightened by a large penis." This fear inhibits Hans from going out into the street in the evenings, and leaves him at times, according to his father, in "low spirits."[3] His father, in his initial correspondence with Freud, wonders whether, along with the fear of large penises, this phobia might also express Hans's anxiety in relation to his mother. It is intriguing to note here that the father sets the stage for what will become contrasting strands in this case narrative: attachment versus desire. Is Hans's anxiety best understood through the examination of how he attaches to and relates with his parents? Or should the interpretive focus center on Hans's sexual desire for his parents, his mother in particular?[4]

Freud contemplates the father's suggestions and offers an initial interpretation that centers on the mother-child bond, in particular Hans's concern about separating from his mother: "The disorder set in with thoughts that were at the same time fearful and tender, and then followed an anxiety dream on the subject of losing his mother and so not being able to coax (caress, cuddle) with her any more. His affection for his mother must therefore have become enormously intensified." Freud concludes: "This was the fundamental phenomenon in his condition."[5] In spite of that, Freud moves quickly to unsettle this claim so as to position sexual desire, not attachment, as primary. He counters by emphasizing that Hans's anxiety began as "every infantile anxiety, without an object."[6] Aim (the push/pull of bodily excitement) and erotic desire, Freud explains, precede object. Hence, the "fundamental phenomenon" of affection or attachment is secondary to (or only follows upon) the yet more fundamental press of sexual longing.

Seeking to illustrate this claim, Freud links Hans's wish for "coaxing" ("or whatever else this young lover may have wanted") with a repressed erotic longing for his mother. He argues that longing can easily be satisfied by the return of the longed-for object: "Longing can be completely transformed into satisfaction if it is presented with the object longed for."[7] In contrast, anxiety, linked according to Freud with repressed erotic longing, lingers and disrupts. Hence the analysis of repression becomes Freud's mark.[8] It is noteworthy that as Freud turns toward his analysis of repression, he presumes adequate or untroubled attachment security: the object (the mother) in this case, according to Freud, was secure.

And so Freud turns to the repression and the primacy of sexual desire, along with an emphasis on the push/pull of bodily excitation prior to the power of parental relations. One can note this stance, as Freud moves next to allay the father's anxiety regarding the possible role of the mother's "excessive display of affection," along with her anxious and threatening response to Hans's masturbatory behaviors. Might, the father asks, these behaviors have contributed to Hans's anxiety? Might these bonds signal some distress relative to attachment security? Describing Hans's mother as "excellent and devoted," Freud sets aside these considerations and once again foregrounds the problematic press of desire and the consequent repress of repression. The day-to-day mother, the mother taken up and into her own fantasies, the vicissitudes of mother-child attachment, and the to-and-fro early mother-child processes of recognition/reflection are seen as less important than the determining power of the symbolic mother, the siren, the object of the boy's desire. Freud says of the mother, "She had a pre-destined role to play, and her position was a hard one."[9]

Building on these claims, Freud then makes his first pass at assessing the horse and, in keeping with the father's first suggestion, views the horse as equivalent to untamed bodily excitement—specifically, forceful and frightening phallic aim. The horse and its phallic body become something of a funhouse mirror, a distorted self-object, and at the same time a frighteningly big other. Freud links this reading with his observation of Hans as preoccupied with his penis, and with masturbatory pleasure. Additionally, he suggests that Hans is made anxious as he judges himself to be inferior to those who possess penises larger than his.

Once again, anyone who has spent time with young boys is sure to recognize the phenomenology Freud captures: masturbatory single-mindedness, castration fears, phallic monism, and the press of phallic exhibitionism. It was not, however, these phenomena per se that most interested Freud. Rather, it was his meta-narrative, which configures "sexual constitutions" first before all else, following as they do upon discrete drives that have purpose and meaning before language, before culture. The psychic states called "masculinity" originate, according to Freud, through "biological function," and for the boy are constituted through the penis: "In contrast to the later period of maturity, this period is marked not by a genital primacy but by a primacy of the *phallus*."[10]

Freud returns again and again to his claim of phallic primacy, charting the psychical energy Hans devotes to his penis, including his countervailing, counterconstructing fear of losing it. Freud positions masculinity (the "true man") as equivalent to heterosexual desire (he employs *heterosexuality* and *mascu-*

linity interchangeably). And while he suggests that the boy's heterosexual masculinity follows on his identification with his father, Freud nevertheless consistently trumps this process of identification through his emphasis on the determining power of the penis, and the boy's instinctual heterophallic aim.[11] As Freud saw it, Hans's lack of education about female anatomy held him back because it did not join up with and reinforce what Freud saw as Hans's instinctual heterophallic aim.[12] In this frame, a boy's body—his penis in particular—initiates and drives his subjective and relational desiring experience. In this frame, the penis precedes the boy.

Indeed, Hans proves a charming font of phallic preoccupation, castration fear, and fantastic solution. The widdler is foremost and forecasting. Consider, from the many examples, his manic phallic monism as it coupled with his optimism about growth and his defense against castration: "And every one has a widdler. And my widdler will get bigger as I get bigger; it's fixed in, of course."[13]

In keeping with Hans's optimistic forecast, Freud attempts in his first interventions with the boy to reassure him that his fears are nothing more than "a piece of nonsense." He instructs Hans's father to tell him that he need not fear castration, as perhaps had been evoked by seeing his mother's and sister's bodies, because "his mother and all other female beings (as he could see from Hanna [his sister]) had no widdler at all." Once again (however fraught with misinformation), this move seems to have been a bid toward assurance.[14]

Assured, though, Hans did not feel. According to his father, both his fear and his masturbatory inclinations continued apace. Freud and the father stayed the course, emphasizing the castration fear evoked by the large horse. But once again the reassurance does not mend, and Hans remains, as Freud puts it, "oppressed by the fear of having to lose this precious piece of his ego."[15] Here we witness Freud's extraordinary theoretical dexterity, as he moves from considering the penis as material reality to considering it as psychic reality—toward the penis as mentally materialized.

It is also at this juncture that he begins to reckon with the limits of reassurance. The anxiety is too deep: "When once a state of anxiety establishes itself, the anxiety swallows up all other feelings."[16] Freud then begins to fashion what will become a central piece of his analysis, once again a significant theoretical move—a move that illuminates what will become a hallmark of psychoanalytic clinical technique: he considers the horse to be not only a real object that provokes (fear, comparison) but a symbolic object as well.

Hans is afraid that a horse will "fall down and bite." Freud reads this "improbable . . . collocation" as follows: "The train of thought . . . was that the horse (his father) would bite him because of his wish that it (his father) should fall down."[17] In other words, this image symbolically couples both the wish (patricide) and the fear that his father was going to punish him for his patricidal wish (through castration). The horse, then, is the father.

Freud applies his deepening appreciation of Hans's fear to his consideration of a dream reported by Hans: "In the night there was a big giraffe in the room and a crumpled one; and the big one called out because I took the crumpled one away from it. Then it stopped calling out; and then I sat down on top of the crumpled one."[18] It seems this dream provoked sufficient anxiety to wake Hans, whereupon he joined his parents in their bed. Treating the dream as a "continuation of his fear of horses," the father interprets the dream for Hans, emphasizing that the big giraffe represented him (the father), the crumpled one his mother ("or rather her genital organ") and Hans's wish to get into bed with his mother despite his father's protests.[19] He was, the father ventures, fearful lest his forbidden wish be seen, and he be met with his father's anger: "He had come up against the barrier against incest."[20]

In a short consultation soon thereafter, Freud reinforces this reading of the boy's fear: "He was afraid of his father, precisely because he was so fond of his mother." Freud also attempts to link the father's appearance (eyeglasses/blinders and moustache/muzzle) with that of a horse. Following the interpretation of the giraffe dream and this consultation with Freud, the father reports the "first real improvement."[21] Freud, in reflecting upon the case, seems to view this consult as key, perhaps *the* key: "The fear which sprang from this death-wish against his father, and which may thus be said to have had a normal motive, formed *the chief obstacle* to the analysis until it was removed during the conversation in my consulting-room."[22]

Yet the lessening of anxiety again does not hold, and in fact the phobia becomes rather diffuse at this point. It transfers to carts drawn by horses, to railway cars, to falling and biting that intermingle with thoughts of urination and defecation. At some point in this diffuse phase, Hans reports the following "thought"/fantasy: "I was in the bath, and then the plumber came and unscrewed it. Then he took a big borer and stuck it into my stomach." The father initially interprets the fantasy as representing the father's privileged enforcement of the incest barrier. Putting the fantasy into the first person for Hans, the father says: "I was in bed with Mummy. Then Daddy came and drove me away. With his big penis he pushed me out of my place by Mummy."[23]

Freud, however, departs from the father's interpretation, and temporarily from his heretofore guiding focus on Hans's incestuous wishes (fueled by phallic primacy) toward Hans's sibling rivalry. He reflects on the bath in the fantasy, bathing, and babies, and guides us toward the consideration of Hans's growing concern with matters of childbirth, and his sense of murderous displacement following the birth of his sister, Hanna, when he was 3½ years old.

Freud observes that Hans repeatedly played with the tale of the stork and developed an elaborate story in which Hanna arrived in a carriage box. In response to this fantasy, Freud suggests that the carriage box might symbolize the mother's pregnant body and Hans's angry response thereto. Freud proposes that the wish to tease the horse was likely a condensed expression both of Han's anger toward the Oedipal father's privilege and of "an obscure sadistic desire for his mother," which Freud then relates to Hans's thoughts about the mother's pregnancy. Hans reinforces this interpretation as he moves in a fantastic riff on beating horses toward his wish to beat his mother.[24]

We come then to see the horse as both mother and father, and their procreative relationship. These considerations lead Freud to counsel the parents to educate Hans about pregnancy and childbirth. Reluctantly the father gives Hans bits of information, and Hans weaves yet more intriguingly fecund birth fantasies involving storks, eggs, and his declaration that he shall have a baby of his own. The father strives at this point to provide Hans with more, and more correct, information about childbirth and pregnancy. These efforts allow the father to refine his Oedipal interpretation, emphasizing the relational dimensions of the fantasy: "You'd like to be Daddy and married to Mummy; you'd like to be as big as me and have a moustache; and you'd like Mummy to have a baby."[25] It also allows the father to further reflect on Hans's fear of falling horses, and to suggest that perhaps the scene of a falling horse is akin to the chaos and fear of childbirth.

The treatment comes to a conclusion around this point. The father reports that Hans has set about to play through/ work through his anxieties with a toy horse: loading and unloading carts, and enacting various scenes. Hans, the father indicates, also ventures outside now with little to no distress.

The father concludes the case report with the final dream of the treatment: "The plumber came; and first he took away my behind with a pair of pincers, and then gave me another, the same with my widdler." The father, returning now to the body, greets this dream as Hans's wish for a bigger behind and widdler; Hans would then be more like his father. With which Hans concurs, as does Freud. He reads Hans's response to the father's interpretation of the dream as confirmation/ resolution, and equivalent to productive identification with the father. In something of a summation, Freud suggests that Hans diverted Oedipus's fate by finding the "happier solution" of identifying with his father and sharing the prospect of generational happiness.[26]

The Graf Family

Before I can take up my rereading of the horse, I first reflect on our expanded understanding of Hans's family afforded by recently declassified interviews with Herbert (Hans) Graf, as an adult, and Max Graf, his father, late in his life. These interviews were conducted by Kurt Eissler in the 1950s and were declassified in 2005 from the Freud Archives.[27] I take this step so that we might reapproach the horse with an idea of family that expands upon Freud's family romance—a family that remains symbolic, but also alive, fantastically alive, in ways that contribute to a boy's gendered personhood.

The family of the case report comes to us as though emanated from Hans's desire and conflict: a family characterized by Oedipal desire, rivalry, and conflict; a family playing their predestined roles in a mythopoetic structural drama. Hans is the main character, and his penis the main organ. The story is about his desires and fears. His phobia is understood as his anxiety in playing his predestined part. The clinical story, structured as a mystery, concludes with the satisfaction of solution.

In contrast, the family of the interviews is marked by marital discord and familial dissolution, a history of significant trauma and loss, and a wary engagement with psychoanalytic authority. Olga, not Hans, is the central character, around whom considerable anxiety circulates, and for whom others struggle to speak. The family of the interviews moves from the liminal spaces of myth and fantasy toward the impress of parental personalities, the force of interpersonal realities and trauma. The story remains one of desire and fear but is much less definitive than the case report, both in the act of its telling and in the mode of its ending.

In the opening of the case report, Freud explains that Hans's "parents were both among [his] closest adherents," and that Max Graf shared his observations with Freud in the spirit of "collect[ing] observations of the sexual life of children." Near the end of his discussion Freud also mentions, in passing, that he had treated Olga as an adolescent for "a neurosis as a result of a conflict during her girlhood."[28] Freud tells us nothing more about this treatment, or about Olga's mental state, or about his relationship with Hans's parents, nor does he tell us anything else of the parents' histories, or their social or cultural conditions.[29]

The nature of Freud's relationship with Max and Olga Graf, as well as their histories, has only recently come to light (and only partially, at that) in the Eissler interviews. Olga was the first to become acquainted with Freud. She was in treatment with him during her courtship with Max.[30] The young couple often took walks during which Olga spoke of her analysis, and Max explains to Eissler that these talks were the impetus for his interest in psychoanalysis. Max also indicates that he and Freud frequented the same coffeehouse, where they often met and discussed psychoanalytic theory.[31]

In his interview with Eissler, Max intones an account of a complex relationship with Freud. Several self-states come forward, but prominent among them is his portrayal of himself as an uncertain young man in search of ideas and counsel. This characterization seems to shadow him as an older man as well, and one can note in the interview what might be described as the kind of regret that haunts an uncertain person. Consider, for example, the indecision that leads Max to consult with Freud before marrying Olga in 1899, and the regret expressed in 1952 as Max reflects back on Freud's advice. Max tells Eissler that Freud advised him to go ahead with the marriage, saying, "By all means marry her, you will have fun!" Max then counters, "Fun I really didn't have, but it is possible I was too young."

One year into the marriage, Max tells Eissler of a consultation during which he told Freud, "Professor, this marriage is not working!" According to Max, Freud seemed surprised but encouraged him to stay in the marriage. It seems that Max spoke of his wish to have children, and his hope that having children would help Olga. He does not detail any advice from Freud in this regard. Hans/Herbert, however, in his interview with Eissler, indicates that his mother seems to have believed that Freud did in fact counsel Max to have children. What is more, Hans/Herbert links Freud's counseling presence in his family with the ultimate breakup of the family, telling Eissler: "My mother still has complaints, saying that Freud was not good in her life, and advising my father to have children, and so forth, etc. It more or less broke up, off, ultimately, the marriage." Max and Olga were married for eighteen years. By his account, Max remained only for the children, saying once again to Eissler, with regret, "Only later did I wonder whether it would not have been better, after all, if I had left already earlier."

In keeping with the uncertainty and unhappiness expressed in regard to his marriage, Max variously describes Olga as "restless," "insecure in the company of others," and "avoid(ant)," and as "a hysteric, [who] was very focused on herself." At one point he suggests that she suffered from a more generalized depression, but then retracts that assessment, and instead suggests something in the manner of social anxiety: "She had inhibitions in her relations with people, to go out." It is as though Max is searching for a vocabulary to describe Olga's states of mind, and her disrupted relations with others. In what seems a particularly anguished description, Max reports to Eissler, "There was trouble between my wife and everybody."

Olga's apparent trouble in mind is foreshadowed by a difficult and traumatic history. Harold Blum deduces from information gleaned from the Eissler interviews, along with what he determines to be a description of Olga in a letter Freud wrote to Wilhelm Fleiss in July of 1897, that Olga's father died during her infancy.[32] Furthermore, Max reports to Eissler that Olga had five siblings, three sisters and two brothers: one sister died young, perhaps of polio; the other sisters are described as beautiful, as is Olga (repeatedly), and both sisters seem to have been performers (a pianist and an actress). One of these sisters—it is not clear which one—made a suicide attempt; both brothers committed suicide by shooting themselves. These descriptions of Olga's siblings are brief and unelaborated. We also learn that Olga suffered a miscarriage before Hans's birth.

How Olga held her history in mind we do not know. How that presumably traumatic history may have been transferred in her relations with her children, we also do not know, or know only at a level of stretched deduction. In this way, Eissler follows and repeats Freud's representation of Olga. We are granted only limited access to Olga within the case report. She rarely appears as an active or speaking subject. Her experience of mothering and her subjectivity are not elaborated, even though one presumes that Freud may have had some insights to offer in this regard. Instead, Olga is most often discussed as a fraught object of desire, and Hans is repeatedly queried as to his wishes and aims where she is concerned. When she does appear, she is depicted as chastising or threatening (in one case castration, in another abandonment), or in contrast seeking or assenting to Hans's affection in the form of "coaxing" or caressing.

Contrary to the case report, Olga dominates the Eissler interviews. Like Freud's "unlaid ghost," she is ever present and ever elusive.[33] As the literary theorist Madelon Sprengnether says of mothers in Freud's theory, "Like the spirit of the mournful and unmourned Jocasta, she haunts the house of Oedipus."[34] Both Max and Hans/Herbert speak of Olga as hauntingly "nervous, always nervous," and describe her as an inconsistent wife, mother, and person.

In keeping with these characterizations, Max responded to a question from Eissler as to whether Olga neglected Hans by saying, "Oh, neglected, that would be saying too much. But that she was involved with him the way a mother is involved with a child, that I wouldn't say." Eissler does not ask Max to elaborate on this assessment, though one gathers from the conversation that Max is referring to his characterization of Olga as often turned in toward herself, preoccupied with her own anxieties, and unable to take in another.

Max and Hans/Herbert emphasize this point in speaking about Olga's relationship with her younger daughter, Hanna, who was born in 1906, when Hans was three and one-half years old. It seems the pregnancy was unwanted, and it is further implied that Olga would have preferred another boy. It appears that Olga may have found it difficult to respond to her daughter. Describing neglect and possible abuse, Max tells Eissler, Olga "behaved well toward the boy. She didn't toward the girl. . . . She discarded her." Max's use of the word *discard* intones a cool indifference, a morbid remove: one discards, throws away, or thrusts aside an object; one abandons a person.

Through Max's interview, Olga's purported neglect of Hanna is discursively linked with information about Hanna's suicide as a young adult. It is tempting to think about Olga's history and her states of mind, and the probable intergenerational transfer of trauma, as it relates to Hanna's suicide. But this manner of deduction is limited in its reach. The information at hand is incomplete and compromised. The members of the family have no way to speak to such interpretations. In particular, Olga would once again become the object of interpretation within a discourse that she had pointedly declined: she wrote to Eissler, saying that Freud "wreaked havoc on us"; she felt that to speak any further on the subject would be too costly to her peace of mind.[35]

It is important to recognize that one is led toward filling in Olga's absence in the case history and her continued absence as a speaking subject in the historical record. In his theory of masculinity, Freud does not position the mother as a speaking subject, or the family as a living fantastic entity. The Graf family becomes somewhat mute in Freud's discussion of the case; this is in contrast to the family voice he captures in the case history. The family in the discussion is rendered as symbolic, but their daily life, the network of attachment and desire as captured in the case history, is not sustained.

In fact, one could argue that the past century's psychological discourse on masculinity hinges on these very absences. I write against a background of work that not only positions the mother as speaking, but as key, as *the* key, to her son's masculine development.[36] I write buttressed as well by the nearly century-long redress of Freud's limited attention to the social-psychological dimensions of parenting, maternity in particular. In keeping with these moves, a child's longing to grow, expressed through the complex interplay of parent-child recognition and emotional attunement, has become an increasingly important aspect of our understanding of child development.[37]

The Horse II

The impress and impact of unconscious fantasy is not at stake here, nor is the manner in which such fantasy may be saturated with symbolic configurations. What is at stake is how we theorize boyhood, and masculinity's origins, if indeed we hold to the possibility of identifying elusive, and overdetermined, origins. Freud's "covering law model," which offers deductive and deterministic cause-and-effect explanations, has been repeatedly challenged, and Oedipal theorizing, both within the annals of psychoanalysis and in the consulting room, has long been on the wane.[38] Theorists point to the ways the Oedipal myth and Oedipal theory are not transhistorical truths but rather a way of thinking, a narrative, a set of concepts. Clinicians, in turn, repeatedly face the ways in which Oedipal narration fails to illuminate as often as it succeeds.

In my view, the appeal of Oedipal myth is the way in which mythic narratives aid us in coping with common problems and patterns (generational difference; the incest barrier; recognition of the other). Oedipal theory provides a symbolic framework for telling the stories that families collectively tell in order to account for their relations—stories that include narratives about parental union, parental sexuality, childhood sexuality, and conception. Narratives, however, come with and install limits. One narrative is not enough.

One of the pleasures in reading Freud's case history of Hans is to track his multiple narratives, his manifold approaches to the feared horse, and his varying approaches to the determinants of Hans's anxiety. Similarly, the vicissitudes and unsettled conditions of masculinity Freud captures through swift-bright empathy is a rare pleasure for the clinical reader. A quality of affection (identification, attachment, love) colors Freud's clinical writings about men—a quality one rarely notes, or at least rarely with such ease, when Freud is discussing his female patients. He moves on in his writings to present a number of men, a cast of characters, an array of emotionally distinct men variable in their masculine subjectivities, and almost to a man well met by Freud.[39]

The range of masculine subject possibilities to which Freud affords attention is perhaps nowhere more apparent than in the notably generative scope of his Oedipal template. The clinical psychologist Kenneth Lewes presents an intriguing matrix of the twelve possible solutions to the Oedipal complex and the consequent variety of sexualities and masculinities that can follow from these solutions.[40] Eight of the twelve Oedipal solutions configure the gendered social stance of the boy/man as feminine, pointing to the profound phantasmagorical potentialities and structural fecundity of Freud's propositions. As Lewes argues, the normative Oedipal outcome—one position out of twelve—is born out of trauma and compromise, as are all of the possible outcomes. The attribution of trauma/pathology to the less expected outcomes follows not on the structural dictates of the theory but, as Lewes suggests, the "disguise [of] moral judgment about what is 'natural' as a pseudobiological argument."[41]

Yet judgment has accrued. Expected and repeated conditions are equated with that which is natural, which in turn is considered equivalent with well-being. The "disguise," however, points to that which is kept behind or concealed (the variability, the malleability, the unsettled) as moves are made to chart the normative (as natural).[42] The "disguise" also registers the power of normative narrative to keep the masquerade in play. Here one is reminded of the psychoanalyst Joan Riviere's employment of *masquerade* in speaking of femininity. Freud, through his employment of a narrative strategy in his report on Little Hans that follows the slow, deliberate arc of a mystery, adopts the disguise of the detective. He sorts through clues, multiple interpretations, and symptoms, and moves toward an explanation that can be "proved beyond a shadow of a doubt."[43] Like any good detective he is charmed and charming, operating as he does through the powers of keen observation and a superior mind. Yet the mystery's element of surprise or the promise of the unexpected never lifts off the page.

One is always aware of the authorial hand, and while indeed the narrative arc is presented as a mystery, it is belied by a tale foretold: "Long before he was in the world, I went on, I had known that a little Hans would come who would be so fond of his mother that he would be bound to feel afraid of his father because of it." Hans was a character in Freud's Oedipal narrative before he was a character himself. Hans was predetermined. And he seems to understand this. When following Freud's comment about his destiny, Hans asks, "Does the professor talk to God, as he can tell all that beforehand?" Freud wisely and wittily indicates that he would be flattered had he not led Hans to such an opinion.[44]

Sidestepping Hans's experience, Freud in his estimable manner perseveres in his effort to capture the intricacies and complexities of his Oedipal theory, and to position Hans as a normative Oedipal boy.[45] But in my view, he does so at a cost:

the enigmas and contradictions so central to psychotherapeutic action (and childhood) are too quickly solved. One can work to hold open the unsettled tensions Freud elucidates through the multiple interpretations he offers. But such a reading is an act of counterwill to Freud's will to honor the normative Oedipal frame, and to privilege his claim regarding phallic primacy.

Consider how Freud moves from his interpretation of the horse as multiply symbolic (father, mother, parental couple, parental coupling) that he and the father offer at the end of the analysis, and the multiple dynamics he addresses throughout the treatment, as well as multiple interpretations that shaped the psychotherapeutic action, toward one explanatory solution. Freud marshals a complex array of information to arrive at his final interpretation and formulation: "Hans really was a little Oedipus who wanted his father 'out of the way,' to get rid of him, so that he might be alone with his beautiful mother and sleep with her."[46] The feared horse, the object of Hans's phobia, is understood in the final, the "chief," analysis to represent the father, who would seek reprisal for Hans's patricidal and incestuous wishes. The phobia is understood as a defense or precaution against the development and expression of Hans's aggressive and hostile desires, fueled as they are by the primacy of the phallus. The dynamics of attachment, the early parent-child psychic envelope, the overdetermined affects that map out the relational contours of this family, and the influencing cultural surround are too quickly glossed as Freud moves to fix Hans as a normative Oedipal boy.

Increasingly, and in response to the narrowing linearity and predetermination of the normative Oedipal narrative, modern theorists and clinicians focus less on the foreshadowed Oedipal outcome and more on the developmental experience of the triangulated Oedipal situation.[47] The task then becomes one of noting a child's erotic desires as those wishes couple with his attachment experiences; in turn, how does a child's attachment experience afford him the opportunity to observe others in relation: How does he wish? How does he reach toward another? How does he see others' desiring and reaching? How does he begin to contemplate the minds and desires of others?

What then, we might ask, of Hans's Oedipal situation? What of the frame built through the bonds of his family? What might Hans have observed from his third position in the triangle with his mother and father? How might his observations have commingled with the desire he felt in relation to his mother and father? How did his experience of third-ness (the third point in the triangle) influence his growing subjectivity and masculinity?

In response to such questions, I turn back to the horse. As a modern reader, given the revised historical record, one is drawn to complicate Freud's symbolic reading by reflecting on the contribution of the parent-child psychic envelope as it, too, may have contributed to Hans's anxiety. Freud also briefly reflected on the force of this parent-child surround. Pausing in the midst of his symbolic reading, he makes a passing remark with respect to the consequences of reality, one that haunts the modern reader, knowing what we now know about the Graf family. Defending against what he imagines to be the common response to Hans's fears—that they are born out of everyday experience—Freud says, "But a neurosis never says foolish things, any more than a dream. When we cannot understand something, we always fall back on abuse. An excellent way of making a task lighter."[48] This remark is made as Freud moves from considering Olga's behavior as a mother toward, a few paragraphs later, casting her as symbolic.

Knowing what Freud knew about the Graf family, this statement reads as disavowal, a gap that engenders a split between the psychic action of neurotic fantasy and the fantastic and interpersonal expressions of trauma. Freud had before him a family in considerable distress—bursting at the seams: a father who came to him seeking his advice on how to live in these deteriorating circumstances; a mother, a former or perhaps ongoing patient, who evidently at this juncture either refused his counsel or was beginning to reject his ideas; and a boy who may indeed have been caught in an unconscious embodied web of maternal desire and a symbolic faceoff with paternal authority (haunted by embodied paternal desire), but nevertheless a boy who was also likely trying to communicate something about his experience of his family as troubled.

Consider in this regard how Hans/Herbert in his interview with Eissler repeatedly emphasizes the "personal misery" of his parents' unhappiness. He suggests that his parents' deteriorating marriage was the single most influential dimension of his young life. Interestingly, Freud gives no account of Hans's despair in his brief postscript description of his consultation with Hans at age eighteen, perhaps further demonstrating Freud's disavowal. Noting the divorce, he portrays Hans as virtually (or even, heroically) unmarked: "Not only had he come through his puberty without any damage, but his emotional life had successfully undergone one of the severest of ordeals [the divorce]."[49]

In my view, Hans/Herbert reports/repeats what he calls his misery to point out how Freud's symbolic Oedipal reading of his family was limited in its reach—even if we accept Freud's claim that Hans's anxiety followed on repressed erotic longing and that Hans was under the sway of Oedipal desire and conflict. For example, one could argue that despite the breakdown of parental desire, Hans persevered in his Oedipal complexities—after all, fantasy need not, and most often does not, follow on daily reality.

Yet the failure to include consideration of the intimate family surround is to leave Hans an oddly romanticized boy, one who is untroubled by the intrapsychic vagaries of relations, other than those that occur in his pursuit of phallic sexualized relations. The flavor of this romance seeps into Freud's proud description of Hans's "energetic masculinity with traits of polygamy," a boundless heterosexual desire that Hans "knew how to vary . . . with his varying feminine objects—audaciously aggressive in one case, languishing and bashful in another."[50] Hans pinned as a cad. This problematic romance results in Freud's underilluminated general theory of masculinity: men and boys are cast as desiring, but the relational yearning that shapes their desires goes unexplored.

Freud's disavowal of the actual active parenting parents, the mother in particular, sustains the Oedipal frame as symbolic and idealized. Yet without a developmental story that captures and theorizes a boy's separation from and identification with his mother, or a theory that postulates a symbolic representation of maternality beyond that of an idealized beauty, or an idyllic plenitude to which a boy returns, boys and men are left to traffic in women, construct them outside of mutual recognition, with little to no acknowledgment of the dynamics of separation and dependence that color, construct, and embroider men's and boys' sexualized love relations.[51]

In my view, Hans's experience of masculinity, as Freud begins to demonstrate, but then whittles away, was built through a complex accrual of parent-child exchanges, social-child exchanges, symbolic-child exchanges, and body-child exchanges, including Hans's experience of his body and genitals, his observation of morphological sexual differences, and the physiological components of sexual development. In accord with modern reconsiderations of child development, this complex matrix starts to operate at birth (or even before birth, now that a child's sex is often known to a parent before birth) and is crisscrossed by an infinite array of conscious and unconscious meanings and enigmatic messages passed between parent and child.[52]

Similarly, symbolization is recast; symbols too are transferred within a parent-child-body-mind-social matrix. Symbols precede us. Their internalization serves to construct us. Yet cultural symbols emerge in and merge with relational exchange. Symbols materialize within play, or in flashes of fear. The horse, for example—the symbol of desire and fear—would by necessity be read as contingent in terms of how the interpretation is offered, how it registers Hans's sexual longings, how it denotes his wishes for love and relation within his family, and how it may signify his growing awareness of the intersubjective network that constituted his family.

With these thoughts in mind, let us return to the horse. Might we read the falling horse as a beast of burden, as the stumbling, falling family, as the relations crumbling under the weight of two children and a deteriorating marriage? Might we read Hans's description of the commotion of the feared falling horse as indicative of his experience of his parents' relationship, witnessed arguments, fallings out, rows (in fact, *row* is the word Hans uses to describe the troubled horse)? Or might such commotion be the swirling hysteria of four people in a family losing hold?

Similarly, one could view the feared horse's bite as the wound of parental discord, or the bite of Hans's taxed state of mind, or the bite of his mother's castration threats, or the bite of his mother's seeming objections to Freud's ideas. Following on the psychoanalysts John Ross and Jerome Wakefield, the horse, especially as Hans elaborates his fantasies of beating it, could be seen to represent a scene of abuse: his mother's beatings of his younger sister. As Ross points out, the "row" Hans describes can be heard as an echo of Hans's description of the "row" Hannah (age eighteen months) makes when beaten by her mother. Or could it be the row of Hans's mind as he tries unsuccessfully to mentally outrun the abuse?[53]

Or might one look, as is my view, upon the falling horse as the faltering fantasy of a family weighed down by the heavy load of reality's cart? Could desire ride? Freud's description of childhood, with its emphasis on the child's sexual longing, underplays children's wishes for others to live within love and desire. Might we read the horse as the symbol of maternal desire or paternal authority that cannot keep their footing, flagged as they are by the effort of going on being? In other words, might the falling horse be desire's breakdown? Was Hans's anxiety less specifically linked with the force of maternal desire and paternal authority, and instead a product of a lack of desire and authority, in particular the authority afforded through desire's going on being?

Masculinity Foretold, Told, Retold

I approach these interpretations as questions because in fact that is all they can be. While I have turned to the text of Freud's original report and the subsequent interviews in order to generate these questions, there is at this point no subject who can respond. Reinterpreting the symbols of this case would be a move yet further from Hans, and would serve to compound a problem that already exists within the treatment as it is reported: a boy read by an authority, a boy with limited recourse to response and limited capacities to elaborate on his thoughts/associations, or to confirm the interpretations offered.

On the opening page of his case report, Freud indicates that the psychoanalytic method utilized in this case rests on the ways in which "the authority of a father and a physician were united in a single person."[54] As the treatment moves forward, however, he does not attend to how such authority may weigh on his patient, or his patient's family, or indeed how it might change that which is thought of as the family.[55]

Consider in this respect Hans's response to yet another of his father's interpretations of his fear of the father, "*You know everything; I didn't know anything.*"[56] Unlike his wise observation regarding Hans's transference to his godlike authority, this response is held forward as confirmation of Hans's humble smallness in light of his father's knowing bigness. However, wouldn't one be suspicious of such a response? Doesn't the affect suggest frustration and pique, as captured by Freud's emphatic representation of Hans's statement? The patient who throws down the gauntlet of his own mind and history ("*I didn't know anything*") is a patient challenging the failure of shared recognition.[57] While the relationship depicted between Hans and his father is colored primarily by the goodwill of attention and recognition, it is also often marked by the incursion of the stubborn authority of didactic interpretations. Hans is told; rarely is he met. He is seldom engaged at the level of fantasy, that is, within fantasy as it is played.

Consistently, the complex and overdetermined nature of Hans's associations and responses to his father's interpretations are read as simple confirmation. One is left to wonder where Hans may have taken us if he had been freer to engage his own associations to his dreams and play scenarios, instead of being always, immediately faced with his father's-qua-Freud's interpretations. Hans greets these interpretations in various ways, from immediate rejection to assent to rote repetition to muddled confusion to dissociation to irritation to the occasional response that moves toward mutual recognition. For the most part, however, the therapeutic exchange is not an exchange; it is given in response to Freud's interpretations and inquiries. Are Hans's responses truthful, or is he responding to the demands and acceding to the claims of his interlocutor? Our regret extends to wondering how Hans might have elaborated on his experience in the context of more consistent recognition. And, in turn, how a theory of masculinity might follow nearer to a boy's experience.

One significant consequence and/or illustration that results from this manner of clinical engagement is the way in which masculinity is foretold. While it may unfold in the back-and-forth of parent-child-social space, it is not told in that register. Instead, it is told, or more precisely foretold, from the superior position of the father, a position powered by the muscle of myth. And heard from the position of the told boy. Masculinity is constructed outside of shared recognition, and bears the indelible stain thereof: the unmarked position, driven (aim over object), heteronormative, homorepudiating, unfettered by contingencies of dependence, propped by power, taking, not needing, and left to dominate through the repeated failure of recognizing the other.

Masculinity is foretold, told, and retold, instated, regulated, and enforced. What a boy is, what a boy does, what a boy fears, what a boy desires, are all introduced to Hans through interpretation. What a boy *is not* is also voiced, as a gender binary is established and employed to police the boundaries of the category.

Now it must be said that Hans appears to have been a boy who, like most boys, did not mind being named as such. It must also be said that Freud and Hans's father were not acting in a manner unlike most fathers. They passed along the cultural terms by which masculinity is normatively recognized, and in this way the case report is a wonderful illustration of how masculinity is inherited. Cultural norms are enacted, introjected and reinforced; they are internalized; they shape psychic reality and the coordinates through which masculinity becomes an identity.

Hans does not reject his inscription as masculine, nor does he reject wholesale the forms of rationality by which he is being made intelligible. Indeed, often he seems to feel cared for through such inscription. And here we come upon an intriguing split between that which is said of masculinity by the father and Freud and that which is transmitted via the emotional resonance of the various exchanges. One reads this case often bemusedly, and with goodwill, a set of feelings that I venture might speak to the experience of those involved. In other words, in my view, Hans may have felt helped and cared for less by what was said than by what was affectively transmitted through the tenor and the attention of the interpretations.[58]

This aura of goodwill and affectionate recognition may have been aided by the fact that Hans was not a boy making a claim to a gender experience other than that which is called "boy." He was not confounded or called out through the principal propositions of masculinity. Nor does it appear that the normative trope offered by his father and Freud was out of keeping with his experience.

Still, Hans does frequently, vigorously challenge his inscription, and the propositions upon which it is based, seeking as he does to broaden the category of masculinity. In so doing he points toward the cost of normative masculine inscription: the repudiation of homosexual desires, the forsaking of fantastic cross-gendered identifications, the diminution of dependence and passive desires, and the phallomanic onus of sustaining aim over object, penis over person.

Freud presents Hans's challenges, often with considerable interest. But in each case he catalogues these challenges and these affect states as temporary, unschooled, and soon to be resolved as Hans moves toward Oedipal resolution and a more normative masculine identity. Hans generally concedes Freud's points/interpretations, yet he does not relinquish his beliefs and affects, not even when Freud presumes that Hans has come to a point of resolution or is on the path thereto.

This underestimation of Hans's view reflects the nature of cultural regulation as carried forward by the father. As a consequence, neither the boy nor the father is adequately illuminated. The complex web of their rivalry and aggression is not adequately perplexed by their experiences of dependence and desire. Once again, there is an intriguing gap between, on the one hand, what is theorized through this case history and discussion and, on the other, the affective resonance (the dependence and desire) that emanates from the pages of the case history in particular.

A theory of masculinity that is forged solely through competition with paternal authority, with little regard for the interplay of identifications, desire, and mutual recognition that seek to establish relations with others outside a dynamic of domination is largely a theory of phallic narcissism–qua–masculinity, and not a theory that can reckon with the range of phallic states beyond penetrative desire, or relational configurations beyond besotted adoration or domination. Freud's narrative of boyhood masculinity, resting as it does on the "primacy of the phallus" narrows the scope of a boy's motivations, underestimates a boy's experience of gender and growth, too quickly systematizes a boy's body, and renders boys as adultomorphic ("Hans has really behaved like a grown-up person in love").[59]

A boy's narcissistic and psychically energized investment in his penis, his rivalries with men, and his trafficking in women trump his relational needs.[60] The point here is not to deny the pleasurable experiences a boy has with his penis, or the exquisite dominance of such pleasure, even the possibility of untamed aim (the push/pull of desire unhinged from love and dependence) when it is in play. Rather, it is to question how such pleasure reflects and radiates, and what and/or who is constructed and encountered through such pleasure. Does it radiate through a boy toward his becoming, as Freud suggests, a "young lover" in search of genital union? Does it dominate and thereby create relations? Or is it created within relational exchange and recognition?

Does the penis precede the boy, or does the boy precede the penis? Or might they move forward together through the interimplication of pleasure, anxiety, and growth? In my view, Hans illustrates over and over again how his relationship to his penis is part of his overarching quest to grow: "And my widdler will get bigger as I get bigger." While I concur with Freud's assessment that "it was as though the child's wish to be bigger was concentrated on his genitals," I read the twice-uttered *bigger* as the operative word in that statement of desire, as opposed to Freud's reading, which emphasizes the dispositional push of the penis.[61]

What does it mean to a boy to be bigger and to have a bigger penis? Freud and Hans's father repeatedly interpret such wishes as expressions of a boy's desire for his mother. Yet Hans repeatedly end-runs such interpretations. He may accede to his father's interpretations regarding his desire for his mother, but Hans's own spontaneous associations are almost exclusively to a father with children, or a father who has access to the outside world. In other words, the longing is to be a big father/man who has children and access to the outside world.

Hans repeatedly indicates that his wish is less genital per se than it is generative. Hans, like many boys in my clinical experience, holds fatherhood in mind as a many-faceted experience, and in keeping with my experience, he holds forth the generality of bigness as topmost. As Hans illustrates so well, a boy's psychic reality is something more akin to an enigmatic sketch, as opposed to the complete drawing Freud proposes. Wishing to be big is wishing to fill in the drawing.

While Freud's structural, symbolic regeneration of masculinity was once seen as the avenue to coherence and well-being, we are left to question the degree to which such an account is an insufficiently problematized romance. The boy who emerges via Freud's account is a boy who is set apart from women, their bodies, and their affect states, yet vulnerable—nay, besotted with their idealized beauty and bounty. He is a boy formed through competition with men and his repudiation of his desire for them. A boy who must endure the oppression of powerful narcissistic men. A boy who is constituted through aim prior to object.

We are left to trouble this account as we cast an eye toward regulatory cultural practices as opposed to structural myths, and work as well toward a less determined theorization of masculinity. Masculinity is being recharacterized as something akin to a force field or chaotic assembly. Sociocultural gender tropes combine with sociofamilial patterns that are further inflected through the contingencies of race, class, and historical epoch. This psychic-sociofamilial/historical construction further intertwines with the intricate unfolding of brain, neuron, bone, hormone, and skin. From this complex and humbled position, we are left to speak with less certainty, reckoning still with the mystery of masculinity, and with the limit of our reach as we move now, a century hence, to consider modern boys and boy hoods.

CHAPTER TWO

Nontraditional Family Reverie
Masculinity Unfolds

"WHERE DID I COME FROM?" HAS NEVER BEEN AN EASY question to ask or to answer. Setting aside the existential uncertainty this question provokes, it often places children and parents alike in the manifold grip of wish, anxiety, and defense. This knot of anxieties has been drawn even tighter with the proliferation of nontraditional families, including lesbian and gay families, multiparent families, and single-parent families: How to speak to children about the ways in which their conception and/or their parents' sexual union differs from traditional family narratives about procreation and parental sexuality? How to introduce and negotiate a child's growing awareness of majority as opposed to minority stories of kinship and procreation? How to explain and express one's feelings about the fact that while two women are capable of gestational reproduction, two women or two men are not capable of genetic reproduction? How to explain, as a single parent, the desire to have a child outside the bonds of marriage and the traditional marriage/love narrative that is often used to explain procreation? How to create a parent-child-donor tri-angulated space? How to contain the pull of guilt and protection experienced by the minority parent and child as they confront normative assumptions and majority expectations?

Add to all this the ways in which many (if not most) non-traditional families employ fertility and reproductive technologies—technologies that are increasingly complex and various. Consider as well the wide spectrum of donor insemination and donor-egg profiles: from the anonymous to the known donor; from the donor who is known all along to the donor who can be known at a later point in a child's life; from the known donor who plays an active role in a child's life to the known donor who is not actively involved; from the genetically related donor to the nonrelated donor; from the single donor to the blended donor—and this is to name but a few. How to speak about technological innovations that perhaps even the parent finds it difficult to comprehend? How to introduce a child to category distinctions that are only now beginning to coalesce (such as the distinctions among a genetic mother, a gestational mother, and a social mother)? Add to that the so-cial/contractual arrangements, including adoption and surro-gate or contractual parenting, that are engaged to establish these nontraditional families, and it is not difficult to see that one is indeed left to be brave in this new world.

But even before the world was this kind of new, parents were notorious for their lack of bravery in the face of procreation questions. Anxious parents commonly turned toward metaphorical obfuscation in order to dodge questions about reproduction or parental sexuality. Hence the cabbage patch, the stork, and the rose. The mystification engendered by comparing a cabbage patch with the process of gestation has become an emblem of parental anxiety and defense. Then again, parents rely on metaphors not only to mystify; they also employ comparisons and metaphors in telling stories to help their children understand complex and anxiety-provoking phenomena.

Stories or "family romances" make up one way a family becomes. Freud first introduced the idea of the family romance in describing adolescents' fantasies, in the service of separation, of having been born to parents other than their own. While Freud situated this experience with the child and with the act of separation, I am suggesting that family romances are also told by parents or between parent and child in the service of attachment. Children often request that stories of conception and birth be repeatedly told as they strive to comprehend reproduction, parental sexuality, and family formation. Heroic and miraculous accounts of birth, for example, are often given a special place in family stories.

Traditionally, accounts of parental union and conception serve as the opening chapters of family bildungsromans. But what about families for which there is no parental union and/or in which conception was achieved with the assistance of someone outside the family? As child analysts and family therapists know all too well, we cannot look either outside or inside our homes and/or consulting rooms these days without having to grapple with our growing awareness of the multiplicity that is modern life.

There is not just one story to tell. Our clinical observations are confirmed by demographic data released by the U.S. Census Bureau in 2008 indicating that only 61 percent of American children live in the same household with their biological mothers and fathers.[1] With these new norms in mind, we are forced to rethink how children and families grow. We need to reexamine our developmental theories that assume a mother, a father, and a child. In concert with such reexamination, we must also look at the ways in which the normative ideal of the biological nuclear family continues to function. In other words, while norms are a way to speak about empirical demographic data, they also function to uphold social ideals or an idealized normative order.

I move forward in this chapter by addressing four constructs that filter through the story-building work of clinical psychoanalysis and that require rethinking in light of the category crises posed by and for the nontraditional family: (1) normative logic, (2) family reverie and the construction of a family romance, (3) the primal scene (a child's fantasy of parental sexual union), and (4) the reproduction of gender through heterosexual complementarity. Guided here by the psychiatrist R. D. Laing's prescient observation in 1968 that "we speak of families as though we all knew what families are," I suggest that the contemplation of nontraditional families and the vicissitudes of contemporary reproduction lead to unknowing what families are—including the ways in which we configure the family within developmental theory.[2] Family stories are central (perhaps most central) to how we conceive of child development. Family stories are also central (perhaps most central) to our clinical endeavors. But: whose family? And once we question what a family is, we are also left to question *how* a family is. How does a family do the work of family? Is that work dependent on a particular or fixed family structure?

Normative Logic

I begin with the crisis of normative logic and the nontraditional family. And I start with the following proposition: no one develops outside a system of norms, but no one develops as a simple mechanical reiteration of such norms.[3] Children and families grow against and within the "logic" of normative social structure. Such structure operates through various forms of social practice, power, and language. No child, no family steps outside this outside world. However, as the political scientist Jane Flax has argued, every child and every family is individualized through struggle with and against these social structures.[4]

For example, children from nontraditional families are frequently reminded of how incomprehensible they are as the law or logic of the dominant culture bears down on them. How might this normative logic be internalized and drawn into a child's consciousness and unconscious? How might we consider the intricate manner in which the psyche is always produced within an outside world, and at the same time keep in mind that along with norms, contingency and chance are also present in that outside world, present and always interacting with norms—thereby creating the possibility of repetition with a difference.

Consider Andy, the seven-year-old son of two mothers. When confronted on the playground with the privileging of the traditional nuclear family in being told that he could not be born to two mothers, he countered with, "Stupid, haven't you ever heard of donors?" Or consider Jade, the six-year-old daughter of a single mother, who when confronted with a similar sentiment simply replied, "Well, a man helped us." Whereupon one of her friends apparently rallied to her defense by pointing out that their mutual friend, Lilly, "came from a dish." At least part of the time they defended their marginality with either seemingly casual explanations or with a sense of entitled defiance. They stood out. But they stood up.

Andy and Jade did not simply or solely suffer in the face of prevailing cultural norms; in their own ways they seemed to understand that norms can occur only with variance, and that their and their mothers' subjectivities constituted a mix of a repetition of certain norms and a challenge to other norms, either through fantasy or conscious action. This is not to suggest that these children lived without conflicted wishes for a family story that reflected the norm.

Andy, for example, experienced considerable confusion, shame, and anger in relation to the butch-gendered surface of RJ, one of his mothers. He could feel especially ashamed and angered by what he perceived to be RJ's incomprehensibility—in particular when and if she was publicly perceived to be a man. Andy's feelings in this regard were overdetermined. One variant of this overdetermination was that Andy could feel incomprehensible as her child. He was not her biological child, and while he bore a clear resemblance to his biological mother, he looked nothing like RJ. Not only was he often in the position of having to explain that RJ, who others often perceived to be a man, was his mother, he was also often in the position of having to explain and comprehend their physical dissimilarity.

In a further complication, Andy also had to reckon with his desire for a kind of active physicality and embodiment that he recognized in RJ and with which he identified. In contrast to Ellen, Andy's other mother, who often experienced and expressed feelings of gender difference in relation to Andy's "boy-ness," RJ regularly identified with and joined Andy in many of his typical boyhood pursuits. They played soccer, they built model airplanes, and they proudly challenged Ellen's squea-mishness when it came to bugs.

As a result, Andy's feelings of anger and his wish to distance himself from RJ were the source of much pain for mother and son alike. RJ often spoke about her gender experience with a kind of ironic pleasure. For example, she enjoyed pointing out that she coached Andy's soccer team and at the same time was one of the PTA room mothers for Andy's class. She was not, however, unmindful of the dilemmas her experience posed for Andy, as well as his feelings of confusion and anger. Help-ful in this regard was RJ's capacity to parent. She happened to be possessed of a vigorous, bodily, and lustful approach to living. She readily jumped into active play. She could intuit and initiate a child's voluptuous pleasure in excess. She could also intuit and fulfill a child's need for comfort, soothing, and structure.

RJ and I worked together to utilize her good-enough par-enting to allow for Andy's wish that, as he put it, he could have a "mom who looked like a girl, but could play like a boy." RJ understood that she could not embody that wish. She could, however, provide a mind that was open to Andy's wish and his corresponding confusion, anger, and hate. Through her reflec-tive capacity to remain open to Andy's affects and his uncon-scious projection of those feelings, a paradox could be created and held: Andy's wish could be recognized. Similarly, his per-ceptions of cultural norms could be recognized, and RJ's cul-tural incomprehensibility could be located in relation to those norms. Andy's dilemma was not solved, nor were his shame and anger erased. Rather, they were held and explored.

Andy faced a similar, though manifestly different, dilemma with his other mother, Ellen. He would often become angry when Ellen made efforts to explain their family to others, which included identifying herself as a lesbian. Andy would press Ellen to remain silent, and to pass as virtually normal. Ellen would at times accede to Andy's wish, but feared that such accession represented collusion in feelings of shame. Ellen spoke of her concern in our first consultation: "Andy is a great kid. I love him with all my heart and I trust he knows that, along with feeling the complications of that, you know, that sort of 'Oh, Mom.' And it has not been difficult to help him understand that I am gay and what that means. He gets that. I think he also understands as best he can, at this point, the circumstances of his birth. But how do I deal with his beginning to understand that I am hated?"

Their family did not always blend into the backdrop logic. At times they were greeted with anxiety and hate. RJ recalled a "hateful moment" when she met Ellen and Andy on a street corner. She kissed them both and they set off toward a restaurant. As they joined hands, a passerby yelled, "Fucking freaks!" Tearfully, RJ described her feeling of dread, anger, helplessness, and sorrow as she watched Andy's happy expression veer from confusion to fear to anger. RJ and Ellen actively resisted the hate that often greeted their sexuality and their family. They promoted ideas of tolerance and discussions of difference. They spoke out against acts of violence and hate. They proactively provided Andy with stories about minority experience. They participated as a family in a supportive community-based organization for gay and lesbian families.

However, RJ and Ellen could see that being proactive and supportive, while necessary, was not sufficient. They were in need of what Ellen called a "more reflective, less reactive space." It was this need that led them to seek treatment. They sought a referral through the psychologist at Andy's school, who referred them to me. The school psychologist reported no significant problems for Andy at school. In her opinion, Andy was a "healthy boy struggling with the ups and downs of living a nontraditional life." He was an above-average student in a competitive private school. His social relations appeared to be good; he had several friends and was recognized as a "popular" kid. The school psychologist pointed out that there were two other children in Andy's class from nontraditional families, and that the teacher and the school made a decided effort to be inclusive.

I worked with Andy and his family for two years and continued to see them occasionally in consultation over the next two years. While I undertook a twice-weekly individual psychotherapy with Andy, I met frequently with his mothers (usually twice per month). I felt that it was especially important to grasp what I could about how they lived together as a family, and how Ellen and RJ lived together as a couple.

Ellen and RJ described their relationship as loving and largely satisfying. Indeed, each displayed an easy affection with the other, and an equal willingness to hear the other out, although early on I noted a subtle tendency to "manage" the feelings of the other in such a way as to ease, but also truncate, what was being expressed. When I questioned them about this, they began to consider what RJ eventually came to label the "circle-the-wagons mode." This dynamic not only infused their immediate family relations but also carried forward into their "tight circle" of friends, and "close-knit" relations with their siblings. Themes around protective silence quickly surfaced and were threaded through this treatment.

At the heart of my work with Ellen and RJ were our efforts to understand how Andy would find a way to contemplate his anxiety about their difference and endure his experiences of shame and hate. RJ, Ellen, and I spent a lot of time talking about how they could use their minds to "hold" Andy: they could hold and contain Andy's emotional states, both good and bad; they could reflect on the feeling; they could contemplate and work to resist their urge to immediately protect or disavow the bad feelings. We strove to grasp how children can sometimes be ruthless in their pursuit of their feelings and needs, and how they need their parents to survive such onslaughts. This can be particularly difficult for some parents when a child expresses aggressive feelings. But as I worked with RJ and Ellen, I kept pointing to Andy's need to experience their solidity in the face of his anger and anxiety.[5]

Ellen and RJ came to see the ways in which their reflective capacities not only held Andy but also demonstrated their capacity to survive the angry and fearful affects that inflected Andy's anxiety. We worked toward understanding that while we wish to protect our children from pain, anxiety, and hate, we are in fact helpless to stop those feelings from entering into our children's lives, and that furthermore, a life without pain and loss would be an impossibly distorted one. They came to understand that Andy would not be without pain or anxiety, though he would have a mind with which to hold them.

RJ and Ellen recognized that their capacities for reflection and reverie, in particular their capacities to reflect on their marginality, had developed over a long period of time. They began to think about how they could help Andy in this regard as a dance—sometimes you lead, sometimes you follow. Sometimes in accord with his anxiety, they would follow Andy's defenses. If given the opportunity, they might reflect on his fear, or on his perceptions of their cultural incomprehensibility, or on their collective wish for the apparent ease of the normal. At other times, they would lead by helping Andy fashion his own minority story.

Family Reverie and the Construction of a Family Romance

Another feature of Andy's minority story was the manner in which he grappled with the idea of a father. In this regard, Andy was cautious and uncharacteristically quiet, as opposed to his more typically lively manner. His reluctance to indulge his curiosity about fathers stood out. I once referred to his "father," and he rather firmly and decisively corrected me by explaining that he did not have a father, he had a donor. I understood that he was repeating what he had been told. But I was also sincerely struck by the integrity of his response. After taking note of my blunder, I asked him whether he ever imagined his donor. He replied by reciting the facts that had been provided him. Andy knew the difference between facts and imagination, and when I pointed out his "just the facts, ma'am" approach, he reluctantly revealed that he did have an idea about the donor. He had it in mind that he could not meet this man until he was eighteen; otherwise, this man might want to keep him.

We came to understand many things about this fantasy, including his wish and fear that I might want to keep him with me. We also examined his feelings of divided loyalty regarding his wish to know this man (and to know fathers in general), and apprehension about how that would affect his mothers. In particular, would his curiosity separate him from his mothers? Would his curiosity result in retribution in the form of being stolen by this unknown man?

At this point in the treatment, I began to work with Andy and his mothers in an effort to bring their collective fantasies about the donor into what I called their "family reverie." It became clear rather quickly that the entire family had worked to silence their fantasies about this man. Andy's mothers had had many discussions that were often colored by rather lively fantasies about the donor. However, those discussions principally had taken place before Andy's birth. Of particular note were the ways in which they had linked the donor with their own histories in what we came to understand as their wishes for genetic reproduction and continuity. Each imagined the donor as similar to the beloved sibling of the other: RJ imagined the donor to be like Ellen's younger sister, whereas Ellen had imagined the donor to be like RJ's older brother. They made these links in accord with information they had about the donor: he had an advanced degree in mathematics, as did Ellen's sister; he played the cello, as had RJ's brother. Another expression of their efforts to make the donor "familiar" was what they recalled as a feeling akin to "falling in love" with him. As Ellen clarified, "Not exactly falling in love, but sort of—at least a big crush. We only had a written description—no picture. But we certainly had him in mind as lovable." RJ added, "We even gave him what I think of as a lovable name, Tim. We of course didn't know his real name."

RJ and Ellen began to see the ways in which their silence about the donor had followed on anxieties that were multiply determined. Principally, however, they were concerned that such open discussion would prove overstimulating and would lead to questions and wishes for which they could provide neither answers nor satisfaction. We worked toward recognizing the limits of reality: there were answers they could not supply; there was satisfaction they could not provide. At the same time, we worked toward that which they could provide: their minds, the possibility of reverie, the stability born of reflection, and the freedom of imagination.

When they recognized how important their fantasies regarding the donor had been to them, it was an easy move to see that the same might be true for Andy. They had provided Andy with the limited facts they knew, though they had not encouraged discussion beyond the facts. They began to see how Andy might have limited his fantasies in an effort to comply with their anxiety. As opposed to their fear that their fantasies would prove overstimulating or separate them as a family, they were able to entertain the possibility of the opposite—the possibility of minds opening onto and into their collective fantasies in such a way as to bring them together as a family.

Andy's dilemma regarding his donor brings me to psychoanalyst Diane Ehrensaft's reflections on "the destruction" of the sperm donor–father. Reviewing the lesbian parenting literature, Ehrensaft notes a tendency to deny the importance of the information about insemination to the child. She argues that by relegating the role of biological father to that of a "nice man who donates his sperm," parents are underestimating their child's need for information about their biological roots. She also maintains that by reducing the biological father to sperm, parents are defending against their own anxiety regarding the role the donor played in creating the child. According to Ehrensaft, such denial obscures a child's need to establish and construct a "whole father."[6]

Returning to Andy, we can note that he and his mothers did not destroy his donor but they did sequester him, and thereby attempted to restrict their own fantasies about a father. Following Ehrensaft's proposition, Andy was having difficulty creating a "whole" father, as opposed to a "part" father—a father who was composed only of sperm and facts. Yet I was aware that in creating a donor-father Andy was faced with a paradox: donor sperm is a disconnected piece or component part given away in this case by an unknown, though presumably whole, man. Andy had an integrative need to know more and imagine more about this man, yet at the same time he was faced with the disconnected role this unknown man played in his conception.

Constructed and deconstructed by material reality, Andy's father in psychic reality was multiply determined. One feature of that multiple determination was the way in which Andy's donor-father was both a part object and a whole but unknown person. Another feature included the material reality that the person in Andy's life who usually took up the activities most often associated with fathering was a woman, RJ.

Sequestering the donor, collectively keeping their thoughts, fantasies, and feelings silent, was a defensive move toward protection; yet in effect they were denying themselves and Andy an internal donor/father (as we spoke of him, "the donor/father in his head") that could be used as he set about to narrate/imagine his life. Such use was further complicated by the fact that Andy could know (imagine) and use this man only internally. He had no access to this man—he could not experience him in reality. He did not have the opportunity to play with this man, make him laugh, make him mad, challenge him, and frustrate him, while observing his survival.[7]

In contrast to Ehrensaft's observations regarding the destruction of the donor-father, I found that Andy did not have the freedom to fully imagine and fantastically play with his donor, up to and including the vigor and verve that sometimes shapes fantasy and play; he was too busy protecting him. This was an especially intriguing feature of his relationship with me. Early on in the treatment I was treated with great care, and there was much anxiety lest I become displeased. He was cautious as he moved around my office, careful not to disturb or upset anything. He treated the toys carefully lest they break. Once, early on, he dropped a toy on the floor, and it left a minuscule dent in the carpeting. He became concerned that I would be angry and not ask him back. I often commented during this period on his carefulness and suggested that perhaps he was worried about what would happen if we "really played." I also commented on his apparent anxiety about repair and resiliency. For example, we were able to see that as the hour progressed the carpet "bounced back," and I took that opportunity to wonder whether he "worried that we would not bounce back if we really played."

Once we began to take up the question of his donor (along with the work I was doing with his mothers), his play became more active and aggressive. I recall my optimism the first time I had to set a limit on his activity level in my office. Themes typical for children Andy's age began to emerge, in particular the theme of the struggle between big and little. This play theme was repeatedly enacted in a race between cars we would construct out of Legos. His car was always the bigger and sturdier one. Mine was always small and less viable. I often reflected on this play by talking about Andy's wishes and worries about "growing big." Around this time, he set in play a game whereby I would measure his height (which, according to Andy, changed) each hour, and we would make a secret notch on the edge of the bookcase to measure his growth. The vigor and assertion of this kind of play, though once again not unusual for a boy Andy's age, nevertheless provided an opening to begin to address his anxieties about growth: Would he grow? How would he grow? How would he grow as a man? What was it like to grow up as a boy in a house with two moms? What was it like to grow in front of me?

Andy would rarely, if ever, directly answer such questions. Instead, I took my cues from the ways in which he responded through play. It was around this time that he began to take greater interest in me, and in my body in particular. During play he would often edge closer to me, careen into me, or jump into my lap. Once while we were looking at a book, Andy reached up and touched my chin. He asked about the stubble he discovered there, which set in play the theme of the "five o'clock shadow" (our appointment was in fact at five o'clock). Andy took great delight in the phrase "five o'clock shadow" and thought it one of the "funniest things" he had ever heard. Throughout the next few sessions, my chin was inspected almost before Andy was across the threshold into my consulting room. This inspection was repeated many times throughout the hour to see whether my beard had grown. I used this play to expand on our discussion about his wish to "grow big" and to "grow a big man's body." We talked about his curiosity as a way to wish and learn. But I also took note of the ways in which the repetition and exaggeration of this play might communicate something of a manic defense, which in turn raised the question: defense against what?

Andy began around this time to expand his interest in me: Where did I live? Was my office my home? Was the couch my bed? Was I married? Did I have pets? Did I have children? And the question that arose most often, why did we have to meet at my office? Why couldn't we go outside and play? Why couldn't we go fishing? Initially, I attempted to make a link between fishing and therapy, and to point toward the "fishing"/exploration we could do within our work together. However, as Andy persisted with his request, I began to see that my initial (all too clever) response was the consequence of a counter-transference defense (an effort to avoid that which I was feeling in relation to Andy).

Indeed, during this phase of our work I found myself entertaining fantasies of going fishing with Andy. I once caught myself in the middle of reading an article about fishing in a magazine—an article that I normally would have skipped right over. As I began to examine my fantasy, I noted the ways in which the wish was largely felt as physical—the rocking rhythm of the boat, the heat of the sun, and the cool darkness of the water. The silence. Hardly the experience of being with a child in a boat. I began to consider this contradiction as a reflection of my effort to deny or silence Andy's wish that I join him in a parental union, up to and including his wishes for sexual union. Here, I considered the manner in which I might be joining Andy in enacting his family dynamic of protection through silence.

I contemplated the ways in which the fantasy seemed to simultaneously convey and contain sexual desire—perhaps a manifestation of my nonverbal efforts to allow yet contain the erotic transference and countertransference. In particular, I reflected on the nonverbal limiting cues I conveyed to Andy about how he could sit with me, or the ways in which I managed his pull toward rough-and-tumble play. But were my efforts also defensive? Here, I believe we come upon an aspect of child therapy that is rarely discussed and insufficiently problematized—the subtle ways in which a child therapist is often in the position of having to negotiate the muscular eroticism of children, up to and including the therapist's own erotic countertransference response. As I believe my fishing daydream expresses, I was consciously aware of and unconsciously drawn to the kind of sensual contact that characterizes parental care: holding, bathing, caressing, soothing. But I was also aware of something more vigorous—the muscle-to-muscle exchange prompted by Andy's efforts to make more aggressive contact with my body. For example, I was aware of the pleasure I experienced in exercising my strength in setting limits with him, and my corresponding recognition of his pleasure in feeling my strength. Or the pleasure I felt in feeling his small body (the fragility of his rib cage, the thinness of his arms) as I lifted him up so that he could reach something on a shelf in my office—a reach he was insistent on achieving. In this light, I viewed my fishing fantasy as a defense, and I had to entertain the ways in which my own experience of prohibition may have been inhibiting the development of Andy's erotic transference. Was I more comfortable presenting myself as a nurturing parent as opposed to an erotic man?

Following upon these countertransference reflections, I

began to interpret more directly Andy's wish to be close to me—to observe my habits, to touch my body, to feel the excitement (muscular eroticism) of rough-and-tumble play. In marked contrast to his usual style of limited verbal response to my interpretations, he was quite eager to disallow these thoughts. As I puzzled over his response, I wondered whether maybe he wanted to be close to me but not talk about it. This did not strike me as particularly unusual for a boy Andy's age. But what did impress me was the fact that by stepping out of our previous nonverbal manner of managing his wishes, I was also stepping out of the wish.

In this regard, I spoke about how he might want to "make me up and play with me" without having to talk about it. At the same time, I began to speak more directly to Andy's efforts to "make up" a father, and how he sought to "make me up as a father." I sought through such interpretation not only to empathize with Andy's mental state (and the sincere difficulty that he faced in imagining his donor-father), but to offer a re-representation that would awaken and afford the developmental action of play. Specifically, I sought to create a frame for play and reflection that would allow Andy to work out his anxieties surrounding the circumstances of his birth and his family life—anxieties that had been partially shrouded by ignorance and confusion, thereby making them more difficult to express and work through.

Gradually, Andy and I began to grasp his disappointment and anger that his wish could not be granted. Pretending that I was a fathering figure (one with a gendered surface that would pass) and pushing for the enactment of that wish did not alter the reality of his family structure, nor did it annul the paradox of his relationship with his father-donor. Andy's arrival at these realizations was not configured solely through loss. He began to think through the ways in which fathers are not only real but also exist in our minds. We began to talk about "the father-donor in his head," which in turn stimulated pretending (not only in relation to fathers), as well as bringing about enhanced self-representation and reflection.

Taking up Andy's disappointment allowed for further exploration of his confusion about his donor's relationship to paternity. At this point, distinct from the silence that veiled his earlier feelings of disappointment (along with the repudiated and threatening fantasies), he and his mothers were able to engage in a mutative process. Instead of splitting off their collective confusions and fears, they were able to create and integrate a set of shared representations with which to play. We can note here, following on the thinking of the psychoanalysts Peter Fonagy and Mary Target, that Andy and his mothers were able to play within a family reverie to contemplate, metabolize, and think through the shared reality of their nontraditional family. I would add that through this "mentalizing mode," Andy and his mothers were able to construct their family romance.[8] Through this developmental exercise, Andy's mothers were able to help him understand his experience of marginality while not denying either the anxieties or the pleasures of variance.

Children conceived through donor sperm or donor egg technologies may have to create a donor-parent between the material reality of their conception, the psychic and material vicissitudes of their own family life, and the psychic constructions produced via their unique integrative needs. These internal parental constructions will hinge on multiple and overdetermined factors, such as the degree of charge of the donor/

object, the degree of turbulence and corresponding defense, and the transforming quality of any given child's mind. How is the missing (is it missing?) donor/object transformed in the child's mental sphere? For example, did Andy destroy his father, or did he grasp the impossibility of knowing the donor? To divide and collapse these phenomena in one direction or the other—toward either the category father or category donor—is to foreclose both the paradox and the multiple forces that inform these children's lives, and thereby to short-circuit the corresponding possibilities for the deconstruction of parenting and reproduction that may allow children such as Andy to realize and construct their variant families.

The Primal Scene

Part of any child's construction of his or her family or family romance is a growing understanding of parental sexuality along with a growing understanding regarding the child's own conception. Central to psychoanalysts' idea of health is the need to come to terms with the "facts of life," along with the ways in which those facts delineate differences between the sexes and the generations. The so-called facts of life have in turn been linked by analysts with a constellation of fantasies known as the primal scene.

Branching out from Freud's original definition of the primal scene as the child's observation or inference of sexual intercourse between the parents, the metaphor of the primal scene has by now accrued a range of meanings, including the child's knowledge of sexuality, the child's understanding of the parental relationship, and the child's knowledge about conception and reproduction. The primal scene has proven to be a problematic construct, given the breadth of its meaning and scope. In particular, increased attention has been brought to bear on what precisely is achieved through the knowledge of parental sexuality.[9] Contemporary reappraisals and theoretical revision have taken a decided turn away from Freud's original proposition, which fixed the primal scene as an expression of phylogenetic inheritance, and as a foundational fantasy that shapes the organization of all fantasy life.[10]

Contemporary psychoanalytic theorists, most notably Lewis Aron and Ronald Britton, have shifted our attention toward what Britton has referred to as the "primal family triangle."[11] While primal scene fantasies are still seen as foundational, the foundation has been shifted, according to Aron, from what were held as primary symbolic structures (before language, before social exchange) to the intersubjective exploration of "the child's perception, understandings, and experience of the parental relationship and interaction."[12] Unlike Freud, who never specifically incorporated his discussion of primal-scene fantasies into the Oedipal complex, contemporary theorists have endeavored to locate primal scene fantasies within what is now commonly called the Oedipal situation.

Several clinical shifts occur as a result of this theoretical reconfiguration: the primal triangle is examined for evidence of the child's capacity to participate in a relationship observed by a third person as well as his or her capacity to observe a relationship between two people; attention is focused on the development of a space outside the self to be observed and thought about; attention is paid to the child's capacity to distinguish between the material and the psychic; less emphasis is placed on how a child may or may not be negotiating psychosexual stage development (so-called psychosexual stages are seen as less fixed, and open to more oscillation); emphasis is now placed on how children can hold multiple relations and contrasting ideas in mind, including the ability to fantasize multiple sexual relations.

It is around the phenomena of sexual and relational multiplicity that Aron has drawn attention to another problematic feature of the construct of the primal scene, the manner in which the "primal scene connotes a singularity or uniformity of desire that is incongruent with the multiplicity of sexual experience/desire not only between individuals but within individual experience."[13] The singularity to which Aron refers is heterosexual coitus.

In fact, most children begin to understand reproduction through the normative heterosexual love narrative that then folds into the penis-vagina/seed-egg reproduction narrative. But as we know, this reproductive reality is open to variance. While reproduction does indeed require a seed and egg, it does not require heterosexual coitus. Sperm or a male reproductive cell may unite with an egg or a female reproductive cell by means other than heterosexual penetrative union. These contemporary realities require that we begin to distinguish heterosexual penetrative union from primal scene fantasies from conception fantasies, which to date have been considered as one and the same, revealing yet again an assumed correspondence between heterosexuality, reproduction, family, reality, and well-being.

Further illustration of the need to distinguish procreation from the primal scene is a recent summation or proclamation offered by the French psychoanalyst André Green that "if any one of us breathes the air and is alive, it is as a consequence, happily or unhappily, of a primal scene . . . between two sexually different parents, whether we like it or not."[14] Green not only ignores the facts of contemporary life and the various forms a family takes, he ignores the fact that primal scene and conception fantasies are open to a range of permutations and possibilities. Moreover, those permutations may inform our lives and build our minds as much as or more than the limited facts of material reality. And why shouldn't they? The problem is not the possibility of fantasy (how is a lesbian primal scene any more or less enlivening than a heterosexual primal scene?) but rather the ways in which those fantasies are either disavowed, debased, or diminished.

Such foreclosure leads to clinical blind spots that do not afford a more complex way to consider the progenitive wishes of a family, and how those wishes, including the manner in which they are enacted, are open to variation. Furthermore, we are hindered in our efforts to understand how those wishes circulate within the family reverie, how those wishes inform a child's procreation narrative, and how those wishes shape the family's romance.

The heterosexual singularity that is instantiated in most discussions of parental union and family formation serves to foreclose our understanding of a child's capacity to form and flourish within multiple circulating narratives. Recent work by developmental psychologists and psychoanalysts has taken a turn away from fixed developmental structures.[15] Key to this reexamination of childhood is a critique of the linearity and normativity that is tacitly implied by fixed developmental stages and tasks. Linear and deterministic accounts of childhood have been shown to be overly general and insufficient to account for the variability and complexity of development. In response, we have begun to refashion our theories of development by moving toward the exploration and integration of relational processes that afford a more complex and perplexed account of child development. For example, Nancy Chodorow has persuasively argued that "we should be wary of clinical explanations in terms of objectivized universal childhood stages or psychobiological drives that determine or predict later psychological experience." Opposed to such universalizing, Chodorow proposes that we begin to look "from a particular subjective childhood and the unique evidence of individual transferences."[16]

Returning to Andy, his understanding of parental sexuality and reproduction was multiply informed and determined. He knew the facts of life relative to both the global regularity of heterosexual penetrative union and the variant reality of his own conception through donor insemination. He understood reproductive biology and sexual anatomical difference at an age-appropriate level. He knew about what he called "s-e-x" as a mysterious and exclusively adult phenomenon, and he often communicated his sense of this mystery through a mix of curiosity, stimulation, and prohibition. Typical of this mix was an exchange wherein he spoke of how he "better not" speak about "s-e-x." When I asked why, he claimed that to talk about it would give him "shivers." I asked whether they were good shivers or bad shivers. He replied that they were bad shivers and launched into a rambling description of how kids at school said that "s-e-x" was bad. He concluded by pronouncing that when he got married he would push his wife to the other side of the bed. I laughed and said I wondered what his wife would think of that. He indicated that he didn't think we should be talking about such things, and he reinforced his position by telling another rambling story about a friend of his who had gotten into trouble that day for saying "b-u-t-t." At which point we both laughed. I ventured that butts and bodies were funny. I followed by indicating that perhaps the fun adults had with their bodies is confusing. Giggling, Andy once again ventured forward with a rambling story about overhearing RJ and Ellen laughing in the bathroom. He blurted out that RJ most likely had farted in the bathtub. More giggling ensued and recurred in fits and starts throughout the rest of the hour.

This exchange, which is perhaps most notable for its typicality, nevertheless communicates Andy's lively engagement with both his and his parents' sexuality. He links Ellen and RJ in a body space (the bathroom) and translates their laughter into a form of bodily fun (farting in the bathtub) with which he can no doubt identify. The interest and interpretation he brings to parental sexuality, typical of children his age, is probably based on his own physical experiences, perhaps even his own experience and desire in being bathed by his mothers. Simultaneously, one might look at the link he makes between parental laughter and anal pleasure (farting) as a defense against his growing understanding of adult genital sex; note also his reference to pushing his wife to the other side of the bed. Here we might also wonder whether Andy was defending against a growing understanding of the difference in his parents' sexual union. Once again, though, this manner of defense is not unusual for children Andy's age as they seek to negotiate their curiosity, excitement, and stimulation with their experience of exclusion and taboo.

How Andy processes and expresses his understanding of

his parent's sexuality is combined with his registration of the psychic reality of his parents' relationship. He represents his parents in a combined relationship that is exclusive rather than rejecting. Andy also represents "s-e-x" as exclusive and prohibited but not rejecting; we had better not talk about it, yet we were; we had better not feel it, yet, arguably, we were, in the form of shared recognition and laughter. Together we could observe and share in his experience. At the same time he could communicate a sense of limit relative to what he could know, or thought it appropriate to know. This limit, however, did not curtail his curiosity, or his robust capacity to "play with" "s-e-x" (to act on it imaginatively).

This robust quality is also reflected, even within this small exchange, in the manner in which Andy moves between multiple stories and wishes. Consider how he moves between speaking about his own imagined heterosexual marriage, his parent's homosexual union, and the simultaneous experience and prohibition of "s-e-x" with his peers, which is then repeated with me.

This play/exchange, which occurred near the end of Andy's treatment, signaled a significant shift in the nature and quality of his willingness to play in contrast with the careful and constricted play he exhibited at the beginning of his treatment. This exchange also illustrates Andy's growing capacity to play with ideas that were imbued with the implication of his own wishes and desires. Instead of carefully disavowing his fantasies and wishes, he could now playfully move between internal fantasies (his own as well as those that circulated within his family reverie) and external reality (both normative and nontraditional) in order to grasp the wishes that produced him.

Heterosexual Complementarity and the Reproduction of Gender

Just as our thinking about how children are formed through the phantasm of a primal scene has been limited by heterosexual presumption, our thinking about childhood gender development has also been hindered by our continued reliance on a model that rests on heterosexual complementarity. It is presumed that like gender produces like gender; fathers produce sons, mothers produce daughters.

Nonnormative families repeatedly come up against explicit anxieties about how the family's network of identifications will influence a child's gender development. Can a boy become a boy with two moms? Setting aside the anxiety expressed via such questions, abundant empirical data have indicated that yes, in fact, boys with two mothers do in fact become normatively recognized boys.[17] I have had occasion to work with a number of such boys, as well as with boys raised by single mothers, and while I have observed with considerable interest that their masculine subjectivities reflect the relational contours of their families, the degree to which their experience of masculinity links up with that which is considered normal has been remarkably unremarkable.

Such was the case with Andy. His masculinity, established as it was in a minority story, psychically specific as it was (as indeed any masculinity is), nevertheless easily fit within the normative social position called "boy." He embodied masculinity and boy-ness with a kind of admirable ease. He was seen as "easy-going" and "regular" by other boys, and was sought out by them. Like his school friends, I, too, was aware of his boyish ease. However, I was also intrigued by the ways in which he was not much interested in many of the activities that bring urban boys together. He was a good soccer player. But as RJ noted, he rather easily "left the game on the field." He did not follow local sports teams, as did many of his friends. He played the computer games that interested many of his peers. But here too, he did not take up the games with the kind of obsessive drive I have noted in many of his peers. He enjoyed movies, and going to movies with his friends, and he enjoyed talking about them. But again he did not recount them with the kind of obsessive detail I have often observed with other urban boys.

Andy's principal interests were less urban. He was the kind of boy who might be seen today as old-fashioned. He was interested in outdoor activities, such as fishing, camping, hiking, skiing, and boating. His descriptions of his trips to his family's country house, where he often took a friend, were the most lively reports he brought into the consulting room from the outside world. He even dressed in this more traditional manner, eschewing the hip-hop style that many of his contemporaries donned. He wore khaki pants, flannel shirts, and sturdy shoes. "He's our nature boy," RJ proudly explained. In fact, Andy did share many of these outdoor activities with his mothers. Through an intriguing gender transfer, these masculine activities (foundational activities undertaken by Boy Scouts) and these practices of conventional masculinity were transferred in this case from mothers to son, or more precisely between mothers and son in the social context of a traditionally masculine terrain.

In keeping with a tradition that has changed little in the past one hundred years, we continue to presume that masculinity unfolds within a psychically specific heteronormative domestic story: dis-identification from a mother, rivalry with a father, and identification from son to father. How masculinity is told from culture through parent to son or, put another way, how masculinity precedes parents and sons has received less consideration. How masculinity may not be a matter of identification with an other, but rather an identification by the other in accord with culturally established terms by which masculinity is recognized (a point the psychoanalyst Virginia Goldner has repeatedly emphasized with respect to gender in general), has figured little in our psychological theories of masculinity.

Analysts' focus on the guiding presupposition of heteronormativity and the so-called balance of heterosexual complementarity has overshadowed the ways in which families and parents—either majority or minority—transfer what the psychoanalyst Adrienne Harris has called "the practices of identity," and along with those practices the symbolic and the cultural regulations that determine those practices.[18] Gender's practices are enacted within a variety of kinship systems, within a variety of parent-child relations, and on a variety of registers: social, symbolic, political, psychological, biological. We live gender suspended between these systems, relations, and registers. And we spill out onto gender's complex field: a field, yes, with a dense median, and an assiduously controlled mythos, but a field nevertheless that demonstrates how multiple acts of gendered address, affect, and embodiment are equally robust and intelligible, however majoritized or minoritized they may be. (Imagine a football field with most people gathered around the fifty-yard line but others scattered here and there across the rest of the field.)

I find that in my psychotherapeutic work with children we spend a lot of time considering the story of how their families came together and what holds them together or fails to hold them together. In my work with children from nontraditional families, I also find that we spend a lot of time contemplating how they have to reach beyond the categories they have been given in an effort to think about what they know about their families and the wishes that shape them.

Near the end of an hour during which Andy and I had addressed his reluctance to unveil his fantasies regarding his donor, he told me about learning to ride his new two-wheel bike. He recounted a scene with his mother on a dirt road near their country home, a scene full of near mishaps and near mastery. As Andy spoke, I recalled a similar scene. I could so clearly see my father and myself in an empty parking lot as I attempted to master that peculiar delicate balance that, once achieved, is so unremarkable, yet at the moment of achievement so grand. My memory/story included a man, my father, who happened also to be my genetic father. Andy's story included a woman, his mother, who was not his genetic mother. I believe Andy may have wished—and sought to communicate his wish through this unconscious communication—for me to understand that he had someone to help him gain his equilibrium as he mastered one more act of separation; as he moved one step further into the outside world, an outside world that is increasingly populated by children from nontraditional families, who in turn are looking to us to reach along with them beyond the narrow categories that have shaped our thinking to date.

Just as Freud had an opportunity to meet with Hans (no longer Little), I had occasion to see Andy many years following our work together. His mothers sent holiday cards and family pictures, as many parents of child patients kindly do. I knew from their notes that Andy was well. I could also see in the pictures that he was growing, especially in the past few years, and that in the last picture he seemed to hover over his shrinking mothers. In addition, there was some overlap in my social world with a friend of Andy's family, who knew of our work together, and who, on occasion, had mentioned how much she enjoyed Andy. So I had some secondhand knowledge of his well-being, and was pleased to think of him moving along in the world.

Then, one evening a couple of summers ago, I was walking down the street of a small New England town where I spend my summers, and a boy on a bicycle giving a ride to a girl on the back fender stopped abruptly and said hello. It took me a moment to register that it was Andy. I smiled, shook his hand, said how good it was to see him, introduced him to my friend who was walking with me, took note of the fact that he was now taller than I, and said, "You look bigger out here." He laughed, and introduced me to his friend.

I was struck all over again by the ease with which he was a boy. He was thin and lanky with long curly blonde hair, handsome by traditional standards, and hale as befitted the New England setting. He explained that he and his mothers were on vacation, and he exclaimed over the beauty of the town. I concurred, and asked whether he had been to some of my favorite spots, including a beach with tidal pools that I thought he might like. I asked him whether he had been fishing. He smiled and said that in fact they had just come in from the boat: "A bust. But we did see a whale in the distance, and that was pretty cool." He added that he and RJ were getting up early the following day to go back out on the boat.

I asked about school (I knew he was attending a high school that was known to be particularly demanding), and he and his friend (who I learned attended the same school) laughed. I said, "In other words you are happy to be on vacation." They laughed again. To which I responded, "Enough said."

I asked about his parents. He said they were "good," enjoying their time away from the city. His friend asked whether I knew where they could get pizza. I gave them directions. And off they rode.

As they rode down the street, my friend exclaimed, "They don't make them more adorable than that." I nodded and silently concurred with her. I found as well that I immediately thought of Freud and Little Hans, and how the nature of our wishes for our patients, but perhaps even more so for child patients, leaves us adoring—a state that can be examined in the context of therapeutic action. I have no doubt that Andy's life is far more complex and contradictory than the Andy I saw that evening. But on a summer night in a seaside town, one is simply disarmed by the charms of youth, and so it should be.

PART II

Boys, Masculinity, and Gender's Divide

CHAPTER THREE

Boyhood Femininity
Masculine Presuppositions and
the Anxiety of Regulation

DURING THE FIRST WEEK OF WHAT WAS TO BECOME a six-year analysis, Jesse, then twenty-two, described his experience as a feminine boy as follows: "There was this sense of otherness. You know, not being the norm, not the normal boy. But I don't know, I feel like civilization has robbed me of the words to describe this." Following on Jesse's sentiment, I turn in this chapter to boys who struggle to lay claim to cross-gendered experiences that are at odds with what is considered normal masculinity; boys who regularly feel unnamed or without claim to the gender name they desire, and without standing as intelligible humans.

A discourse has accumulated around feminine boys, constructing them as nonconforming, extreme, and disordered. This diagnostic discourse provides a particularly interesting opening through which to examine regulatory norms and how these norms rely on unquestioned presuppositions about not only (1) that which constitutes masculinity but also (2) that which constitutes gendered coherence and (3) the relation-ship of said coherence to psychological well-being.

Descriptions of feminine boys unfold almost exclusively within discussions of gender identity disorder (GID). These descriptions take different forms and follow upon differing motivations—from the claims of empirical neutrality within developmental psychiatry to the theological claims and ex-plicit activism of Christian psychology.[1] Whether the focus is on the psyche or the soul, the presuppositions of masculinity remain the same. Unquestioned.

Regulatory Anxiety

Despite the many modern considerations of gender, no effort has been made to critically theorize gender with respect to feminine boys; gender is as gender was. As such, this body of work bears the mark of a kind of generation gap: sage experts tuning out the queer rap of postmodernism, feminism, and queer theory. Consequently, we are left with modes of diagno-sis and treatment that are out of sync with modern social life; modes of care that proceed from an inadequate understanding of the range that is masculinity and the mutability that is gen-der; modes of care that cannot see beyond expected norms to the possibility of mobility and transformation.

Illustrative of this tie to outmoded norms is the concern that has surfaced recently regarding the planned revision of the *Diagnostic and Statistical Manual* (*DSM-V*) and the psy-chologist Kenneth Zucker's prominent appointment as chair-man of the workgroup overseeing the section on sexual and gender identity disorders. (Zucker, a noted GID theorist, along with the psychiatrist Susan Bradley summarily dismissed "social constructivists" as the "contemporary gadflies of psychiatry.")[2] In a twenty-first-century variant on "Off of the couches and into the streets!" we are witnessing a move from hand-painted protest signs to the Web, where there has been a flurry of accusation, much of which bears the understandable anxiety of nonnormative people faced with the authority of the *DSM*. Zucker and the American Psychological Association have responded to these concerns, reframed as "confusion," through an appeal to their dedication to ending discrimination, by detailing the inclusion in their task force of a diverse group of scholars, and by repeatedly invoking their commitment to empirical science as the route to a fair and balanced review.

Indeed, Zucker is noted for his persistent and extensive empirical investigations of cross-gendered phenomenon, with the significant exception of treatment effectiveness studies. Nevertheless, his data serve to distinguish him from many of his clinical colleagues, who offer a different perspective on cross-gendered life and whose work is less often represented in empirical terms and more often recorded through the rhetorical strategies of the case report. Difficult though it may be to reckon with these differing modes of data collection, it seems to me that the dominance of empirical data (data that are most often reduced to behavioral terms, that in turn reflect the behavioral dictates of the treatment strategies employed by Zucker and his colleagues) has skewed our vision, and may not afford the kind of complexity that is necessary to understand cross-gendered phenomena.

But more important, in my view, are the ways in which these empirical findings follow on numerous unquestioned presuppositions and claims about gender. This matter seems especially important when taking up pleas for social change made by nonnormative people who are rarely supported by empirical findings. In this light, are empirical findings where we should be looking? At this juncture, might we not benefit from a departure, a deconstruction, and then move from there?

A social or developmental lag has opened between the formal written discourse (empirically based) and the day-to-day clinical work that is undertaken with feminine boys. Within my professional and supervising experience there is a greater appreciation for variety, and even something of a clinical grass-roots movement that promotes the possibilities and potentialities of childhood gender variance.[3] A particularly interesting example of this movement is the Children's National Medical Center in Washington, D.C., a national outreach group that began in 1998 for parents of gender-variant children. Summarizing the overriding ethic of the center, Edgardo Menvielle, a child psychiatrist, recently stated, "The goal is for the child to be well adjusted, healthy and have good self-esteem. What's not important is molding their gender."[4]

This modern shift in the clinical approach to boyhood femininity has been largely undertheorized. This gap may not signify much beyond the time that lies between the forces of social change, clinical redress, and our reflections on such change. Time ticks, though, with a relative tock, and given the remarkable advances of feminist theory and the impact of such theorizing on psychology in general, one is once again reminded of the strong arm of regulatory anxiety as it muscles masculinity, keeping it unquestioned.

Binary Force

Masculinity advances largely by appeal to the necessary reproduction of discrete and complementary genders: masculinity and femininity. The claim of this binary precedes any boy: boys will be boys by not being girls. As Robert Stoller put it, "The first order of business in being a man is don't be a woman."[5]

The claims of the binary are so powerfully compelled that they are unthought as natural and essential. Gender is routinely conflated with anatomy, and gender is routinely conflated with that which produces our desires and personality traits. Male traits are linked with the desire for female traits, in keeping with the model of heterosexual complementarity, and so it goes. Social order, it is claimed, rests on the reproduction of this masculine-feminine gender complementarity. Boys become boys through the reproduction of fathering, which is presumed to follow on heterosexual desire. It is presumed that a life lived off the rungs of this normative ladder—nonheterosexual, nonmatrimonial, non–child rearing, nonbinary—follows on pathology, and will result in despair.

The punishments for not heeding the demands of this normative compact also compel our belief in the binary's natural authority. Retribution for gender crossing can be extreme, even deadly. Recently, in a case that garnered national attention, fifteen-year-old Lawrence King, a boy who wore makeup and fingernail polish, was shot and murdered, allegedly by a fourteen-year-old boy whom Lawrence had asked to be his Valentine. Taunting, abuse, and disruption had, it seems, become a way of life for Lawrence, who at the time of his death was living in a group home and treatment center for "crisis" kids. It seems his alleged murderer also had his share of troubles, including a history of family violence. Taunting and abuse can be a daily feature of adolescent life: homophobia and misogyny run through school halls. Clearly, though, something went fatally awry in this case. And one is left to ask why there was no one, why there was no social system to do a better job of helping Lawrence and his alleged murderer.

I am reminded here of Mitchell, a boy I saw after his kindergarten teacher told his parents during a midyear parent-teacher conference that "this *kind* of boy" didn't fit in "this kind of private prep school." It seemed he was "too pudgy," "too colorful," had "too much to say," often in a "most animated way," and that, above all, he felt too much; "sometimes he even cries." Mitchell's parents brought him to see me as they considered moving him to a different school, and because they were concerned about the lingering effects of the teacher's disdain. As Mitchell's father put it in our first meeting, "How much of her hate did he take in?"

The parents spoke directly about their son's femininity, and while they were concerned about his welfare, they were not especially troubled by his gender variance. They were quite clear that they were not seeking a consultation to correct his gender; instead, they wanted to know how to help him feel less injured by the ways others experienced him.

They found him to be a "sweet, loving boy," whom they understood to be "overly sensitive." His mother reported that Mitchell had always been sensitive to noise, color, and smells. She said, "It's like he is a sensation magnet." He could in fact easily become overwhelmed, though this was abating somewhat as he got older. They wondered about how his increased sensitivity might have influenced his gender experience. For example, they thought that Mitchell might gravitate toward girls as playmates because they were less rough and more accepting of his sensitivities.

In my first consultation with Mitchell, after we spoke about his school ("It is so strict"; "The toys are so boring"; "Music is so good; do you know Bach?"), he set out to draw a cake. He "decorated" it with bright pink frosting and "orange sprinkles." I commented that it seemed quite the opposite of how he was talking about his school. He replied, "Oh, no, Mrs. R. [his teacher] wouldn't like it. Anyhow, cake makes you fat." He then drew a series of blue stripes beginning at the top of the cake and running down to the end of the paper. I said that it looked as if the cake was crying. He replied, "No, cakes don't cry." I then asked whether the cake was in jail. He looked at me curiously and said, "Cakes don't go to jail!" I said that in fact that was true, but that sometimes pink boys did get in trouble. And that sometimes boys who are in trouble cry.

Another curious look. Another drawing. This one in pencil: a rather well-rendered metronome, accompanied by a rambling story about Bach. As I listened, I began to wonder whether he thought his music teacher *was* Bach, but no matter, he was quite taken with the idea of music making. I asked him whether he knew the word *Baroque*. He did not. I explained that Bach had lived during a time when people liked a lot of color and were extravagant with their sprinkles. He allowed that that would be "nice."

I saw Mitchell for three more sessions. During those visits Mitchell played with a range of toys, including ones that many boys would have disregarded or shunned, like dolls and a dollhouse, which he enjoyed rearranging. He drew miniature pictures and carefully taped them to the dollhouse walls. The play was quite creative and involved many elements and story lines that principally involved domestic and aesthetic concerns—narratives one might normatively link with femininity. During this play Mitchell never "named" his gender. He did not refer to himself either as a boy or a girl, and I was not sure whether it was much on his mind; was he sincerely lost in the play, or was it avoidant?

When I brought his lack of gender naming to his attention, he said that sometimes kids made fun of him and called him names. He reported these interpersonal experiences as though he was somewhat confused by how he was perceived. But curiously, he still did not name himself "boy" or "girl." I found myself wondering whether he did not feel himself to be "mixed" rather than binary. Was he also confused that there is not a way to be seen as such? He said that kids could be "rigid"—a word that I was sure was not his own, perhaps one he had gotten from his parents—but, I allowed that it was hard to feel judged, and that sometimes a person did not feel like he or she fit with the rules. I suggested that sometimes creativity even led some people to change the rules, and linked this thought to an art book in my office in which he had shown interest—a book that illustrated the progression in painting from realism to impressionism to modern nonfigurative painting and minimalism. (One of his paintings for the dollhouse was Pollockesque, another mimicked Agnes Martin's signature lines.)

When I met with his parents after these consultations, I concurred with the decision to move Mitchell to a different school. I gave them some information about parent support groups for gender-variant children. We talked at length about how to hold open a space for Mitchell to reflect on his experience of difference. I suggested that they might want to be especially keen to take note of those times when Mitchell might feel shame. Mostly, though, I listened to them and felt assured that Mitchell was protected and loved, and that their reflective capacities were good enough to help this boy. They seemed possessed of the ability to read the social life of gender and to look for those moments of social transformation and malleability that would allow this boy to find his variant way.

I found, though, that I kept coming back to the metronome. I even went to the *Oxford English Dictionary*, where I found that *metronome* derives from the Greek *metron*, to measure, and *nomos*, law. To be measured by the law; was that what Mitchell was trying to tell me? That the tick of the law had entered him? And the question that followed for me was How do we help children grasp the contrapuntal (as Bach might have it) discourse of law?

Yes, the social order of the binary rules; it is the law that ticks loudest. But modern reconsiderations and shifting social forces have ticked in return. Gender is being rethought, and newly lived. And binary schematics are insufficient to account for this new life.[6]

Gender identity—the internal conviction regarding one's gender classification—is no longer positioned as a fixed essence at the core of a person. While gender is constructed as a rigid binary, and while many people freely identify themselves as masculine or feminine, their experience nevertheless roams, in the language of chaos theory, as a free radical, policed by norms though it may be. As the psychoanalyst Adrienne Harris puts it, once again using the language of chaos theory, gender "softly assembles," and is open thereby to shifting states, iden-tifications, and social expectations.

All identifications are part of a complex system wherein identifications stimulate intricate feedback loops. (Imagine a loppty-loop Rube Goldberg machine that illustrates how seemingly simple structures are always the product of convoluted pathways.) Consider how genders are constructed through the transfer of various traits (long hair, short hair), codes (dresses, pants), behaviors (sensitive, rough), and fantasies (surrender, domination). Once transferred, these internalizations come to rest (to the degree that any internalization comes to rest) in exquisite, unique, inner worlds, the staging ground for significant personal patterns and differences. (Imagine an attic you cannot keep orderly no matter how hard you try.)

This turn toward the chaotic complexity of gender speaks to the place within masculinity for feminine masculinity (the place in the attic where dresses and cowboy hats end up in the same box). Such contemplation also invites the reconsideration of the supposed link between gender coherence and well-being; there is much more latitude than has been previously presumed, and surely more latitude than that which directs the diagnosis of GID.

Still, modernity's march in the name of difference and variation has been, at best, inconsistently successful. Boys and men blurring the binary continue to stick like a fish bone in our psychological throat. We cough in accord with the dictates of the binary. We struggle still to clear our throats of a legacy of exclusion and grievance, despite what is by now seventy-five years of feminist critique of the masculine-feminine divide and almost twenty-five years of the queer dismantling of gender.

A striking example along these lines can be taken from the literature on feminine boys, and the language used to diagnose them. Consider how the psychoanalyst Richard Friedman identifies a group of boys whom he says are suffering within the "syndrome" of "juvenile un-masculinity." He describes these boys as feminine but not so feminine as to qualify for a GID diagnosis. George Rekers, a psychologist, also employs this descriptor, providing an intriguing example of the discursive intersection between the traditions of developmental psychiatry and Christian psychology. This "syndrome" of "juvenile un-masculinity" corresponds as well to what Zucker and Bradley coined a "sub-clinical manifestation" of gender identity disorder. Variance becomes "sub-clinical" via ex officio medical rhetoric. Gender is fixed as a binary system of conformity, variance is erased, and the marginal, even the marginal marginal, boy is deemed pathological.[7]

All genders are plagued by anxiety. All genders lack coherence. All genders are colored by defensive operations and fictive performance. In particular, genders follow on the ways in which we split our selves and others into rigid gendered patterns that follow in accord with cultural dualisms, as the psychoanalyst Muriel Dimen has often pointed out.[8] The regulatory regime moves with particular vigilance and diagnostic overdrive in the face of feminine masculinity. Throughout the discourse on feminine boys, masculinity is not queried; masculinity *is,* and is therefore diagnostic. Justice and expert judgment do not proceed through an account of masculinity's social and historical construction. Variance is read as disturbance or illness; rarely is variance recognized for the ways in which it speaks to the range of that which is normal, and never is it read for its potential, or relished for its ideality.

Femininity as Symptom

The diagnostic rhetoric that corrals feminine boys propagates and perpetuates the anxious assessment of a boy's bonds with his parents. Is the boy properly aligned? Has he identified with his father? Is that identification robust and competitive? Has he separated from his mother? Is that separation secured through the proper degree of dis-identification from that which is maternal and feminine?

For the feminine boy this separation is disrupted by his continued attachment to and identification with his mother. Traditionally, this maternal/feminine identification has been read as a symptom.[9] The dis-eased transfer of femininity to a boy has most often been depicted as coming from an arresting mother. As the psychiatrist Richard Green advised, "You've got to get these mothers out of the way. Feminine kids don't need their mothers around."[10] Green's blunt advice follows on the ways in which psychologists have repeatedly posited a course of development that presumes early trauma and forecasts maturational difficulties for boys who identify with their mothers.

The arresting mother remains remarkably constant given the ideological differences that separate the traditional theorists who have written about feminine boys. Differing and even contradictory dynamic explanations are offered for this psychogenic mother, and yet she remains on the whole consistent, whether she is depicted as lacking proper maternal empathy or as excessively symbiotic, whether she is overgratifying, and thereby intensifying separation anxiety, or overbearing, resulting in poor social conditioning, whether she traumatically transfers unresolved trauma catalyzing separation anxiety and aggression, or lacks social proficiency and adequate affect regulation, fostering an insecure mother-child bond.[11]

However this pathogenic mother is configured—through lack or profusion—she arrests, consumes, and disorients. Traditional developmental theory does not afford the possibility that a boy could try to construct a feminine identity along with his mother (and others). Rather, he is seen as stopped and subsumed within his mother's troubled being-mind (her traumas, her anxiety, her depression), and his femininity is interpreted as a snared regressive lack of separation.

There is no consideration given to relational transfers that are not the result of dominating or traumatic intromissions. There is no consideration given to the possibility that a boy could identify with his mother and through processes of internalization and gender mobility constitute his own feminine subjectivity. There is no consideration given to relational exchange or relational bids (the reach, the transfer from one to another) that are founded in a loving mother-son bond. As to matters of separation, I do think that feminine boys often experience difficulty in separating from their mothers and attaching to their fathers. I do not, however, agree with the presumption that this mother-son father-son configuration is necessarily pathogenic, nor that these boys are on the margin only as the consequence of trauma or relational insufficiency.

Trauma as seen through the lens of the norm may actually be a mistaken perception of the variant human's quest to undo the norm. As Judith Butler so eloquently puts it, "There is a certain departure from the human that takes place in order to start the process of remaking the human."[12] The departure of the feminine boy is routinely taken for trauma; but trauma for whom, him or the normative order?

Pain's Registration

The urgency of a clinical discourse that theorizes social regulations beyond the impress of punishment, or the reductive rhetoric of social roles, is perhaps best illustrated in discussions of pain as advanced by traditional theorists of boyhood femininity. Pain as described by Nicolosi, Rekers, and Green is the social pain of punishment, humiliation, and shame, pain that is seen as coming from outside social forces. And although they do not theorize the internalization of such pain, they do warn of the pain of difference, the pain and shame felt by the feminine boy in the face of social force.

Pain as it is described and theorized by Zucker and Bradley, and most comprehensively by the child psychologist Susan Coates and her colleagues, includes the pain of social punishment as well as the pain of difference, but it also includes trauma that is transferred from mother to son; pain that is distinguished as intergenerationally introjected and is seen to be the catalyst of boyhood femininity. Coates and her colleagues claim that GID follows on the ways in which a boy's mind is ensnared by a traumatized mother. The boy is thereby robbed of his sovereignty and his own autonomy.

Pain in one instance is seen to reach socially from outside in, and in another to reach psychologically from inside out. In one case, gender results in pain, the pain of difference that follows on normative injunction. In the other, gender is the result of pain, the pain of the interned. At stake here, as Butler points out, are considerations of the feminine boy's mental freedom. On the one hand, freedom—the expression of gender difference—garners pain (the pathologization that greets the feminine boy). On the other hand, freedom is curbed or disturbed by pain (the recruited mind).

Surely we must remain open to the recognition of pain in another. Yet the traditional discourse fails to reckon more fully with the social, and thereby too easily conflates pain with resistance to normative regulation. How the feminine boy challenges social order is too easily mistaken for pain. The resistance and play of the nonnormative are too easily seen as lacking in freedom, as opposed to granting more autonomy to the categories we employ toward understanding the human. The fantasy play that colors nonnormative sociality, and the closets within which nonnormative bonds are forged, are not affirmed as legitimate ways to imagine (boys, it is said, fantasize *this* way, not *that* way).

The clinical risk of pathologization calls for a more perplexed and humble approach, one that does not mistake social consensus for well-being, and one that is not so assured in its attribution of pain. If one follows basic psychoanalytic presuppositions as to the ways in which fantasy is intertwined with formative relationships and the making of a body, and if it is also accepted that genders evolve in a relational world, then one would have to be open to considering the ways in which bodies and genders are open to a range of fantastic expressions and relational dynamics, including traumatic intromissions, as well as nonnormative openings. Furthermore, if one accepts that relational dynamics create varying intimate relationships and spaces through which genders emerge, spaces that are more or less coherent and more or less organizing and loving, spaces that inflect the manner of the transfer of gendered fantasies and attributes, then one also has to be open to considering the ways in which the construction of gender is open to a range of well-being and coherence.

Yet on the other hand, if one accepts that the human is never outside social regulation (even before birth, even in resistance), and if it is further accepted that genders are formed and constituted by cultural norms, then one is left to question the attribution of originary pain. There is no pure psychology of the protagonists (mother and feminine son). There is no pure authority of the past. Intromissions, both traumatic and nurturing, are always and already socially and historically under way and open to a variety of nuance and complication (even contradiction). We cannot speak, as do the traditional theorists, of boyhood femininity, with such psychic specificity.

Without a theory that locates the perception and assessment of pain within the constituting frame of the social, we are left with no social demarcation for this clinical scene. The ethical insufficiency that issues from this lack is that it leaves the therapist inadequately prepared to question whether counterresistance or counteranxiety is being repeated through normative presumption and reactive pathologization.

Paradox, Norms, and Variant Possibility

Here it is imperative to reflect on the fact that there can be no empirical norm without variance. Norms have morphed into that which is considered essential and essentially coherent, shadowing our ability to appreciate variance, to reflect justly, to respond with empathy, and even to respond within the pleasure of play.

New sustaining ideals are being articulated. New possibilities for recognition are in play. The rigid necessity of the social order has been called into question. Psyches need not be fenced in the same old cage. Genders need not follow on the same old identification with the same-sex parent. Paradoxical bodies may stand as such. These new ideals have been slow in coming to how we think about children's attachment patterns. Boys, it is still said, identify with their fathers and separate from their mothers. We are now left to ask whether this assessment is overestimated as the ground upon which masculinity is built (through a kind of one-to-one identificatory correspondence; boys will be like their fathers, not like their mothers). Masculinity is just as likely to be transferred from mother to son as it is from father to son. Femininity is just as likely to be transferred from father to son as it is from mother to son.

Gendered codes, behaviors, and traits circulate and transform through mini–social intromissions within modern families—families that, in turn, are part of a larger and more complex social field. As the psychoanalyst and family therapist Virginia Goldner has repeatedly suggested, the family is less a fortress, more a clearinghouse, open to the currency of social forces; the "outside" society is indelibly "inside" the family.

The "outside," though, has remained largely outside the attachment theory and the social learning theory that underscore the traditional psychological discourse on boyhood femininity. While "social" does indeed qualify the learning in social learning theory, the society that appears is whittled down to normative order. Consider, for example, that Zucker and Bradley telescope the social into "social reinforcement," concentrating on "parental gender socialization" and a parent's ability to encourage "psychosocially appropriate gender identification."[13] Through this manner of behavioral reduction—which is amply reflected in the works of Nicolosi and Rekers—social and normative forces are uncritically reduced to one and the same. There is no complex social field. There is no complex family. There is no variance. There is no resistance (only impropriety). There is no paradox (only pathology).

Perhaps even more troubling, though, is the absence of the "outside" in attachment theory, as it has been applied toward our thinking about feminine boys (arguably the most influential epistemology within the traditional discourse on feminine boys, and children in general). Attachment-inflected relational theories coupled with feminist theory and critical theory (hence, the social) have been employed with considerable élan toward our modern understanding of femininity, and of gender development in general.

Theorizing about feminine boys has yet to take such a turn. Attachment as a discourse and research tradition has, remarkably, not considered gender as an identity category. Attachment-inflected developmental theories more often than not move in step with normative gender presumptions. The family in these attachment-inflected theories is the traditional family that has always held center stage in psychology. (Tronick's recent work is a promising shift, as he begins at least to examine attachment as shaped by culture.)

Relational-attachment patterns and styles are gendered: Boys separate, girls attach. And they do so via affect states and relational bids that mimic traditional presumptions regarding masculinity and femininity: girls cling via hysteria and brightly colored sentiments (sugar and spice and all things nice). These feminine "symptoms" are often read as indicative of relational breakdown and distress, and in turn they are routinely linked with disorders of separation and regulation. Boys bolt via obsessional control, aggression, and muted emotions (snips and snails and puppy dog tails). These "behaviors" are less often read as indicative of relational trouble, but when they are, they are linked with disorders of attention and attachment.

Masculinity as Mantle

If, as Joan Riviere has suggested, femininity is a masquerade, one that is ingenuously carried forth with a bright mask of emotion and rests on the repression of aggression, then masculinity might be looked upon as a mantle, worn with the appropriate expression of aggression abetted by emotional and sentimental restraint.[14]

Depictions of feminine boys rest in large measure on accounts of their conflicts with aggression and what is seen as their countering emotional sensitivity. They tumble too little. They feel too much. Feminine boys' reluctance to fight, to tussle, to risk injury is read as a harbinger of a compromised masculine identity, impotence, and failed phallic heterosexual adulthood. Consider Rekers's depiction of Craig, a four-year-old boy, who "displayed high rates of pronounced feminine mannerisms, gestures, and gait," "was dominated by feminine topics," and "avoided boyish play, being both unable and unwilling to participate in rough-and-tumble games of other boys his age." Craig "declined to defend himself when with his peers, and he expressed fears of getting hurt."[15] Craig's disinclination to play with other boys is characterized by Rekers as compulsive and rigid. One could wonder whether Craig might have suggested the opposite, had he been able to: that boys' persistent pursuit of rough-and-tumble play was compulsive and rigid, and moreover open to escalation that often culminates in violence. What, too, Craig might have asked, about the gripping expectation that boys endure pain while not expressing it as part of play?[16] Zucker and Bradley in their overview of the phenomenology of GID speak of the ways in which feminine boys "appear to have trouble distinguishing between rough-and-tumble play and intent to hurt."[17] A curious assertion given that hurt does often occur in rough play, and is often intended (however unconsciously). Might they be confusing "trouble distinguishing" from trouble dissociating, trouble keeping quiet, trouble not naming the hurt, and trouble enduring pain?[18]

Aggression must be displayed, activity must be maintained, and passivity must be repudiated. These lessons have traditionally been situated between father and son; masculinity follows on the transfer of aggression between father and son. From there, the dilemma plays out further between boys and boys. Sadism and mastery (threads of the mantle) are often relational gambits. In this way, boys wrangle toward their proper phallic stance: aggressive, active, heterosexual, not receptive, not passive, not homosexual.

The clinical psychologist Joseph Nicolosi, for example, pointedly tells parents of a feminine boy of the "statistical probabilities that their son would eventually involve himself in homosexual behavior."[19] He then makes a direct link to the necessity of an active father-son bond as a means of preventing homosexuality. This bond is given limited illustration beyond what could be called paternal behaviorism (the modeling and reinforcement of traditionally masculine activities). While the active and aggressive bond of fathers and sons is put forward as a means of working through, the dicey terrain of such effort is never actually described. Aggressive prescription, dire warnings, and punishments are detailed, but no working through, belying the role of unmetabolized aggression and sadism in the construction of normative masculinity.

Behavioral Paternalism and Melancholy Consequence

The legacy of this aggressive regulation is well illustrated in the treatment of men who suffer through internalized behavioral paternalism. I have had the opportunity to treat many young men, who come into treatment in conflict over their jobs. They are typically in high-paying traditionally patriarchal jobs, in which they enact a false self-competency, sometimes with spectacular results, but fall simultaneously into a dulling depression that over time, like a slow-moving arthritis, can have crippling effects. Analysis almost always reveals that the young man forswore a more creative and less traditional career route that he felt to be inadequately masculine.

Consider my patient Ted, who entered treatment just as he became a partner in an architecture firm. He presented a litany of physical complaints, most prominent among them headaches, back pain, insomnia, and impotence. Soon into the analysis a full-blown clinical depression surfaced. Much could be said about this treatment and how we came to untangle Ted's despair, but of particular note in this context were our efforts to sort through his finding himself in a realm of work that he described as "old-boy-boxed-in."

Ted had a degree in art history from a well-known liberal

arts college, and had been encouraged by several of his professors to pursue a career in art. In addition to studying history, he also painted. His understandable anxiety about whether he could make a living as an artist or as an academic was compounded by the unexpected death of his father shortly after Ted finished college. In what we came to understand as one of the consequences of Ted's melancholic incorporation of his father, he quickly applied to and was accepted at an architecture school, which happened to be at the same university where his father had studied law.

More precisely, we came to understand that long before his father's death, Ted had effected this melancholic incorporation. Early on, he had rejected his father but simultaneously incorporated him as a model of never-possible perfection. His father was imposing, handsome, authoritarian, and accomplished. He found Ted's femininity troubling and often "coached" him in more normative boyhood activities. Ted often came up against the shadow of this object, at once desiring it and rejecting it. In keeping with the psychoanalyst Richard Isay's analysis of father-son dynamics for homosexual men, it seemed likely to me that the rejection that colored this father-son relationship had been mutually constructed. Father and son together worked to manage (disavow, repress, dissociate) not only Ted's femininity but also the desire this gendered identity spoke—a desire that slipped the knot of the homosexual taboo that underscores Oedipal resolution.[20] The desire is thereby foreclosed, shut out, and closeted. As Freud would have it, "By taking flight into the ego, love [a love that cannot be named or given up] escapes extinction."[21] This flight, though, casts a shadow, and under the shadow of this foreclosed yet not forsaken love, melancholia blooms.

It was of course important to analyze how this melancholic incorporation colored and constricted Ted's relationships. But it was equally important to understand how this paternal incorporation operated to constrain Ted's creativity and daring. Repeatedly, Ted found himself working on large-scale corporate projects, office buildings principally, and working in turn with the corporate clients who retained his services. While he found the scale of these projects exciting, he tired of them as formulaic (foreclosed).

Slowly, we began to make links with the ways in which Ted was living through his incorporation of his father, and how that incorporation shadowed his work life. Slowly as well, he began to shift his focus. He joined forces with a new female associate at his firm, and together they won a competition to design a theater. That partnership blossomed, and one day as he was recounting the pleasure of a project on which they were working, he recalled his efforts at rebuilding a playhouse on his family's property that had been used for many years by his older brothers. When his brothers moved on to other interests, the house fell into his hands. Laying claim to the house, Ted set about redecorating, as he described it, "a la *Bewitched*, an homage to Samantha, very sixties housewife." He made curtains, he painted, he decorated the walls with appliquéd daisies; his crowning achievement was wall-to-wall shag carpeting made from remnants he had salvaged from the trash. He undertook this project in secret, wishing to unveil it to his family upon completion. Unveil it he did, and Ted laughed as he said, "Can you imagine? They were horrified—amused, but horrified."

As we spoke about this project, Ted insinuated that domestic creations were evidence of a faulty boy, one who was weak and mediocre. But his childhood projects, such as the play-house, hardly struck me as mediocre or weak. As I pointed out, such projects, and the manner in which he completed them, seemed to be fueled by complete seriousness and passion. One does not stitch wall-to-wall carpeting out of remnants without drive. Eventually we began to see Ted's wish to demean his visions as a defense against his love of extravagance and flam-boyance. As Ted put it, "You notice, I wasn't interested in June Cleaver; it was Samantha who did it for me."

It became important to understand that Ted's visions were not solely domestic. In fact, he often set out to undomesti-cate the domestic. Along these lines, Ted and his partner took on a pro bono job creating the set for a charity drag ball. He brought in pictures to show me what they had created. He had never done this before, and I was mindful of the unveiling of the playhouse. As I looked at the photos, I laughed over their outlandish aspect and the zany enthusiasm they seemed to convey.

I noticed, though, that Ted seemed eager for me to hand the photos back, as though we should not linger over the images. I brought this to his attention, and with some reflection he agreed with my observation. As we worked to understand his response, he revealed that he was concerned that I was too permissive. But in addition, he feared that my permissiveness would implode and that I would pull away from my enjoyment of his creations. It was in this way that we began to understand an important family dynamic. It seems that his parents and his brothers, his father in particular, often appeared to take pleasure in Ted's capacity to create larger-than-life spectacles. But after a while, Ted felt them grow self-conscious about such enjoyment and pull away. In fact, I realized that what I was enjoying was that the photographed images were extreme and foolish in their fantasy, and thereby more enjoyable than everyday fantasies. As Susan Sontag has suggested, such visions are liberated from moral relevance, duty, and seriousness.[22]

Vision that sees around everyday regulation is regularly met with regulatory anxiety. The moral commitment of what might be called regulatory rationalism is privileged. And normativity that is mistaken for cohesion is enforced and internalized. Repression and depression often follow. I have found it to be the case, as I described with Ted, that analysis of this depression frequently leads one toward the melancholic internalization of the paternal. This internalization need not be solely based on a boy's experience with his father. In fact, I think it more likely that this introjection is a distillation and combination of many voices that speak and act through a kind of behavioral paternalism. In other words, this internalization that is distilled as paternal is a combined voice including father's, mother's, sibling's, teacher's, coach's, minister's, and so on. This social intromission voices a behavioral command or a demand for adaptation by which the boy must comply in order to avoid cruelty, condemnation, and pain. This voice is unconsciously reinforced as a never possible perfection, one that is simultaneously desired (for its strength), admired (for its normative moral privilege), and grievously rejected as unloving.

With these ideas in mind, in the course of an analysis, one is then in the position of understanding the frequent and turbulent pattern of a man's quest to embody the paternal, to secure the paternal through desire, and to reject the paternal as unloving. The analysis of these paternal dynamics is often at the heart of our efforts to understand the difficulty men encounter in forming lasting attachments with other men, and as I have illustrated in my discussion of Ted, also aids in the understanding of men's ability to establish a satisfying work life.

The therapeutic work I described with Ted is to some degree a redress of the traditional presumption that masculinity is a site of emotional disavowal. Feminine boys present a challenge to that ideal, and certainly it is not without meaning that most often such boys come to the attention of mental health authorities because it is felt that they are too sensitive, they cry too easily, they are too flamboyant; in short, they are too expressive in a variety of ways. They upset what the philosopher Arnold Davidson refers to as the "affective geography of gender."[23] The colorful, sentimental, and hysterical themes that sometimes inform the play of feminine boys threaten the rugged, tight-lipped, stoic terrain of masculinity.

Psychologists routinely fault feminine boys for their emotional states. Feminine boys are described as "whiny," "mincing," "weak," "just like a girl." Such modes of address not only signal the demeaned status of these boys (one is entitled to speak of them in such degrading ways, just as one is entitled to demean girls) but they also illustrate that anguish (the grievance of the melancholic) as a bid toward social redress is shunned.

The psychological discourse on feminine boys is a staging ground for the regimented regulation of masculine expressivity. In an intriguing collection of writings on narratives of masculinity and emotion, cultural studies theorists Milette Shamir and Jennifer Travis argue that this turn from masculine sentimental expression is in keeping with the work of separating genders "along the line of emotional expressivity: a feminine mode marked by effusion of sentiment and its representational conventions, in contrast to a masculine mode where affect is presented negatively, in terms of disavowal and repression."[24]

One is left to question the goals of adjustment that shape the traditional therapeutic techniques employed with feminine boys—techniques that generally rely on behavioral desensitization. For example, the gradual and often coercive removal of toys and activities associated with femininity. This attempted erasure of the feminine is coupled with coaching the boy in normative masculine play. Yet have we exercised adequate sensitivity to the pain and humiliation faced by feminine boys? Have we too quickly overlooked and failed to relish their particular idealities? Can we create a holding environment for these boys? Can we dedicate ourselves to creating an ever larger and more variegated culture? Do our current theories even begin to approach the changes made within modern families, and the moments of cultural malleability that are open to the feminine boy?

Such malleability rests, at least in part, on our ability to question that which we have considered psychic coherence. Perhaps psychic coherence is not all that it is cracked up to be. Too often analysts have looked at variance and called it illness. Too often analysts have failed to note the ways in which the pain of fragmentation is simultaneously the variant construction of a way out. Too often we have looked upon the trauma of difference and sought to cure it through the clumsy application of similarity.

Transforming Nexus

My clinical experience with what is by now scores of feminine boys and their families, along with men, such as Ted, who have a history of boyhood femininity, has afforded me the opportunity to consider how feminine boys and their parents create moments within which the social order of gender is challenged. Within such moments a transforming nexus of gender transfer and malleability is created. Gender is resignified through collective fantasies and terms; bonds are forged. These bonds, this challenge to the prevailing order, can be created through a wide range of relational dynamics, fantasies, material conditions, and beliefs (as is true for any parent-child bond). Slipping the symbolic can occur through freedom as well as through alienation. Moments of malleability open through loving protection, just as they open through malignant seduction. Speaking to power may follow mental freedom or mental anguish. How, and whether, a transforming nexus is fashioned is as individual as any parent-son pair.

The creation of this transforming nexus is undertaken with both parents, but it may have a particular significance for mothers and their feminine sons. In direct contrast to Richard Green's suggestion that feminine boys do not need their mothers, it has been my overwhelming clinical experience that those boys who can, along with their mothers, create a holding environment fare much better as they move into the outside world. Across time, this mother-son dialogic is internalized and comes to serve as a voice that privileges the boy's peculiar ideality, offers solace in the face of normative cruelty, and holds out the hope these boys need to imagine themselves otherwise. This internalization is not solely based on a boy's experience with his mother. This introjection is more likely to be a distillation and combination of many parental voices, including grandmothers', aunts', sisters', teachers', father's, uncles', television characters', and so on.

Again, in contrast to Green's assertion regarding the need

to separate feminine boys from their mothers, I have consistently found it to be the case that those boys who cannot establish this holding transforming nexus do not fare nearly as well as they move forward into the world of school and others outside their family. Many permutations of this parent-child breakdown can occur, and many psyches follow. But one pattern that I have had frequent opportunity to analyze is of abject young men caught in a web of loss; this melancholic condition is usually accompanied by a narcissistic presentation.

Consider Kyle, a young man who came into treatment following a string of affairs with mostly older men that had all ended in turmoil. Kyle felt undervalued, the men overburdened. These affairs where often fueled by the use of various intoxicants, principally amphetamines and euphorics, leading to periods of orgiastic abandon and a fleeting sense of richness and expansion. The affairs ended as Kyle, fearful of an encroaching separation and state of dissolution, sought more and more attention and care, presumably overwhelming the object. Enraged and unable to link his anxieties with his own state of genuine abjection and internal emptiness, he focused on ensuring and enhancing his exterior desirability.

Kyle was a traditionally handsome young man, and with the effort of exercise, diet, and the equipoise of the unfashionable fashionable, he garnered a great deal of attention. However, I was immediately struck by the ways in which this attractive surface seemed forced and perhaps supercilious. These were not welcome countertransference responses. I questioned my own experience of envy. I questioned my own vulnerability to encroaching age, mortality, and waning desirability. Yet over and over again as Kyle's efforts to garner attention did not hold, we began to understand that there was something about this narcissistic surface that in fact was born not out of desire but rather out of lack. This was not an embodiment made in or played in the presence of another. The fantasies that might come into play in the stylization of embodiment were surprisingly shallow. Indeed, Kyle's gender experience was strikingly empty, only spoken of as purchased, and dictated by the hierarchy of designer cachet. Similarly, outside of the sexual abandon of euphoric merger, he preferred the quick release of masturbation that was achieved while watching pornography and seemed rather indiscriminate and largely void of underlying fantasy.

Through many years of what was at times a remarkably turbulent analysis, marked by periods of rage in the face of felt neglect and anxious demands for more and yet more, I began through my countertransference experience of Kyle's efforts to dissolve any boundary there may have been between us, to understand that there had been no truly maternal space for Kyle as a child. Key here was my feeling of near constant intrusion. At times, it seemed that Kyle was everywhere: at the theater, the gym, the pharmacy, the restaurant, the lecture, the museum. He avidly followed the public career of my partner, eager to discuss dimensions of my personal life seemingly before I had had time to experience them. This feeling state was encapsulated in a dream I had in which Kyle was peering through the glass doors that open into the lobby of the apartment building where I live. My associations to the permeability of glass, the wish not only to see in, but the desperate and fantastic effort to get in, reinforced my growing feeling, paraphrasing what the philosopher Slavoj Zizek might have called the object that came too close, an ominous seductive object that suffocates.[25] This association helped me to understand, in accord with some of what Kyle had begun to describe about his early life, that he had had both too much and too little of his mother, who seemed enshrined in her own melancholia.

Kyle's mother was a young South American woman who had married a somewhat older Englishman. Soon after their marriage, they immigrated to America. She seemed always to be in mourning for her past, her country of origin, and a life that was consistently held forward as better, more cultured, and more civilized. She lived in a cloud of neurasthenic illness: headaches, vertigo, palpitations, and tremors. Kyle's father was positioned as a failure and a boor, and together mother and son, in something of a narcissistic merger, ruled the father insignificant. This merger, however, was not an opening but a depressive melancholic withdrawal.

The pull toward this melancholic position was palpable and powerful throughout much of Kyle's analysis. There were moments when I questioned my ability to go forward, to continue in the face of his pressing despair and desire. The pull and suck of a merged collapse were truly overwhelming. The emergence and recurrence of periods of abject dissolution only reinforced my doubt, as Kyle faced what the philosopher Elizabeth Grosz has called "the absolute mortality and vulnerability of the subject's relation to and dependence on the object."[26] Time and again we were pulled into a vortex of fragility, as Kyle's narcissistic defenses gave way to his experiential emptiness.

Key to allowing this melancholic position to emerge in the treatment, but not giving in to its darker pull, were our efforts also to grasp the sensual and generative desire for another; this is the progressive push of melancholia. Our work in this regard accrued, and over time we were able productively to move from this progressive wish to better understand Kyle's abjection and narcissistic defenses. Our analysis of this maternal melancholia gradually afforded Kyle the opportunity to imagine, approach, and to some extent begin to construct an encounter with innerness that he could bring to another, an innerness that spoke of possibility as opposed to abjection.

Similar to my experience with other young men like Kyle, the analysis of these maternal dynamics afforded the opportunity to grasp that genders and desires are a mode of becoming, a constitutive possibility. Outside a maternal/parental space within which a feminine boy may become, he is left to construct a narcissistic approximation, caught as he is in the poignant pain of that lost space. The marginal boy is left with very little in the way of a safe return. While he may be able to turn toward a shadowed melancholic retreat from the world, he is given little in the way of a progressive push, or the license of imagination through which he might hope and work toward securing more productive attachments.

In contrast, my clinical experience suggests that feminine boys and their parents who can establish a holding transformative nexus fare much better as they move into the world. Key here is helping parents to allow and reflect upon their child's needs for gender practice, gender construction, the performative play of gender theater, and the concomitant normative counterreactions that cross-gender play evokes. Parents who can keep one foot in the play and one eye toward normative counterreaction allow their child to bring into this nexus his experience of reactive shame and/or hate. He then has an opportunity to reflect on normative force and its anxious regulatory push, and to gather strength in order to push back.

Contrary to the various prognostications regarding a feminine boy's difficulty in separating from the family, my clinical experience with feminine boys, especially those who have been able to form a transforming nexus with their parents, suggests that separation does take place, and with the same degree of success and failure that one notes for most everyone. As is the case with all children, the feminine boy leaves home, is met with regulatory practice as meted out by his peers, and more often than not is motivated to make some accommodations to sustain peer relations. This is not to say that these accommodations do not lead to ways in which these boys subordinate their feminine subjectivity to avoid cruelty and pain. This is not to say that regulatory rationalism does not animate the pain of depression and create a legacy of shame. But accommodation does not stop with a one-way adjustment. There are also ways in which these boys seek to preserve their feminine identifications, to seize moments of mobility, to join forces within minority communities, and to imagine their ways into a world where the social life of gender is more malleable.

CHAPTER FOUR

Trans States

Feminine Boys and the Therapeutic Scene of Address

OVER THE PAST FIFTEEN YEARS, I HAVE REGULARLY met with parents of feminine boys, sometimes on their own, sometimes in conjunction with seeing their son. Usually, these parents find their way to me when their son has been diagnosed with gender identity disorder—a psychiatric diagnosis, based largely on the persistent belief that one is the gender other than his or her sex. By and large, these parents find the diagnosis disorienting, disturbing, and humiliating; more than one parent has referred to it as an "accusation."

Frequently these parents have gone online or to the library and have read about GID, often from multiple points of view. Typically, they know that I am a clinician and theorist critical of the GID diagnosis. They come to my office seeking a therapeutic space where they can express the ways in which they do not recognize their son, his experience of gender, and his relative well-being within the frame of gender identity disorder.

They come for consultation confused and angry, often searching their minds, questioning their motives, desires, and histories, looking for the trauma that is presumed in the diagnosis, looking for the repudiation and poor relational skills that are attributed to their son. Most often they come up empty, and even when trauma is at hand, which has been rare (I can recall two consultations in which that proved to be the case), the parents are alarmed at the treatment options offered for their child. These recommended treatments presume a social order and a regulated range of gendered experiences the parents find to be outmoded and old-fashioned.

The majority of these parents see their son as having not a psychological problem but rather a social problem: their son does not fit the social category "boy." Rather, he is a category crisis. He breaks normative dictates, and as such, his very being seeks a new social order. To the extent that they see repudiation, they see it as a matter of their child's opposition to cultural norms, not as a matter of psychological shutdown, not as a psychotic or neurotic turn from social order. It is, however, in this social zone where parents locate their son's, as well as their own, distress, as their child makes a bid to remake social categories, to seek accord from others who often recoil, relying as they do on the structure provided by normative regulation.

We might schematize this interlocutory exchange as follows:

Boy: You see me as a boy. I feel myself to be a girl, or variously girly. I ask you to recognize my subjectivity, my experience, my psychic reality, and to name it accordingly.

Other: I see you as a boy. I see you in accord with the rules of social reality. These are the normative rules by which we live. You upset the rules/roles. You upset me. I don't trust your psychic reality. You have to adapt, not me.

Not surprisingly, many of the parents I meet are confused with regard to their boy's need to adapt, and fearful of the consequences lest he not. How much should they support their child's experience of difference, and how much should they encourage by way of a more normative adaptation? How can they (should they) look toward a future?

Their worries, however, are almost always tempered by their experiences of their child's adaptation, seasoned often with daring and perspicacity. Yes, their son is sometimes faced with exclusion and hate. And yes, to see one's child repeatedly met with anxiety and resistance is indeed painful. But these parents also report that their sons rather quickly learn that their gender experience is a challenge to others' ways of thinking. Such learning probably rests at least to some degree on processes of repression and depression, further fueled by the subordination of their subjectivity (or more precisely, an aspect of their subjectivity) to the will of the majority. This is no small mater.

But at the same time, these children understand themselves to be unexpected, and sometimes unwelcome. They broker these experiences of social dissonance in a variety of ways: sometimes they adapt, sometimes they acquiesce, sometimes they create bonds with more like-minded intimates, sometimes they forge ahead by queering the conflict, putting their "queer shoulder to the wheel," as Allen Ginsberg might have had it.[1]

These queer efforts that challenge regulatory norms could be variously read as manic (gender in high relief is often manic), and hence, read further as evidence of a defense against depression or melancholia. Indeed, one might read Ginsberg's ecstatic verse in a similar manner. Or in contrast, and perhaps more precisely, in convergence, as determined, and borne forward by resolve, put into play through the bravery of difference, and the storm of mental freedom. Ginsberg found "angelheaded hipsters burning for the ancient heavenly connection to the starry dynamo in the machinery of night."[2] Bedazzled feminine boys reach for less lofty stars. Still, the pop, the sparkle, the dynamo must be seen as unconsciously overdetermined, as well as consciously practiced, flurried, in your face, and variously motivated.

There is a long queer tradition, perhaps best embodied by Wilde's conscious ideological aestheticism, as Sontag suggested, of queering the narrative through parody, irony, and theatricality.[3] There is, in short, a long tradition of being silly and extravagant—states that, on the one hand, seem quite in keeping with childhood and yet, on the other hand, become suspect as too arch, too precocious, too performed, too defensive. Perhaps. Irony is routinely employed to defend, to ward off, and to negate the will and/or ill will of another.

But irony and theatricality are also routinely employed as a challenge to established meanings and tacit rules. Might these boys have something to be theatrical about? Many of the boys I have seen over the years go on to develop interests in art, music, and dance, often with considerable talent and invention. Or might these boys learn early on that irony is a way around the grip of the regime?

Might we also see here an example of the privileging of defense, in accord with the dictates of the gender binary: obsessional defenses are more accepted, indeed often valued, in contrast to hysterical defenses. Obsessional (read masculine) defenses are less theatrical, less relational, and in turn valued for their turn "in" and their lack of demand on the other. Hysterical defenses (read feminine) are seen as less acceptable, less "well," as the theatrical hysteric reaches out toward the other, performing, reaching for relation, making a demand.

Questioning these normative views often leads parents to my office, and together with them and their sons, I have had the opportunity to rethink our clinical approach to feminine boys. There is much that I think we still do not know. But over and over again, I am struck by how these boys require us to re-think the future—especially given the ways in which the act of diagnosis is to some extent an act of predicting a future. Think-ing the future is a leap to be sure, and in this case a leap made all the more difficult by the ways we have failed to record the past. As the literary theorist Ann Cvetkovich has suggested in another context, we have no "archive of feelings," and without such an archive it is hard to bring the horizon of these boys' adulthoods into sight.[4]

We have, at this time, a limited historical accounting of boys who will be girls as they move on in life. We do not even know how early boyhood femininity is embodied and lived as these boys transition into adolescence and adulthood: For some the femininity is a mere trace; as they move into adult-hood, perhaps they are seen as particularly loving fathers. For some the boyhood femininity may be the harbinger of adult homosexuality, and the femininity that gave voice to their early desire may evolve into a variety of gendered fantasies and em-bodiments, ranging from those that are typically coded as feminine to those that are coded as masculine. For some the femininity may hold fast, it may deepen and develop toward a transgendered subjectivity expressed through a range of iden-tities, fantasies, and bodies imagined and made.

This matter of a trans future provokes considerable anxiety;

trans fantasies, trans states, trans acts, trans bodies are consistently met with fear, and with prognostications laced with fear. We have yet to find a way to speak of trans states—from the fleeting to those that linger—outside a discourse marked by a split between phobia and advocacy. We have yet to find a way to speak about nonnormative genders outside of therapeutic explanations that rely on claims of individual (psychically specific) trauma. I struggle mightily with the children and families I see to hold open a therapeutic space between the bedazzled ideality of trans play, and the pain that inflects the life of the unexpected—pain that is rarely individual and psychically specific, pain that is far more often a blend of sociopsychological trauma.

My efforts to hold open a therapeutic space wherein we might see these boys more fully, and thereby craft a more efficacious theory of boyhood femininity, is further complicated by the ways in which the vast majority of these children move on to lives that cannot be measured by the norms that mark how we typically understand maturity and well-being: genders that match a masculine/feminine binary, heterosexuality, marriage, child rearing, and typical bourgeois citizenship.

At stake here is nothing less than how we measure the well-being of our fellow citizens, and how much that wellness hinges on genders that coincide with normative expectation. Perhaps norms are not all they are cracked up to be? Is the person who resists the expected social order lacking in well-being? No. In fact, we know (over and over again) many people, many of whom are looked upon as the *most* alive, who live at the margins of our social order, live well enough, and live with good enough psychological well-being.

Sometimes mixed gender or cross-gendered humans are

simply being human. Not to recognize their humanity is to ignore the tempering work of human variation, and the possibilities of more inclusive conditions within which a wide variety of peoples can live. Genders both in their central and marginal expressions open out into lives that are led through many ways of being and feeling well. Yes, the very idea of well-being is open to debate—debate that largely centers on the question of how we disentangle the intertwined psyche and social. How do we untangle that which cannot be untangled? We can't.

We can only reckon with our location on the border of a nonnormative community in search of the imaginary space through which communities are formed. We can only strive to hold open a potential space wherein we can attempt to assess and/or assist. We can, as is our charge as psychologists, help those who cross our threshold to live lives relatively free of psychic suffering and pain. We can work with our patients toward their having good enough capacities to reflect on their complex inner worlds. We can open a space for contemplation and recognition.

We can, and I think we must, when called upon, assist nonnormative people with their experiences of social difference; while it may not be possible to divide the social and the psychological, either in theory or in the act of living, one can nevertheless reflect on a person's experience of social force and normative expectation. For example, the minority person may not be able to escape the force of being hated. I suggest, however, that the minority subject who can reflect on that force, who can hold that force in mind, who can redress that force with good enough well-being, is someone who may fare better as both a social and psychological being/citizen.

Over these past fifteen years, many different boys and families have crossed my threshold. Here, I focus on two families, and in particular I attend to the clinical work of consultation. I do so because one is often in the position of consulting with parents with regard to their child's need for treatment. In the vast majority of these consultations, I have not recommended treatment for the boy. But I have often gone on to meet several times with the parents to think through the anxiety of regulation.

I also seek to illustrate something about the therapeutic action of consultation, an often overlooked dimension of clinical work. Consultation requires something perhaps more active and more direct than that which is offered within the classical psychoanalytic frame, though such distinctions are always troubled, always worried like tattered flags left too long in the wind, markers of an aging nation-state whose citizens have grown too old to take the flag in at night. Frayed arguments about depth and technique aside, parents often come seeking consultation, not treatment per se, and in the action required on my behalf, I have felt something being distilled that seemed worthy of contemplation.

Paternal Coaching

With these thoughts in mind, I turn to a series of consultations I undertook several years ago with a father of a feminine boy. I have chosen to write about my work with this particular father because, unlike the parents I was just describing, he was less—as he put it—"liberal" in his view of his son's cross-gendered identifications, and more "troubled," though, importantly, not less loving.

In many ways this fellow was not unlike John Updike's Rabbit Angstrom, a man caught in the web of time and class, a misogynist, no doubt, but a man who also loved women, or tried to—their bodies, their sex—and similarly loved his son, with whom he made mistakes, many. But even at his worst, Rabbit never abandoned his son. Even when he dropped him, he picked him back up.

I have chosen this material because this man came to me asking what was to be done about his son, who felt himself to be a girl. This man was not closed to processes of thought and reflection—in fact, he was often quite thoughtful and aware—but he made it clear that he was looking for more immediate action. His son was five, and the clock was ticking. He did not share his son's gendered experience, nor did he always enjoy his son's efforts to bring him into his games and fantasies. He wanted something different. He wanted to feel, to love, to relate to his son in ways that his son did not seem to grasp or desire. He understood that these interpersonal spaces and internal states were consciously informing, and more important, unconsciously informing, his relationship with his son. He worried about the consequences of their limited empathy and shared desires, and he didn't feel he had the luxury of time in reaching toward repair.

The Call

I received a phone call from a woman in a neighboring state, requesting that I consult with her husband, who was experiencing some difficulty in adjusting to his young son's expressed identification as a girl. As the phone conversation progressed, she indicated that her sister, who was a mental health professional, had heard me speak at a conference and thought I might help her brother-in-law come to better terms with his son's gender experience. The mother went on to explain that she too found her son's proclaimed identity as a girl to be trying at times, especially as she attempted to negotiate his identity outside the home. "Sometimes," she said, "it is just impossible." And then, in the manner of a tumbling associative chain, she went on, "I can't explain fast enough, or I don't know how to explain, or I don't have the time, I just want to get something at the grocery store, not explain why he's wearing bracelets, you know, sometimes you have the time, or sometimes you have another mother or a child who seem open, sometimes you don't, sometimes you have your wits about you, sometimes you don't, not that I even have the same feeling day to day about this girly thing."

She felt, though, that she "weathered" the anxiety of difference better than did her husband. "He doesn't have the words," she said. "He kind of freezes, and I am really worried for him—for them." She explained, "I don't really know how to say this, but I think somehow I am better prepared . . ." and then she paused for some time, and said, "You know, I realize I just stopped myself from saying that I am better prepared to be embarrassed." She paused again, and finally said, "I guess by gender." She paused yet again, and said, "And frankly, I don't even know what that means. But I guess as a woman, gender—or I don't know—is it shame that I have had to face? You know, the tyranny of a makeup counter." And then, she laughed. And then, there was a long silence. I actually began to wonder whether somehow the call had been disconnected. Or was it that I got lost in the silence, trying to take in what she had said, how much she had managed to convey in such short order. Finally, she said, "Clearly, I am in need of someone to talk to. You probably got that. But I have someone." She explained that her sister had referred her to a local psychologist, whom she liked and found to be helpful.

I asked then whether, or why, it wasn't possible to find someone local to speak with her husband; perhaps she and her husband could speak to someone together? She said that she thought that was a good idea, though she added that she also thought her husband could benefit from speaking to a man who was an "expert." I always flinch in the face of such idealization, and I immediately began to wonder what it concealed: Was I to take him off her hands? And who was the "him": her husband or her son? Was I supposed to give him expert words for "this girly thing"? Were we supposed to collude in some fantasy that, unlike her husband, she had it in command? She had the words. She was somehow beyond the indefinite noun (the "thing") she used in reference to her son. Was I to embody the good son, the good-enough grown-up sissy, and hence ease her husband's anxiety? And if so, was that such a terrible thing? Or was there something about this man's shame that was so significant that he had to cross state lines? Was there some degree of family distress that she was trying to finesse by sending her husband to an "expert" in a neighboring state?

I asked why was she calling, and not he. She responded, perhaps rightly, that that was part of the problem. I took her point, catalogued my reservations, and suggested that she tell him that she had given me a call, and that if he wished to set up an appointment, he should call me, and I would be happy to go from there.

In fact, in a couple of days he did call, and in a very brief conversation said that he preferred to come in to see me, to sit down and talk, as opposed to saying much on the phone. He indicated that he was troubled by his son's identification as a girl, but didn't know exactly what to say beyond that, or at least on the phone. We made an appointment for the following week.

The Consultations

He arrived on time, and as we walked the short distance from the waiting room to my office, I was immediately struck by how much he reminded me of the suburban dads of my childhood; I wondered: had they not changed? The khaki pants, the neatly tucked poly-blend blue oxford cloth shirt, the 175 pounds, the trim hair. As we sat down, I thought it best to acknowledge my conversation with his wife, and made a particular point of repeating her concern that he did not have words for his son's experience. He shook his head and looked at the carpet, sitting as he was on the edge of his chair. I thought for a moment that perhaps he would get up and walk out; or might that have been my wish?

Eventually he looked up and said, "You must think I'm a monster." I was so taken aback that I am pretty sure I shook my head, if only to cast off the flood of affects. I reflexively said, "But I don't know you." I may even have held up my hands, as though in a stick-up. And he looked at me as if to say, "But you do. *You know you do.*" There was a long pause, something of a stare-down, and eventually, I said, almost in the spirit of conceding, "OK, you're a monster. That's where we'll start."

And so we did. He and I met five times over the course of three months (three of the meetings were double sessions).

A host of feelings, states, and stories came forward. We even managed to laugh a couple of times. But the overwhelming experience was one of grief, and his stubborn anger in the face of what Freud might have called "reality's verdict." Over and over again he said to me, "But I don't want a daughter. I want a son." Over and over again I tried to chart a course that recognized his sense of loss, while attempting at the same time to move him toward his need to reckon with his grief, including questioning how entitled he was to such grief: after all, was his son not the sovereign of his own identity? To which we both had to concur that the answer was complicated. Yes, children have an undeniable right to their own mind, but parents surely play an operatic role in the shaping thereof.

He argued, wasn't it his right, may it not even be a manifestation of his love for his son, that he pass along masculinity, that he pass along paternity? He explained that the passing of the masculine baton had been a vital aspect of his own relationship with his father, who had died suddenly two years before our meeting. As he spoke about his father, I began to reflect on his tone, the plaintive bid of the melancholic; something was lost, and he was monstrously, aggressively not only registering his privation within himself, as does the melancholic, but also projecting his loss into his son, bringing them both into a landscape of suffering and abjection. In this way, the loss is taken in but also projected into others, held therein, not clearly seen and, more important, not surrendered.

He had not lost his father; he had lost his son. I suggested that he had lost his own experience of being a son, an experience he consciously proclaimed he wanted to refind, but in fact was rather determined to hold onto as lost.

But did his son's femininity register something about this

loss? Some melancholic impingement? Some dark closure? Or was the boy's femininity a bright binary rejoinder to his father's melancholia, the feminine other, who would bring him back to life? And where was the mother in this story; had she given her husband over to her son, as I felt she may have wished to hand him over to me? Did her experience of femininity involve tyranny beyond the makeup counter, and if so, might her son be answering to her plight as well?

I clocked these questions, and mulled them over as I tried to bring this boy into mind, and to consider how his gender emerged within a particular and particularizing psychic-social-family terrain. His father's melancholia and his mother's femininity undoubtedly influenced his gender experience and subjectivity.

In my view, though, the extent of parental influence remains a necessary mystery. The looping network of internalizations, identifications, and implantations, created through the relational excess of human life, is too complex to deliver and execute originary explanations. In this respect, I take the following comment by Stephen Jay Gould as a bit of supervision: "The details are the story itself; the underlying predictability if discernible at all, is too nebulous, too far in the background, and too devoid of hooks upon actual events [and I would add fantastic events] to count as an explanation in any satisfying sense."[5]

Gender has been an easy target, held in sight by the telescoping anxiety of a normative regulatory regime. Feminine boys have been an easy mark. Their psyches have been plundered and exposed. And in the bright light of examination complexities and complications have been found. These boys became the necessary other, the unintelligible, as opposed to the necessary variation that comes with any normative enterprise. We have been too quick to presume gender to be a cohering internalization and identification, as opposed to a complex and enigmatic series of internalizations and identifications that may "cohere" much less than has traditionally been assumed.

We have been too quick to categorize, too quick to diagnose, and insufficiently attentive to the complex and perplexed relations established between individuals and cultural mandates. We have been too arrogant in our presumption that we can distinguish, or need not distinguish, the anxious work of cultural regulation and normative force as it intertwines with anyone's relational history, or as it maps anyone's internal world.

Parents now come to me with these thoughts in mind, even the father to whom I have been referring. In the first consultation, as he wondered out loud whether his son's cross-gendered identifications might express some manner of psychic distress, he countered his own question with his perception of his son as a "pretty OK kid." He was hard-pressed to see his son as psychologically troubled in any deep way. In fact, he found his son to be more open, more expressive, indeed, often more lovable than he found his older daughter, whom he described as more remote, "brainy," and something of a loner. In short, he found her to be more like himself. His son, on the other hand, more often sought him out, looked toward him for aid and comfort, and in many ways he liked the intimacy until it became entangled with his son's cross-gendered wishes.

When I raised the matter of how his son's gendered address ("girl") might be a response to the father's own melancholic state, he entertained this idea, and it became an idea with which we worked. But he shifted the intent of my question from one of causality to coloration—from why to how. He said, "But he was that way before my father died. It seems he has always been that way." And here we come upon yet another of gender's mysteries, the complex congress of psyche, blood, bone, neuron, hormone, and chromosome. Surely the body speaks. Yet we have been too quick to privilege the body as essential, as opposed to matter that can then, as Judith Butler explains, be seen as "a process of materialization that stabilizes over time to produce the effect of boundary, fixity, and surface."[6] I believe in the necessity of sustaining an instructive uncertainty regarding bodily and psychic origins. I strategically foreground idiosyncratic narratives as opposed to originary reasoning, and in league, I do not employ the determining vocabulary of biological elaboration. I move from why to how.

And in the manner of how, at some point in one of our meetings, my patient moved from describing his son dancing with a scarf, twirling and laughing with his older sister, to speaking about his own father. The move—the association, if it could be called that—seemed abrupt, and I brought it to his attention. (In my mind I began to think of this boy as a butterfly in a cemetery, though I didn't bring that thought forward.)

We contemplated his frequent interruption of his son's play by pulling himself out of the experience, out of the fantasy, out of the potential space, and in toward his own landscape of privation, which was then projected into his son, morphing in its arc toward shame, in this case unconsciously. Rarely did he openly reject or castigate his son. He entertained my position, he even granted it merit. And I don't propose that such insight, if one can call it that, was deep, or internalized in the same manner as self-reflection that is born of time and therapeutic space that allows patients to construct their own interpretations.

But we moved forward, looking further into his projection of lost masculinity in the context of play with his son. He was not a man who was necessarily or immediately impatient with a child's controlling push and demand in the context of play. He was familiar with those states, having experienced them with his daughter. So when at one point he exclaimed, "I cannot take one more princess dance," we set about to examine who he was asked to be, and whom he was asked to grant, to recognize, and to acknowledge in his son's games. He was to be the admirer of his son's femininity, the artifice, the folly, the masquerade, and as the admirer, he was also called upon to be the desiring subject, the vessel of the gaze, as his son as girl became then the object of desire. It is here that he balked. Most often he "tuned out"; occasionally he declined, sometimes with frustration. Other times he tried to institute a new game, a more traditionally masculine one. Sometimes his son would join him, sometimes not.

I suggested that perhaps the masculinity that was lost in those moments was his own, not his son's. If he became the subject of desire, and the object of his son's desire, did he remain a man, or at least a heterosexual man? His imagination, his will, went straight as his son pushed to go queer. Clearly he was not, is not, alone in this position. He stands in a long line of fathers and fathering figures who relate to their cross-gendered sons through what might be called paternal behaviorism.

Paternal Behaviorism

Consider, for example, how this manner of behaviorism guides Greenson's 1968 account of his work with a feminine boy. He begins his essay, "Dis-Identifying from the Mother: Its Special Importance for the Boy"—widely regarded as a classic in the psychoanalytic developmental literature—by asserting that "the male child in order to attain a healthy sense of maleness, must replace the primary object of his identification, the mother, and must identify with the father." To illustrate his assertion, Greenson described his therapeutic work with a feminine boy, who enacted a princess fantasy with Barbie. Greenson entered the play as an admiring suitor: "I followed the princess and told her how beautiful she was, how much I wanted to hold her and dance with her, and that I loved her." Eventually, the boy offered Barbie to Greenson, thinking that Greenson's pursuit was an expression of his identification with Barbie. Greenson intervened, correcting the boy's apparent projection by saying "I don't want to be the princess, I want to dance with her." According to Greenson, this intervention, which was not an observation of the boy's projection but rather a corrective/behavioral form of modeling (in other words, "I do not wish to be a princess, and by my example, neither should you"), led the boy to inquire whether Greenson danced with and loved his wife. Greenson replied in the affirmative. By Greenson's account, this information was sufficient to send the boy "deep into thought" and henceforth to forsake Barbie and his feminine identification, taking up, instead, a "strong [read, masculine] identification" with Greenson, which in turn, as Greenson would have it, ushered the boy into the "phallic Oedipal phase." Minus the love of eccentricity and the comedy that follows thereupon, this case moves with the narrative arc of a

Victorian novel: all's well that ends well—in marriage and the reproduction of matrimonial relations.[7]

Still, the regulatory anxiety that appears to have guided Greenson's therapeutic hand continues to hold sway in various quarters of the psychological community. Rekers and Nicolosi, for example, through a curious blend of fundamentalism and behaviorism, advocate for direct intervention in an effort to undo cross-gender identifications and the pathological homosexuality they believe follows therefrom.[8] Their therapeutic techniques are largely based on behavioral modeling and what might be called paternal coaching, not unlike the exchange reported by Greenson. Coates and Zucker, the standard-bearers of the traditional developmental psychiatric approach, also incorporate behavioral techniques. Both theorists recommend a kind of desensitization to femininity and feminine desires. Parents are cautioned to gradually restrict toys, activities, and modes of dress that are associated with the feminine, as they encourage their sons toward more traditionally masculine ways of looking, playing, being.

For Greenson, along with Rekers and Nicolosi, and Coates and Zucker, the behaviorism that underscores their techniques remains typically unnamed, even disavowed, through Greenson's and Coates's identification with psychoanalysis and Nicolosi's, Rekers's, and Zucker's vague though implicit alignment with supportive psychotherapeutic techniques. Rekers and Nicolosi are, of course, also distinguished from Coates, Greenson, Zucker, and the majority of their colleagues by their advocacy and direct employment of Christian ministry and religious conversion.[9]

Much could be said about the theoretical insufficiency, malignant clinical seduction, and ethical morass that encircle and shroud conversion therapies. I am, however, not going to take up that discussion at this juncture.[10] I focus instead on what might be called the pervasive behavioral paternalism that finds its way into the therapeutic techniques used with feminine boys. Perhaps this drift toward gender behaviorism or the anxious interrogation and threat of gender regulation only serves to further illustrate that gender is socially produced and reinforced, and "exceeds us," as Butler has suggested, "in its generality and power."[11] Or perhaps it points to the vulnerability of masculinity, to the flagging phallus, and the ways in which masculinity is little more than the social supports through which it swells.

Perhaps this manner of paternalism also serves to illuminate the influence that is inevitable in psychotherapeutic exchange, influence that is in turn influenced by social forces as they enter the consulting room. Yet a basic tenet of most forms of psychodynamic psychotherapies is the necessary pursuit and examination of these forces as they enter the room. In other words, therapists and patients cannot live outside of social force. But we can strive to understand how we might lean into social force when we are made anxious by difference. We can strive to understand, as perhaps Greenson should have, why our imagination goes straight when, in following the patient, it should have gone queer.

Imagination and Conclusive Assurance

Which brings me back to my patient. I brought up the matter of imagination, and went so far as to suggest that imagination is not simply a confrontation with reality but a means of altering it; that imagination is actually an instrument for the elaboration of reality; that freedom is dependent on social conditions that can be refashioned by acts of imagination and will; and that pulling away from or pushing against his son's imagination was not simply a matter of challenging his play but also a matter of dropping his son's psychic reality, and in turn his son's bid to alter social constraints. I did not go so far as to suggest, as I believe, that normative masculinity is particularly bereft of imagination, caging boys within a dull fence and making melancholic monsters of far too many men. No, I didn't go that far, because I had gone too far already, and he let me know it.

"I'm not as liberal as you," he interrupted. "I find it hard to be as permissive as you suggest. I'm not fucking Gloria Steinem," he barked. "You got a problem with Gloria?" I tossed back. It was one of those rare moments in which we actually managed to laugh.

His assertion forced me to grapple, though, with how therapeutic ideals about similarity and the importance of empathy can too easily underplay the ways in which the complicated congress of anyone's identity and inner world is built and managed not only through recognition but also through opposition, and even failures of recognition. Affect states, relational configurations, identifications, memory, and convictions regarding one's experience of self (however we problematize the boundedness of self) are all shaped to some extent through failures and lapses, which need not only be constructed as hateful. There can and must be space for difference.

We came then toward some middle ground. He came to understand, or perhaps more precisely began to work toward understanding, that he could want something different. He did have other wishes; he did not necessarily have to share his son's desire. But he (as the parent, as the adult) could not decline to take responsibility for the effort of mutual recognition, the examination and explanation of difference, the repair of failure, and the relative safety of love. He had to step out of the plaint of the melancholic and step back into the possibilities of life, even the possibilities born through difference, which are a world apart from the death of disavowal. He began to grasp that it was his responsibility as this boy's father to lessen the anger, the edge of persecution, the denial, and most of all the disavowal. In his own way, he understood what Fairbairn called a child's need for "conclusive assurance"—a child's need to be loved, loved uniquely, and to have his love accepted in return.[12]

Our work came to a conclusion around this point. My patient indicated that he understood that what was before him was just that: before him, that he felt he would need help to make use of what he had learned with me, but that he wanted to work together with his wife on these matters. She, he explained, had always been helpful to him "when it comes to emotions," and he thought he could now take what he had garnered from our meetings and go to a family therapist in his own city, recommended by his wife's therapist. I told him that I considered that a fine plan, and wished him well, indicating that he could be in touch with me as he wished.

As was his courtly custom, he shook my hand at the door, always saying "Thank you." But this time he took my hand in both his hands and said "Thank you," adding, "I really mean it, man."

We ended, then, with a gendered address: the "man" of exclamation, the "man" of gratitude, the "man" of recognition, which I took to be his conscious and sincere intent. But also the "man" of the gender binary, the "man" of a common set of idealizations that bring people together; and the "man," in his case, who set him apart from his beloved son, the "man" they were faced with having to redress, readdress.

Maternal Trauma, Maternal Attachment

While identification and coaching are the central features of the traditional discourse as it relates to boys and fathers, trauma and attachment are at the heart of discussions about feminine boys and their mothers. I move here to discuss a series of consultations undertaken with a mother and her six-year-old son. I saw both mother and son intermittently over the course of two years. I also consulted with the mother's therapist and with the therapist to whom I referred the young boy. Due to factors both of cost and travel, I referred the boy to a colleague, whom I saw for supervision, and who had an office nearer the boy's home. They met once per week for two years, and on an occasional basis the following year.

Ms. R.: Mother-Son Considerations

I recall, with particularity, the weather the day Ms. R. arrived for her first consultation. It was early spring. But it was surprisingly, freakishly hot. Ms. R., it seemed, had dressed like most of us, prepared for a different, colder day. She, though, had made no adjustment to the sudden change in weather. Ms. R. sat in her chair in a coat too hot for the day.

She promptly reiterated her reason for coming to see me, indicating as she had in a brief phone conversation that she had come in order to talk about her son Lincoln, whom she described as a "boy who believes he is a girl, or at least openly identifies with girls." She described herself as being of "many minds" in relation to her son's femininity. She both "did and did not" worry about the soundness of Lincoln's feminine identity: hence the consultation.

A few months before our meeting, she and Lincoln had met a child psychiatrist who had diagnosed Lincoln with GID. Ms. R. had found that consultation "troubling" and the diagnosis "hasty and too determined." She had gone home and begun reading about GID and had become "more alarmed" with the ways in which she felt the diagnosis "captured yet distorted" her son.[13]

She was further troubled by the descriptions offered of overbearing or traumatizing mothers. She indicated that she knew she was in need of some help with Lincoln. She knew herself to be anxious, and she was sure her anxiety had an impact on Lincoln but that it was "not nearly as extreme" as that described between mothers and sons in the GID literature; or so she thought: "Of course I can't be objective." Trying to explain further, she spoke of her relationship with her son as "generally good" and added that "overall" she did not find his femininity to be too troubling. Most of the time, she felt that she didn't think about it much: "It's Lincoln," she said, affectionately intoning through her summation that his femininity was an indelible aspect of his personhood.

There were times, though, when she found "the negotiations" trying. By way of illustration, she described an incident that had happened earlier that week. Lincoln had asked that she buy him a toy, one of those small toys near the cash register in many stores that seem designed to ignite a child's greed and a parent's irritation. The cashier interceded, saying, "That's for a girl." Ms. R. quickly replied, "It's a toy, a toy, not a gender," as she plunked the toy down on the counter and paid the bill.

"But I hated the toy," she continued. "It was cheap, gaudy. It is probably already broken. I would have normally said no. But I hated the whole scene." Pausing to look up, she said, "So I'm giving this woman a lecture in gender theory. Not good."

As it turns out, gender theory is something about which Ms. R., a young academic, knew a fair bit. As she put it, one could not be a graduate student in her cohort and not know gender theory. What she knew, though, and what she believed, "sincerely believed," did not inoculate her from the confusion, anger, and guilt she could feel in the face of her son's femininity: "Sometimes he can be so insistent." She paused. "But I don't know, maybe it is me?"

She went ahead to say that her therapist, who had referred her to me, had begun to talk with her about the difficulty Ms. R. found in turning out toward others, and her tendency often to turn in toward her own thoughts, her own world. "I can be quite absorbed," she said. (I thought about her coat, and her seeming lack of adjustment to the day.) Ms. R. then linked her difficulty in taking in others with her experience of parenting as more difficult than she had expected. By her lights, she "too often" felt under demand and fatigued. Questioning herself, she asked, "But is it just that Lincoln is trying to get me to see what is on his mind?" Then she questioned herself again, "But should it feel so embattled?"

When I asked her to elaborate on the battle, she spoke more generally about their daily lives, and the course of their life since Lincoln's birth. She explained that she had unexpectedly become pregnant during a relationship with a man she did not wish to marry and who had no plans to marry her. Ms. R. did not speak of this relationship with acrimony but rather with certainty: they had made the right choice. Her choices with regard to pregnancy were perhaps less certain, or at least moved toward less certainty. She had not necessarily been looking to have a child at the time she became pregnant. But she decided rather "easily" to have the child. It was not until well into her pregnancy that she began to register the "commitment." Continuing, she said, "Foolishly, I thought it would be easier."

The pregnancy and birth were relatively uncomplicated. But the task of caring on her own for a baby proved overwhelming. She ended up moving from Manhattan to an outer borough in order to be closer to her parents and a younger brother, who play a significant role in the collective child care. According to Ms. R., Lincoln adored his grandparents, his grandfather in particular, with whom he spent each day after school, and her brother, who saw him several times a week. The battle, or "more like one of the battles," was in being drawn back into "daily family life." Ms. R. explained that while she was grateful for her family's help, she nevertheless felt "disconnected" from "her world." She spoke of hoping to return to Manhattan when Lincoln got a bit older.

I found myself thinking about Ms. R.'s seeming problem of location: in her own world, out of her own world. And as though she was calling me out of my own world/reverie, she recalled our attention to the matter of Lincoln's femininity. Or did she? Was there some problem of location there as well? Over time, I would, in fact, begin to think of this problem of location as a central theme in conceptualizing this clinical exchange. Where do we locate her son's femininity? Do we "see" it in a social register or address, or do we "find" it in psychological space?

She reiterated, "There is some battle there." And in the manner of a defensive preface, she restated her feeling that Lincoln was a generally "agreeable" kid. But she was troubled at times by what she called the "push" of Lincoln's femininity—his persistent and insistent interest in stereotyped, almost parodic femininity ("pink, pink, and more pink"; "everything is princess this and princess that"), a kind of femininity that she as a feminist found troubling ("I get girly play. I'm not above it. But does it have to be so pushy?"). She spoke about how sullen and angry Lincoln could become in the face of confrontations regarding his gendered wishes. "Sometimes there is too much hate in it," she went on, "both from him, or, so it seems, from me, and back and forth it goes."

As Ms. R. was speaking, I had, in fact, begun to reflect on how often she had used the word *hate* in a relatively short time. I thought about hate and hot (radiate); I thought again about her coat. I thought about something I had recently re-read, a passage from Susan Coates and her colleagues on gender identity disorder: "In a variety of ways boys with GID express feelings of self-contempt or self-hatred."[14] I wondered then, as I had when reading that passage, whence did the hate radiate? Coates locates the hate, founded in trauma, with the mother, or more precisely within the intergenerational transfer from mother to son. The trauma (the hate, the heat, the pain) is seen as catalyzing the boy's femininity.

Was Ms. R. drawing our attention to such a network of traumatic intromission? Her therapist, as I learned in a subsequent conversation, had paused over the same thought, although, in keeping with my assessment, Ms. R.'s therapist could find no evidence of the kind of trauma described by Coates. Yes, Ms. R. did experience ongoing discord with her mother, struggles that implied a history of disquieted attachment and separation, struggles to which Coates often points. But Ms. R.'s therapist held, and I concurred, that Ms. R.'s relationship with her mother was not so very different from those of many such relationships, especially those involving single mothers living in large cities with limited child care options, financial constraints, and inadequate social supports. Nor was Ms. R.'s struggle with separation so very different from those of many of her cohorts as they brokered their feminist-inflected identities with mothers who might not share their worldview. Were we willing, Ms. R.'s therapist asked, to speak of all these women as traumatized?

She went on to say that she thought the first three months of Lincoln's life had been "shaky." The therapist indicated that she thought Ms. R.'s introduction to mothering had been "tough," "anxious." She described the anxiety as part of a depressive response. And, yes, she thought it likely that Ms. R.'s state of mind, which had led her to her therapist, did have an impact on Lincoln. But again, she balked at calling it "traumatic," feeling as she did that there was adequate family support to offset the mother's anxiety. Ms. R.'s mother had stepped in immediately to help—help that came with its own set of conflicts, but help that Ms. R. accepted and appreciated nevertheless. The therapist also indicated that Ms. R. had responded well to treatment, and that the initial overwhelming anxiety and depression had subsided rather quickly.

Ms. R.'s therapist was more interested in the overall impact of Ms. R.'s limited reflective functioning, and the effect it might have on Lincoln's experience of attachment, his own capacities to reflect on his own feelings and thoughts, and his growing sense of self. Ms. R.'s therapist, with a hint of affection, described Ms. R. as the kind of "brainy mother," surrounded by books, who forgets to make lunch, feels terrible when she recognizes her lapse, and then by means of repair makes some complicated French recipe for dinner, when really the kid just wants pizza. "She does not always get the adult-kid divide," her therapist summarized. It did seem that there was a shared anxious attachment across this mind divide; might Lincoln's femininity be a manifestation of that anxiety, or an anxious bridge across the divide?

Then there was also the matter of Ms. R. as a single parent. In keeping with something that Ms. R. had mentioned briefly in our first meeting, her therapist explained that they had spent a lot of time wondering about what impact Ms. R.'s single-mother status had on Lincoln. Surely it must have an impact, but what? In particular, they wondered whether it influenced or informed Lincoln's femininity. Were we posed with a hallmark diagnostic marker referenced in the literature on feminine boys: the absent, or detached-hostile father?[15] Ms. R.'s therapist was quick to point out that Lincoln spent a lot of time with his grandfather, probably more time than many boys spend with their fathers, and that he also had a very close relationship with his uncle, who seemed a playful fellow who related well to children.

And then how might we entertain, did we need to entertain, Lincoln's mixed-race identity? Did Lincoln's trans states speak race through gender? Was this his way of being mixed? Ms. R.'s therapist voiced her doubt about this question, even as she asked it, saying that she thought it likely that Lincoln looked like many kids in his neighborhood and school: "I doubt that he stands out. I'm sure he looks like many of the kids at his school," adding, "I've seen pictures, he is a very good-looking little boy."

"So do you think any of this has had an impact on Lincoln's gender?" the therapist asked. I began my reply by saying that I was little concerned with the father's absence given the roles of significant men in Lincoln's life, and furthermore that the assertions regarding a missing father and a boy's femininity had been called into question even within traditional reasoning about boyhood femininity.[16] Absent fathers were a fact in many boys' lives, and could not reliably be correlated to boyhood femininity. Tagged onto that short-order assessment, I added that that didn't mean we could so easily set aside Lincoln's fantasies about his biological father, and I wasn't sure what role if any that played in his gendered and racialized life. How his fantasies included his grandfather and uncle would also be important to pursue. But such thoughts invited the question of whether therapeutic inquiry was necessary, and that was not at all clear to me. For example, I pointed to her thoughts about Lincoln's experience of race and suggested that his life was led in a community, and that to some extent this was a social/community phenomenon, and maybe the community was doing a good enough job. But then again, I did not think we could be so certain. Surely, this was a boy who probably had some understanding of racial categories and discrimination; how did he feel the impact of such social forces?

With regard to the mother's influence, I said I thought we needed more time to sort that out. But in a word, "yes." And then I ventured forward with a jumble of thoughts about how gender is shaped (at least in part) in relation to one's parents (including a parent's absence). But then again, I went on to say that parent-child relationships are structured by the larger cultural surround. "So, yes, in answer to your question, I guess," I said, and then laughed (self-consciously) at my inarticulate expertise.

This was certainly not the first time I found myself in this inarticulate position. Clumsy as it may be, as inexpert as it may be, I feel my uncertainty is in keeping with the perplexity of gender's expressions. Gender should sometimes leave us inarticulate. We are tongue-tied in speaking about gender, as we slip up between the social and the psychological. Though we have made a practice of speaking of gender as psychically specific, we now recognize that, yes, gendered identifications are invested with a psychically specific history—every person is a specific person with a unique family story—but that history (that psychic specificity) cannot be disentangled from the social "outside" that immediately becomes "inside," blurring any effort to distinguish the two.

Lincoln: The Therapeutic Scene of Address

I found that I paused over this social-psychic interimplication often, along with frequent considerations of the question of pain, in my initial consultations with Lincoln, and later in supervisory sessions with his therapist. These questions were in evidence almost immediately in the first consultation. On reflection, I found I thought a lot about gender and the therapeutic scene of address.

When I first met Lincoln, he was not happy to see me. He slumped in a waiting-room chair with his arms crossed over his chest and said he "didn't want to come" to my office. He was "hot" and "tired." Sweat was in fact budding on his brow, his long loosely curled hair damp with the heat of the day.

He did "not like this place." I said that I thought that a lot of people felt that way. I offered that his mother could join us, if he wished, but he didn't want that either. I asked whether he and his mother had talked about coming to see me. He shrugged. His mother said they had. I began to feel the heat of what I attributed to the un-air-conditioned waiting room, which was no doubt the flush of my own anxiety. I made an admittedly desperate plea for the air-conditioning in my office.

Lincoln allowed that it might be "OK" to take a look. He dragged his feet, his sandals shuffling across the carpet. I noted that his feet were quite dirty. Chipped pink nail polish poked through. On his right arm he wore several bracelets, which he eventually told me were "Indian," and from his "favorite store." On his left hand were several rings.

Upon first impression, he struck me less as a girl and more like a beautiful miniature hippie boy, a mixed-race Donovan, even a bit of Jim Morrison. Oddly, given the difference in our ages, I found myself thinking of boys who were older than I; college kids (when I was in high school), who were freer to embrace the adorned late 1960s and early 1970s.

In some region of my mind (not foremost), I was also contemplating Lincoln's racial identity. Indeed, as Ms. R.'s therapist had suggested, he did look like many modern urban children, though as I indicate, I was immediately aware of his beauty and exoticism. In hindsight I wonder, following on the literary theorist Anne Cheng, whether I may have been "caught" in my gaze either in the "promise of substitutive whiteness" that exoticism may offer or in witnessing how exoticism unsettles both gender and racial binaries; where then, might these experiences have led this little boy in front of the mirror?[17]

Once in my office, he chose the basket of dolls and limply

dressed one. I asked him whether he knew what a mood was. He replied, "You mean a bad mood." I said yes, though there could be many kinds of moods, it did seem that perhaps he was in a bad mood. He denied my assertion and said he was just tired. We sat for a while in silence. I found that I was feeling cross, somewhat trapped, and wondered at my own bad mood.

I paused over whether I was being pulled into a stalemate. Eventually, I said, "Well, this is going rather poorly; isn't it?" Lincoln looked at me curiously, and for the first time registered something beyond peevishness. But switching back to peeve, he told me that my Barbies were "a mess" and in need of "new clothes." I concurred, they were a tad ratty: "It would make us feel better if they were prettier?" "Yes," he replied, as if it were self-evident.

He repeated that he was thirsty and tired. I offered him a glass of water, which he gladly drank. More silence. Then he told me while lifelessly redressing Barbie that today had been the last day of school. "Well, no wonder you don't want to be here!" I exclaimed with a laugh. I went ahead, "You know, the freedom of the last day of school."

More silence. Within which I found myself wondering about what I had just done: he thought I was part of the regime, and I had disowned his projection/perception—in a move of manic defense. I then said that I was "sorry," surprising myself in so doing. I stumbled and explained that I thought it seemed that he might want to celebrate his freedom and not find himself at a doctor's office. He told me that his class had spent "the whole day" at the park (hence, the dirty feet), and that he had eaten three pieces of pizza. He burped. I laughed. And for the first time we both softened a bit.

It was at that point that he told me about his bracelets, and his best friend, Maya. She was going with her mom to get her nails done. "And you had to come here. Drag." And in one of those moments that seem to happen in slow motion, I realized that I was doing it again; I was dismantling my power. I was not the normative authority. I was the hip one, the "drag" one.

Lincoln was (as I would learn with time,) a boy whose mind was often turned in toward wary contempt, and he could turn out in kind, with fear, anger, and brittle regard. Over time it became important to be able to speak of his tendency, as he put it, to be "an unfriendly friend." But in keeping with the graduated understanding that can happen across a psychotherapy, it was important in these opening consultations to grasp and maneuver around some of the fear that fueled Lincoln's unfriendliness. (It was this fear-anxiety that led me to refer Lincoln for treatment.)

Lincoln would explain in a subsequent consultation (about a year or so later) that he was afraid of "boys he did not know." In our opening consultations, I was one of those boys, and as such I was seen as someone who could potentially hurt him, most likely by taunting him, calling him a "bad name," or telling him that a boy could not be a girl. I knew from Lincoln's therapist that this was a matter they had discussed at length, and that this kind of conflict was a consistent trope in his play. There was almost always a shunned character, a character caught and called out, who at times sought revenge, though most often was cast aside and left with no voice. With time, my colleague found a way to speak with Lincoln about this character as "turning away from others, and turning in—being mad at himself." Or "being mad with no way to speak." This, then, became a way for them to begin to look at the "harsh things" in Lincoln's mind, as well as his experience of voiceless social humiliation.

In these opening consultations, and in the face of Lincoln's anxiety and "unfriendly" defense, was I overcompensating? Yes, to some extent I believe I was. As well, though, I was walking the tightrope of initial consultations, trying to keep open potential space, a space that might be filled with powerful affects and projections, and at the same time to move in accord with a patient's defenses, noting them all the same.

Lincoln knew why he was in my office, and his anxiety about the scene struck me as reasonable. How could he address me, and how was he going to be addressed? Did he expect something in the way of a clinical interview? Would he face diagnostic questions like, "How often do you wear dresses? Female undergarments? How often do you wear male underwear? How often do you play with cosmetic articles?" Would he be the object of such scrutiny and shame? Would he be subject to a "behavioral play assessment procedure in which two specific sets of masculine and feminine toys are made available"? Would he be scanned for such "cross-sex-typed gestures and mannerisms" as "limp wrist," "hand clasp," or "hyperextension"?[18]

Even in Lincoln's short life, he knew how normative "assessment" operated. He knew the push of anxious regulation. He knew how to push back. He knew what to expect, and it wasn't simply a matter of embellished paranoia. While he made an appeal to be addressed as "girl," he knew it was more likely that such address would be diagnosed and directed at him. "Girl" in those moments spoke "failed boy." Did he risk that shame here, the shame of being seen or diagnosed as having

failed at, or lost hold of, his proper gender? Was I the manifestation of some form of punishment for who he was not, who
he should be?

In direct contrast with most theorists who have written
about boyhood femininity, it has not been my experience that
these boys so willingly or easily or unthinkingly "display" their
femininity. They are guarded, inhibited, shut down, and often
angry, as it seemed Lincoln was. They know what it is to be
the object of scrutiny. Contrary to reports of these boys as extreme, flamboyant, and pinkly unhinged, I have found them
to be cautious to the point of dull. Their play is halting and
unelaborated.

Given a therapeutic space that is more open than a directed clinical interview or behavioral assessment (one that
affords them the opportunity to be the gendered subject as
much as the object), they do not quickly identify themselves
as feminine. In fact, at times they seem to go out of their way
to deny it. (I have seen more than one boy who did not go
near the dolls during our consultation, cautioning us that they
"were for girls.") Even when they choose toys that are typically
of interest to girls, they do not play with them in a lively manner. These moments of fantasy and performance are infused
with contradictory affects: the "play" in play (the freedom, the
liberating reach, the range of affect states that open in play)
is countered by hovering anxiety and regulation; how far can
they go? They watch me. They watch the clock. They serve
their time.

I am mindful here of the characterization by Coates and
her colleagues of the inhibited play of GID boys as "inflexible"
and "lack[ing] the joyful characteristic of play." This "frozen"
play is read as indicative of the "compulsive management of

anxiety," the enacted expression of separation anxiety and un-metabolized aggression—not the anticipatory anxiety of one who expects to be harshly judged, or is uncertain of his welcome.[19]

To be sure, over time it was important to address Lincoln's aggression, his "unfriendly face," but I found that it happened in accord with his experience of the possibilities of address offered in the treatment, and followed in accord with his experience of freedom, or lack of freedom, in gender performance and gender practice. As he felt freer to express and practice his femininity, as he felt less in peril of humiliation, or better able to anticipate and reckon with normative shame, space opened wherein he and his therapist could more freely address his mental states. The anger that came forward had more to do with his experience of impingement and shame—internalized (constitutive and constituting) shame.

More important, though, by bringing the matter of social address and the scene of address into the play, by speaking to a boy's will to be a girl in modes of gender practice and performance (that presumes an audience, an other), one is granted a different purchase on what has been previously interpreted as a manifestation of the intergenerational transfer of trauma or disrupted attachment. We are offered a more complex view of the trauma of normative regulation—a view that leads to the contemplation of melancholia versus trauma.

In my view, the predominant causal explanation for GID, what could be called an individual trauma theory, speaks to a minority of nonnormative gendered peoples. This does not mean that I do not think it possible that a feminine boy could develop through disrupted attachment, or in response to trauma, perhaps even the specific intergenerational transfer of trauma from mother to son. But I think it is quiet rare—more rare than Coates and Zucker take pains to make clear.

In distinction, the social trauma of being disavowed and of being hated is ubiquitous, as are the melancholic lives lived in the shadow of persistent social oppression. A theory that offers insight into the workings of melancholia as it builds the feminine boy affords us a robust set of ideas through which to contemplate not only the individual psychically specific boy, but also the sociopsychological formation of these nonnormative identities. We are granted, in turn, a more complex view into the sociopsychological network of relations, affects, and internalizations that help make the feminine boy.

We also come upon a better avenue of psychotherapeutic action and repair—one that does not only presume individual trauma and employ behavioral strategies that reinforce social exclusion and normative force. We move with the boy from melancholic plaint toward reflecting on his forsworn desires and identifications, and from there we are in a better position to help him articulate, as opposed to enact, his disarticulated grief. Grief, then, as Robert Frost might have it, is "a form of patience"—a position of fortitude and endurance through which different, even unexpected modes of living may open.[20]

With Lincoln, as with several other boys with whom I have worked, it was important to entertain, following here on the work of Judith Butler on gender melancholy, the ways in which his gender performances expressed the coupling of melancholia and mania. As Freud remarks in *Mourning and Melancholia*, "The most remarkable characteristic of melancholia, and the one in most need of explanation, is its tendency to change round into mania." At another juncture he refers to these sudden turns as "a circular insanity."[21]

Let us consider how transgendered states and fantasies come up against the taboo of the binary (upon which Oedipal development proceeds, just as Butler has pointed out relative to the homosexual taboo). Let us then consider the ways in which trans desires are met with regulatory refusal. Boys who will be girls are repeatedly ordered (both consciously and unconsciously) to relinquish their desire. The boy is then caught in a painful and untenable frame of mind. He is torn by the command to lose a desire, an identity *that is taken away from him, but not lost in him.*

The crushed boy comes to live and love, paraphrasing Freud, in the shadow of this forsaken desire. And in this shadow, a complex revolt unfolds, colored by self-reproach, hate, depression, self-exposed (repeatedly enacted) shame, and the constant plaint of one who has unfairly lost his way. Freud spoke of how melancholics, in the heat of revolt, "make the greatest nuisance of themselves, and always seem as though they felt slighted and had been treated with great injustice."[22] In an intriguing overlap, traditional theorists of GID often speak of boys who will be girls in a similar manner—"pushy," "difficult," "whiny," "bossy," "demanding."

Traditionally these noisome affect states have been interpreted as evidence of the boy's struggle to free himself of his mother's traumatized/depressive grip, or as a failed masculinity occasioned by paternal absence. One must remain open, of course, to the psychic specificity, and the specific family that circles any boy's life. Yet I find these psychically specific attachment-based interpretations lacking. Such interpretations misplace gender as only interior or relational as opposed to situating gender as the boundary phenomenon that it is, poised between the psyche and the social. They miss what in my view is the boy's relational bid through these pained states to call our attention to his melancholic snare. Missed in turn are the ways in which such a boy's desire is forsworn but remains alive and trapped within him.

Consistently and repeatedly I have witnessed boys who will be girls perform a kind of melancholic femininity, a femininity of grievance: "See me, I am the lost object of desire"; "See me, I am the lost desire"; "See me, I am the grieved, the cheated one"; "See me, I am the scorned one"; "See me, I am the debased one"; "See me as I sadistically attack the debased one"; "See me as I masochistically throw her aside"; "See me as I hate me." And often, as Freud suggests, these performances take on a manic and narcissistic edge: "How loud, how colorful, how bejeweled do I have to be before you will see me?" "How loudly do I have to suffer—how much do I have to hate before you see me?"[23]

Establishing a reliable holding environment affords the opening for the reflection necessary to contain and work through these troubling melancholic states. But as I learned with Lincoln, it is vitally important to take up these states in the context of the social scene of address. In my second consultation with him, he discovered that I could draw, and asked me to draw some mice, which I did. He colored them (six pink, one green) and cut them out. He seemed less pleased with the green mouse, which he crumpled but then attempted to uncrumple. He did not animate them, give them voice, or "play" with them per se. He held them, shuffled them, and admired them. At the end of the hour he put them under my radiator, where, as it turned out, they lived for the next two years. During his occasional visits to see me over those years, he would immediately go to the radiator, check on the mice, but never move them. He always seemed pleased to find them, though he did not say much about them.

I pondered the mice in many ways. Were they an illustration of majority rule—one odd man out? But the majority in this case was pink. Was that his way of pushing back? Were the mice closeted? Were the contrasting colors some way for Lincoln to register his identity as a mixed-race person? Was the darker green mouse his darker unknown father? Was the green mouse the shunned character that would later appear in his games? Or was the green mouse, the melancholic one as I mostly came to think of her—the aggrieved, the diminished, the shamed, the mouse crumpled by self-reproach; the one who could not speak her identity—the one who might paradoxically take refuge in suffering and, through a kind of circular insanity, ward off her suffering through the manic display of her difference: "See me, I am green"; "Look away, I am crumpled."

As I pointed out, Lincoln said little about them, and in the end, I found that I, too, said little about them. It was their security that appeared to matter most, and once they were secured and sustained, it seemed enough. It seemed in some sense a pledge. In retrospect, I wonder whether sheltering the mice did not serve as an opening gambit and an ongoing marker of the task at hand—creating a secure space, one that holds but does not immediately or perhaps ever fully articulate a complex set of affects, instead serving to open unto the practice to come.

Gender Practice

I speak of practice, to denote the practice of psychotherapy but also in this case the practice of gender. Probably the most

salient theme that developed between Lincoln and his therapist were what we came to think of as "scenes of practice." Lincoln spent much of his first year in treatment dressing and un-
dressing Barbie dolls, commenting on the success of Barbie's
various outfits, making alterations to her hair, and eventually
making alterations to her clothes. Initially, these scenes inevitably came to chaotic and aggressive conclusions. Lincoln
would undress the dolls hurriedly, casting the clothes aside;
the contents of the scene would be scattered and rendered "a
mess." His therapist and I began to think of these scenes as the
"mess" of shame, the self-reproach of melancholia, and the
curtailing wreck of practice.

The stylization of embodiment and aesthetic practice are
often center stage in the play of feminine boys. They have a feeling for artifice, beauty, and style, and their bodies frequently
become the avenue for this mode of aestheticism. They dress
up. They accessorize. They masquerade. They decorate. They
seek a desiring and confirming gaze, a manner of narcissistic
pleasure that is most often policed as feminine. These performances and their reception shape the intersubjective space
where genders, bodies, and desires are made. These fantasies
create the visual, tactile, emotive, and discursive network that
constitute a child as they come to be.

Consider in this regard a comment made—and, I would
suggest, a sentiment offered—by a mother of a boy in Green's
group of cross-gender-identified boys. She says of her son, "He
loved beautiful things. There was just so much he could do
with girls' hair and a girl's dress and her body. He just liked
pretty things."[24] I speculate that one can discern in this comment the mother's acceptance of her son's love of beauty, and
perhaps even some pleasure taken in his capacities. How she

made sense of what was expressed through her son's sense of beauty and his relation to the feminine, we do not know; Green does not provide that information. And though this, too, is speculative, I nevertheless do not read in her comment either the alarm that Green notes about the danger of the mother as she engages her son's femininity, or the alarm Stoller advances relative to what he might have termed this boy's "lovely sign of pathology."[25]

I emphasize this matter of tone, as it reveals the work of behavioral paternalism as it moves to curtail (to shame) the potentialities of cross-gender practice and play. This paternal tone is in keeping with the belief that such play will only deepen an already troubled maternal attachment. Again, I have found just the opposite to be true.

This observation was borne out in a facet of the transference between Lincoln and his therapist. As the therapist set about to engage Lincoln's doll play, and his interest in the practice of dressing, she began to point out that he seemed to pull away from his interest and ruin his creations. They began to speak about the fear and anxiety that his play stirred up in others, and about his own fear. And in an intriguing move that revealed the therapist's internalized shame as well, she "confessed" that she had helped Lincoln learn how to sew so that he could better realize his creations. Initially, she spoke of being concerned that she was acting in a manner that was "too supportive," but she soon realized that that too was a defense. Play therapy often involves some level of teaching or instruction or help. Instead, we began to consider her shame in crossing the normative order, and entering into the development of a nonnormative gender. Key here as well were her thoughts about what it meant to support a boy who was seeking the kind of narcissistic confirmation (the desire of the object of desire) that has traditionally been reserved for women and girls.

Femininity and the Other

Lincoln's therapist's reflections on her shame in crossing the social order and promoting the narcissism of the beckoning object proved helpful in working with Lincoln's mother and her experience of similar shame. Reflecting on the therapist's use of her countertransference and on her approach to Lincoln's feminine experience also points to an important distinction in her approach to that of traditional therapists. The dynamics of crossing and the constituting practice of gender are not addressed in the traditional discourse on feminine boys. Instead, these states are pathologized, treated as psychically specific, and never theorized within a social scene. Within the traditional developmental psychiatric clinical approach, a boy is never met as a feminine other; he is seen only as a mimetic mother. Similarly, he is never taken up as a social feminine other. The variety of affects and dilemmas that arise for the feminine boy in his quest for social recognition are not examined as socially constructed or located. Rather, they are seen as the manifestation of a specific psychic pathology. They are not seen as honorable social, relational bids; rather, they are seen as troubled psychic enactments.

Consider, for example, Coates's reading of feminine boys' anger. She describes boys who are locked in persecutory compulsive imitations of their mother and interprets these enactments as the boys' efforts to simultaneously express and disown their desperate attachment to their mothers. Distinct from Coates's observations, I noted with Lincoln, as I have with other feminine boys, that the anger that emerged in the treatment was not directed at a traumatized and unavailable mother; rather, the anger that emerged in the transference and in various play themes was anger at a mother (at an other), who could not consistently help him metabolize his variant subjectivity, caught as she might be in her own anxiety about his difference, and more important about the relational bid his difference speaks: "Join me in girl-ness."

Lincoln's anger almost always voiced the plaint of grievance, what one might call the dialect of the melancholic. Complaints ("She's messed up"; "Her hair is nasty"; "Her shoes are ugly") inevitably imploded, and sad rejection/withdrawal emerged (Barbie was undressed and dejectedly cast aside). It was important to follow this character that met such rough justice and was left with no ally, no voice. At one juncture Lincoln spoke of the unclothed "messy" Barbie as a "girl who wanted too many things," adding, "She deserves to be punished," revealing yet another feature of the melancholic's tendency to self-reproach and self-hatred. When Lincoln's therapist initially tried to compare this character to Lincoln, and to wonder whether he too might feel like this, he was adamant in his refusal (and she backed away from her inquiry). Several weeks later, though, Lincoln came back to a similar scene, and this time, unprompted, began to describe the shunned character as "tired" ("That's why she is lying down") and "mad" ("That's why she is naked"). His therapist inquired whether she might not be "lonely." Lincoln said, "She was too mad." The therapist persisted, indicating that one could be lonely and mad. She pointedly voiced a connection to Lincoln's experience of his wish to be a girl. His reply was, "Stop talking." And so she did.

I was struck by this response, and by the ways in which it

might capture the abjection of melancholy: "Don't disturb my angry withdrawal"; "Don't disturb my self-reproach"; "Don't disturb my shame." Through these emotional states the melancholic guards his lost love/identity. But slowly Lincoln and his therapist approached his melancholy. She began to give voice to the shunned character's sense of loneliness and abjection, and he did not interrupt her. Eventually, they began to approach the shunned girl, and were able to redress her, comb her hair, feed her, and let her rest.

In my final consultation with Lincoln I had the enlightening opportunity to question him about the "harsh things" in his mind. We were drawing together, and he was using colored pencils to draw an underwater scene, one that I recognized as mimicking the world of the "Little Mermaid," a character that intrigued Lincoln, as she has many of the feminine boys with whom I have worked. I said that I wondered whether he liked Ariel only because she was pretty and had long hair, as he had previously indicated, or whether it might also be the case that he felt like her, "caught between two worlds." Ariel is caught between the world of the mer and her desire to join the earthly world of humans. I wondered whether Lincoln might not feel caught between the world of boys and girls. He sat silent for a while looking at his drawing, and then handed it to me. He said it was "a present." I thanked him. And then suggested that sometimes presents cover over pain, "kind of like a trick." I went on to say that Ariel feels a lot of pain and sorrow.[26] I wondered further whether sometimes his "bright girl play" was not only fun, and, well, bright, but also a trick to disguise the anger, sadness, and pain that he felt. He was quick to remind me that "Ariel is happy in the end"—fortified as he was by the Disney camp romance that colors the studio's *Little*

Mermaid. I acknowledged that that was in fact true, but added that day-to-day life does not always work out as well as does cartoon life. He gave me one of those looks children often do, in the manner of, "Yes, yes, you adults and your reality." He did allow, though, that sometimes he felt "sad" and "mad"—states that he was so very reluctant to recognize during our first consultation.

It was important to hold open a complex therapeutic space, one that afforded Lincoln the opportunity to express his wishes, along with his melancholic anger, and the lack of security he felt—with his mother, but also within social address. It was also the case, in the spirit of modern efforts to reframe child therapy, that such space had to be opened for his mother as well, perhaps even more so. The work undertaken by Ms. R. and her therapist proved very helpful in not only shoring up the attachment bond between Lincoln and Ms. R., as Ms. R. became more emotionally available (and less anxious within the work of child rearing), but also in helping Ms. R. to negotiate the disruption she felt in relation to Lincoln's femininity.

By definition, the nonnormative disrupt. They challenge, sometimes with the frustration (the grievance) of one who has gone unrecognized, and sometimes simply in the act of being different. This proposition seemed especially helpful to Ms. R., who began to better appreciate how Lincoln's difference put him in the near constant position of making a melancholic plea for the redress of social conditions that governed his experience of freedom and autonomy. She could see that his freedom was often denied, curtailed, and corrected, driven once again into a shadowed shame, a place where his scorned desire must live (angrily, reproachfully) in hiding. As Ms. R. began to contemplate these swirling dynamics, she recognized that "Lincoln must grow tired" of pushing, and grasped as well that she too felt these states via his projections—his fatigue, his frustration, his fear (I thought back on my feeling states during my first consultation with Lincoln: fatigue, frustration, anxiety). In this way, she described feeling "sandwiched" between his push, his anger, and the push and anger of normative conscription.

We came to recognize, as she indicated upon first coming to see me, that the social scene was often "impossible." She could not change it, or change it quickly enough, but she could have a mind that afforded her the opportunity to reflect upon and speak with Lincoln about the dilemmas they faced. She might not always be able to provide shelter (either from the incursion of the outside or from her own internalized shame), but they could reflect on the storm. Via such reflection she could help Lincoln to begin to develop his own reflective self-functioning, a skill that he could then apply toward a better "theory" of his own mind and the minds of others.

Of equal importance were our reflections on a child's need for gender practice, once again stimulated by Lincoln's therapist's countertransference experience. Following a session in which Ms. R. and I thought together about a child's need for an improvisation space, a space of multifaceted dispositions and fantasmatic license, Ms. R. reported, several months later, that she and her therapist had spent a considerable amount of time reflecting back on Ms. R.'s own experience of gender practice. She had recognized that her experience of femininity was in an important part constructed in relation to her father. The import of these considerations had to do with her observation of a similar dynamic between her father and Lincoln.

Ms. R. spoke of her father as a gregarious fellow, a musician, who played in a band on weekends. She linked his musicianship to his seeming ability to sincerely enjoy the creative enterprises of others: "He can play, and bring others into the play." He and Lincoln had recently begun "writing" songs together. Lincoln wrote the words—largely princess "dreams." Her father "played along." As she was observing this scene, she recalled how she and her brother used to put on plays that their father would "score." She recounted that she used to dress in elaborate costumes, and that there was always a "big dance number." She went ahead to talk about learning the pleasures of exhibitionism, the pleasures of being the object of desire, and about the importance of those feelings in her experience of herself as a woman.

Aside from the clothes, many of which came from her mother's closet, Ms. R. could not find her mother in these memories. Ms. R. went on, "She was likely upstairs reading. We were too noisy for her." Comparing herself with her mother, Ms. R. spoke of her as less social than her father, more internal, and given to vigilant worry: "sadly, perhaps more like me."

As she thought back on her "subject construction" (as she put it), she indicated that she was grateful for her father's part in her femininity: "It was a good part." And grateful as well that Lincoln also could enjoy that space of gendered practice.

Ms. R.'s reference to a "part" of her experience proved helpful to me, although it was not something I discussed with her directly. I came to think, following here on the psychoanalyst Muriel Dimen, of the ways in which Lincoln's femininity was in parts, multiply expressed and inflected, as are all genders. I also came to a similar position regarding Lincoln's racially inflected gender identity. I regret to say that this was a feature of the work that was underanalyzed. I found along

with Lincoln's therapist that we could not develop much trac-
tion around this facet of his identity, either with him or with
his mother; it seemed not to be much on their minds. Perhaps it will come into their minds and into the light of analysis
at another juncture. In particular, I speculate that Lincoln's
experience of exoticism may prove to be something that he
will need to better understand as his life moves on. The narratives we pursued, though, were in the service of his and his
mother's need to establish better attachment security and reflective resonance. Surely, there were other narratives. Surely,
there are other parts. And just as surely there will be future re-
contextualizations, relations, and fantasmatic spaces through
which Lincoln's gender will reweave.

We did not move within this treatment toward a summarizing originary explanation. The treatment moved, if anything, toward less fixity, and toward the construction of reflective space that could hold the probity of many origins within
a different spirit of social comity. This move follows on my belief not only that normative gender regulation leaves us un-
prepared to face the realities of lived gender variance, but that
the anxiety of regulation also serves to inhibit another order
of things. Psychic and social coherence do not reside only in
normative expressions of masculinity. But unless and until
potential space that is open to a range of subject positions is
actively created, a more variegated culture will not enter the
consulting room.

PART III

Boys, Masculinity, and Phallic Narcissism

CHAPTER FIVE

Faggot = Loser
Phallic Narcissism as Defense

FAGGOT HAS BECOME THE ALL-PURPOSE PUTDOWN. "When we grew up everything was a faggot," a young man tells the playwright Marc Wolf in *Another American Asking and Telling.*[1] Or as Ben, a high school student explains when asked by the social scientist C. J. Pascoe what prompts someone to call another person a "fag": "Literally, anything. Like you were trying to turn a wrench the wrong way: 'Dude, you're a fag.'"[2]

Faggot = anything. Faggot = everything. The ubiquity of *faggot* redoubles its meanings, and at the same time diminishes its meanings, or at the very least blunts them through sheer repetition. *Faggot* is rather like a tennis ball left too long in the game. It has lost some of its velocity. It has become an empty term, a marker, perhaps more akin to punctuation than to speech. One cannot presume the meaning of *faggot* based on the word alone; the meanings are carried through the emotion of the punctuation.

Faggot is a missive/missile for hate, irony, monotony, fear, aggression, affection, scorn, shame, amusement, contempt, ennui, rivalry, and defiance, to name but a few. *Faggot* can be a taunt, a tease, or a trauma. The attribution can linger and attach, or it can be glancing and practically meaningless. The stakes can vary from the nip of play to the bite of battle.

I focus in this chapter on one expression of *faggot,* as it is employed to register failure and loss. Even Ben, Pascoe's research subject, who does such a good job of capturing the ubiquity of *fag,* nevertheless illustrates the word by noting a moment when something went "wrong," when some norma-tive expectation went unmet (a dude should be able to handle a wrench). In particular, I am interested in the ways in which *faggot* is used to mark and manage experiences of failure and loss in moments of rivalry between boys: faggot = loser.

Consider how Eminem embeds his definition of *faggot* within a description of manhood as rivalry:

> Faggot to me just means . . . taking away your manhood. You're a sissy. You're a coward. Just like you might sit around in your living room and say, "Dude, stop, you're being a fag, dude." . . . It does not necessarily mean you're being a gay person. It just means you're being a fag. You're being an asshole or whatever. That's the way that the word was always taught to me. That's how I learned the word. Battling with somebody, you do anything you can to strip their manhood away.[3]

Eminem renders *faggot* as a salvo, and manhood, in his view, is configured, at least in part, on the dynamics of winning or losing in relations with other men or boys. However unex-pected the pairing, Eminem's view is shared and illuminated in the feminist-inflected modern discourse on boys.

This midcentury rereading of masculinity follows on Robert Stoller's assertion that masculinity takes shape and meaning as a boy separates from his mother. Distinct from Freud's theory of masculinity, this rereading focuses less on matters of rivalry and desire than on boys' experiences of attachment and separation.[4] The mother-son bond is key. The psychoanalysts Jessica Benjamin and Nancy Chodorow linked this mother-son dis-identifactory push to the development of "not me" difference. This not-me, not-feminine stance then helps to inform how boys separate from girls, and how boys/men dominate girls/women.[5] A number of theorists, most notably the psychologist William Pollack, have built on this frame to suggest that boys are pushed to separate prematurely from their mothers, leaving boys to detach or separate from their feelings. Consequent upon this premature separation, boys are vulnerable to depression and alienation that are, in turn, acted out through unchecked aggression and disorganized attention. Boys and men are also depicted as less open to psychological thinking—turning in, reflection, and the consideration of others.[6]

Masculinity has been reexamined with respect to the relational fault lines that stem from boys' limited capacities to recognize others and build relations through mutual give-and-take. Consider in this regard boys' self-satisfaction based on their overestimation of the penis, phallic pride, and narcissist exhibitionism. The psychoanalyst Michael Diamond summarizes this exhibitionism as follows: "Figuratively speaking, extending, thrusting, and penetrating become paramount, along with the associated personality traits of assertiveness, aggression, strength, and potency."[7]

Moving from a view that saw this exhibitionism as dispositional and anatomically determined, midcentury theorists instead began to examine this narcissistic display as defense. This new understanding of masculine defense was used to critique

Freud's theory of masculinity as default phallic narcissism. As the psychoanalyst Ethel Person puts it, "The fundamental sexual problem for boys is the struggle to achieve phallic strength and power vis-à-vis other men."[8] Note here that Person problematizes a boy's experience of rivalry with other boys and men rather than presenting these states as presumptively formative. Nancy Chodorow makes a similar point when she suggests that "for some men, and in some cultures, masculinity is cast as an adult-child dichotomy: being an adult man versus being a little boy; being humiliated by other men."[9]

The struggle for boys is to be big, not small. The preservation of bigness is posed as virtually equivalent to masculinity. To be a man is to be big. To be a man is to win. Boys don't lose.

I center here on a clinical moment during a game in which a child patient called me a "faggot." I situate this exchange within the broader frame of my work with this boy and his family. Central to this boy's treatment was his experience of himself as small and losing, not big and winning. Particular attention is given to the defensive function *faggot* played in relation to this boy's effort to disavow smallness and losing as he sought the agency of bigness and winning. To be big, to win, was not to be in a position to express his experience of neglect, or his need for parental love and recognition. I utilize his specific dilemma, and the manner in which it was refracted in his particular family, in order to consider the more general boyhood quest to be big and winning, not small and losing.

I also examine the momentary microrelationship created during the "faggot" exchange. I reflect not only on my young patient's subjective response but my own as well. I do so in order to illuminate the ways in which individuals and genders are always made between (from one to the other, and back again). There is never just one boy, never just one masculinity, there are circulating relations and affect states that speak, to some degree, through generational transfer: the boy, the boy he wishes to be, me as a boy, the boy I wish to be, his father, my father, his mother, my mother, his brother, my brother, the boy in his father's eyes, me in my father's eyes, the boy in his mother's eyes, me in my mother's eyes, the boy in his brother's eyes, me in my brother's eyes, the boy in the social order, me in the social order, our families in the social order.

Boys Don't Lose

I use the terms *small* and *losing* as virtually equivalent. My work with young boys has led me to consider these states as symbolically linked, indeed often conflated within the psychic reality of boyhood. My work with young boys also leads me to posit the wish and effort to be a big winner, not a small loser as a central boyhood theme.[10]

Consider the predicament of losing illustrated in the following clinical material taken from a play therapy session with a six-year-old boy. This young boy, Josh, was referred for treatment following repeated outbursts of aggressive behavior at school. These disruptive outbursts were often followed by equally intense periods of sullen withdrawal and apparent sadness. His parents described similar behaviors at home, and in particular noted that these behaviors were more pronounced in relation to his much older brother.

In many ways, Josh's family was a house divided. His parents brought him for treatment upon the suggestion of their couples therapist. In our initial consultation both parents spoke of their fear regarding the "breakdown" of their marriage, and how their relationship colored their relations with their sons. For the past two years, the father had been traveling a great deal; he was away from home at least two weeks of every month. The mother felt angry and overwhelmed that the lion's share of parenting responsibilities had fallen to her. She was equally dispirited by her efforts to balance her own work with the demands of family life. She became especially anxious when the two boys fought. In her eyes, these fights represented the "breakdown" of their family life. The father, for his part, expressed a mix of guilt and divided loyalty. He was grappling with having "abandoned" his family while wrestling with his "selfish" desire for the worldly pleasure provided by his work.

Both parents recalled greater harmony in the early years of raising their first son. In effect, they described a first-versus-second family divide. The two boys were separated by eight years. Along with the added responsibility of a second child, they described the ways in which their careers had become more demanding. While they enjoyed a greater degree of economic freedom (and in the father's case a greater sense of accomplishment), they described having less energy and "mental space" for the children. This lack of energy seemed especially apparent in response to Josh's aggression: the mother described herself as implosively turning in and away, while the father reacted with a kind of overbearing silence.

The hour I am going to describe began in the waiting room, with Josh's mother instructing him to return a toy that he had apparently taken from my office. Josh sheepishly produced a blue plastic knife from his front pocket that did in fact belong to my toy kitchen set. I nodded and said that we could talk about his having taken it when we got into the office. Once inside, I suggested that he must have really wanted to have the knife for his very own. He concurred with a nod of his head. I asked whether he might be embarrassed, to which he also concurred with a nod. He then suggested that we play a game with which he had been preoccupied for many sessions.

The game comprised the following roles: Josh was a spy, who always had the plastic knife in his rear pocket, partially visible. I was given the role of the spy's younger brother, whose primary motivation was to get the knife. Josh would direct us through this drama in a variety of ways. Today the plot centered on the younger brother's efforts to trick and distract the older spy brother, so that the younger brother could make off with the knife. But the younger brother was never to succeed; he was consistently foiled and left empty-handed.

As I inquired about the younger brother's feelings and motivations, so that I would know how to play his part, I became aware that Josh was more interested in embodying the role and motivations of the prepossessing older brother. He was not interested in talking about the younger brother's experience. I was, at this point in our work, quite familiar with the role of younger brother, and gave voice to "my" experience of frustration at not having and not being able to get what the older brother had. I sputtered angrily, I pouted, and I bitterly complained about the state of being small.

I also suggested that the younger brother might feel embarrassed to be seen as so angry and upset—that he was mad about wanting so much, upset to be seen as wanting, and possibly embarrassed to be caught trying to take what he wanted. I knew these more abstracted comments would not have the same effect as those that could be expressed within the play. But I wanted at least to hint at a move from the play to Josh's experience of having taken the knife from my playroom.

At this point in the hour, Josh turned from the knife drama and suggested that we play a board game that is intended for older children. I explained that the game might be difficult, but Josh was insistent. So we set about playing. He quickly grew frustrated and voiced his fear that he was going to lose. At one point, as I moved a game piece toward the finish line and it seemed that I was going to win, Josh muttered, "Faggot."

There was a pause, one to which I will return, but I go ahead here to record the clinical exchange, and to discuss the treatment arc.

Eventually, I said, "I guess you really wanted to win."

Josh tersely replied, "It's just a word."

There was another pause, and then he added, "My brother calls me that."

I said, "I see." Then I asked, "Why does he say that?"

Josh responded, "I don't know."

I said, "You don't know. But how do you feel when Jed calls you that?"

"Mad," Josh answered.

I said, "It's a word that makes you mad. It sort of stings, doesn't it?"

"Yeah," Josh replied.

"When Jed calls you that, do you also feel bad—sort of small and bad?" I asked.

Josh nodded.

I added, "Sort of like me in the blue knife game."

Josh nodded again.

I ventured that he might feel hurt and mad when he was put down.

He concurred, saying, "I hate him. He thinks he's the boss of everything."

I replied, "Your brother sure does make you mad," and then I added, "But do you think you also might want to be like him—big like him? And be close to him? Like in the blue knife game?"

Josh allowed that he was mad, but was adamant that he did not like his brother nor did he wish to be like him.

I asserted here that it was hard to figure out how to be big, especially if you have a big brother and an even bigger father.

At this point, Josh asked to play a game that had become a mainstay of his repertoire. We called this game "block tower baseball." Josh was the batter. I was alternately the fielder, and the sports announcer who would interview Josh about his accomplishments at bat. The interviews would focus on his prowess and his strength. He would swagger over to the mike and grant terse recognition of my praise.

Today, as usual, Josh built a block tower and then with a large long block he toppled it. The number of blocks that fell was equal to the number of runs scored. Grand slams were especially sought after, and would necessitate an "instant interview." Early in today's game, Josh scored a grand slam. During the instant interview, I suggested that he wanted to show those blocks "who was big—the big boss." He puffed up his chest and said, "Yep."

During this phase of the treatment, I was primarily focused on parsing Josh's defenses: his defense against loss, his "big" puffed-up defense against longing and the expression of ne-glect. In a similar vein, I made only occasional links between

Josh's experience in the play and his own family experience. I felt it best to wait for him to provide such linking. It was some time before these links were made. When they did occur, I believe they followed, in large measure, on work I did with his parents (which I describe below). Poignantly, when Josh did begin to speak more directly about his father and brother, he said at one point, "They don't understand, I wanted to be the biggest."

Faggot = Loser: Panic, Defense, and the Third

I turn back now to the "faggot" moment, not only as I worked to understand my patient but also as I worked to be conscious of my own experience of what the psychoanalyst Gillian Straker calls "the anti-analytic third," those moments when hate enters the consulting room (think here of hate as a third entity that comes between the patient and therapist).[11] I emphasize that not only was Josh constituted in that moment as a speaker, but I too was constituted as the object of his speech act. Working from and through my construction as the "faggot," I show that my own history, and my own experiences of masculinity, informed our relationship in that moment.

When Josh muttered "faggot," my thoughts and feelings reeled in several directions, and then again went nowhere. At first, I experienced the stunned blankness of injury—an injury that nevertheless has a history, and is therefore not blank, rather temporarily held at bay through the defense of shock—not exactly dissociation, but rather a blanketing drone, the blank of too much. I have been called faggot or queer or sissy any number of times, and with a variety of inflections. Mostly, this naming occurred in my childhood. I venture that my peers were speaking to their perceptions that I was a proto-gay boy, but also to their experience of me as oddly able, and then again, not: bookish, obsessive, artistic, "too sensitive," reticent, verbally quick; physically quick as well, fast and agile, athletic in a way, yet easily overwhelmed by too much aggression; shy and exhibitionistic in equal measure.

Faggot, therefore, carries a particular and embodied history for me. *Faggot* not only was a formative dimension of my identity; it continues to sustain that identity. Paraphrasing Judith Butler, the word entered my limbs, crafted my gestures, bent my spine, and shaped my mind.[12] Power relations, my status as a loser, no matter my victories, were and are brought into being and enacted over and over again. Defensive relations, obsessive, overly determined, competitive, and verbally aggressive, countered by wordless withdrawal, were collected and enacted over and over again. The offensive and defensive give way and meld into one. This psychic grammar of power and defense was abetted by a troubled, embattled, and dependent relationship with my young father, as distant in his psychic remove as was Josh's father through his physical and material remove.

By the time Josh got around to calling me faggot, I, luckily, had had many opportunities to reflect on my bent spine/mind. This is not to say that I could escape my constitution as the "faggot" in the clinical moment, or that I was somehow above defense in my response to him. Following the brief pause (and as we well know, a great deal can be communicated in silence, even brief silences), I suggested that Josh must have "really wanted to win." In so doing, I was following the theme of the hour: recall that Josh had turned to the game following my comments about the angry younger brother in the blue knife game, the brother who was mad about not winning. This theme also returns following the "faggot" moment.

However, given the charge of the moment, was I responding to Josh's anxiety or rescripting my own panic, as the psychoanalyst Donald Moss asked in an online colloquium of this clinical moment?[13] Was I speaking to his wish to win, or was I reiterating my own panic as the faggot/loser? Was this moment more discursive and less forceful than the desire suggested by my interpretation? As Josh says, "It's just a word." In this vein, one could formulate the exchange as follows: His speech was anxious. My response was panic.

Following this line of inquiry, one would then be left to question, as did Moss and the psychologist Stephen Frosh, whether the direction of my intervention offered too little room for either the modulation or expansion of Josh's fantasies. For example, was Josh, as Frosh and the psychoanalyst Steven Cooper asked, practicing the fag discourse of boy-ness? Might my intervention have curtailed such practice? Did I fail in that moment to adequately absorb something about Josh's desire for affirmation, in particular, his longing for a father who could see and prize a boy's wish to grow and be like him? Cooper posited that "the boys will be boys bravado and aggressive protest is not only a response to the threat of smallness, but also a response to loving feelings that need to be affirmed." Formulating his idea in Josh's voice, Cooper elaborated, "I need a man who wants me to feel and be like him. I'm alone with my needs to have and be like my father. These longings toward my father make me feel humiliated."[14] Hence, did "faggot" encode something of Josh's humiliation turned outward, turned perhaps toward me? Did it speak the humiliation of the younger brother about whom I was speaking in the game before this one?

I find merit, some helpful post hoc supervision, if you will, in this line of inquiry. I think it is without question that my response was informed by panic. How could it not be? I silently stumbled, attempted to regain my footing, and made my best effort to reflect on what had occurred. My best effort to reflect on, or organize the affect states that collided in that moment were undoubtedly colored by my experience of what Gillian Straker calls "the disorganizing presence of a noxious social discourse."[15]

Disorganized through the determining force of *faggot*, I found myself weighing the rightness of the attribution: Had Josh perceived that I was gay? And, however illogical, did his recognition signal that I had failed to properly embody the presumptive heterosexual male analyst? Had I thereby lost hold of my proper gender, my proper and authorized sexuality? Was I a "faggot" for trying to empathize with his experience? Was I a "faggot" for mistaking a nip for a bite?

In yet another neighboring region of my mind, I came up against my anxiety over being a man who works with children, and an openly gay one at that. Some time ago, a father of another child, in a moment of intense feeling, expressed his concern that I was a pedophile. Stunned and stung, I once again felt the force of hate. And once again I weighed the hateful perception: Did he understand that I was gay, and did he therefore make the unfounded and irrational link with pedophilia? Had I expressed some inappropriate degree of affection for his child? (I recalled touching his son's head in the waiting room as I said good-bye.) We came to understand that this "moment of hate" (the father's phrase) was born of the father's

envy regarding my apparent ease with children, and my willingness to engage them at their level. We came also to understand that he did suspect that I was gay (a fact that was then
confirmed when aspects of my private life were made public
through a newspaper article). In the spirit of our psychotherapeutic endeavor, we worked with his projections and perceptions to better understand his relationship with his son, and in
this respect our work was not extraordinary.

There is, however, an extraordinary vulnerability for men
working with children, which is even greater for gay men
working with children. This vulnerability is overdetermined
and highly idiosyncratic. My experience has led me to reflect
on how this vulnerability, built as it has been on my own experience of being hated, requires a particular kind of countertransference forbearance—a particular capacity to sustain
multiple states of mind that allow me to experience the shame
of being hated while simultaneously (or probably retrospec-
tively) thinking through the shame of being hated.

There is indeed the inescapability of our constitution
in social discourse(s); yet in the act of analysis, the analyst
is also constituted through a variety of procedural working
models and theoretical templates. The analyst leans into those
working models as he or she strives to regain the therapeutic
action that has been disrupted or compromised. Indeed, the
deconstructive action of the analyst's mind, the "standing in
the spaces," as the psychoanalyst Philip Bromberg might have
it—that is, standing apart while still in the action and trying
to assess what is at hand, what is being felt, and by whom,
and moreover, how such feeling states came about in the first
place—is what some might suggest is at the very heart of the
psychoanalyst's contribution to the therapeutic endeavor.[16] As

Straker posits, "If we subscribe to the value of psychoanalysis, then we are entitled to hope that holding in mind its concepts and ideas can at times restore thought when it has been lost."[17]

So, yes, there is panic, there is the possibility of missed opportunity and inhibition, projections are exchanged, there are thoughts lost, but there is also ongoing holding, repair, recovery, and the possibility of reflection. There is the possibility of moving toward a third position (imagine a triangle, and the opportunity afforded by looking from one point of the triangle at the relationship created by the other two points; a point of reference and reflection; a point of contemplation outside/aside the action), one that affords the reinstatement of reverie or play.[18]

Here, in my view, given the arc of the hour, and the play that followed upon my interpretation, we come upon the ways in which interpretations most often have multiple registrations. We come as well upon the analyst's function to hold and track the hour. In this early phase of my work with Josh, I was particularly keen to understand and name his defenses—heading toward how one then speaks to what the defense defends against. In light of this post hoc discussion, I can see that I may have missed (in that crevice of panic) an opportunity to go a step further and speak to Josh's humiliation and feelings of neglect. Luckily, analyses rarely if ever turn on such micromoments; rather, they are held and built in a different experience of time—a web of contingent associations and an ever expansive relay of construction and reconstruction that moves unhindered through past, present, and future, such that an interpretation can be offered before the association, or an intervention can drop a stitch and pick it back up in the next thought or association.

Through this work of holding, the analyst strives to establish enough of a third—enough play in the play—to afford recovery upon inevitable failure. Consider in this regard how Josh redirects us. After his declaration that *faggot* is just a word, he nevertheless gives the word a history—his brother calls him "faggot"; from there we move forward to further consider his concerns as a small boy who feels neglected, who feels himself to be lost, losing, and longing. And then, in league with the power of his defenses, he takes us a step further, and a step back, into the action of block-tower baseball; we return to Josh's wishes to be admired as a big winner, as we will over and over again, in this phase of the treatment.

It strikes me that parents and other parenting figures, such as teachers or therapists, are often in a similar position of striving to hold open enough potential space for masculinity to coalesce in relation to regulatory norms and the psychically specific forces that collect in any given boy, but not to simply accede to these forces. Feminists have marshaled a nuanced and socially powerful analysis of how difficult it is to hold open that space for girls.[19] A similar discourse is beginning to shape our thinking about boys, and key to this body of thought are ideas about boys' efforts to defend against longing and need.[20]

Heading into Battle, and the Work of Defense

I have purposely chosen an hour from the beginning of Josh's treatment in order to illustrate that the predicament of bigness was expressed or solved through battle and the defense of splitting: one either was big or small, strong or weak, a winner or a loser. Firm lines were drawn. As the session illustrates, Josh spent much of his time during this period of his treatment either struggling to represent bigness and strength or struggling to win bigness and strength—even if it had to be stolen. Play was rigidly scripted so that loss was always on the other side. Such scripting required a loser—the role to which I was consistently assigned (as in the blue knife drama). When loss did occur (as in the board game) it was shed and turned out— projected into the other.

Loss was lodged in another, as Josh moved toward a valued (though clearly conflicted) identification with his brother. He stole *faggot* from his brother, just as he strove to steal what he saw as his brother's strength. A similar move can be noted in his apparent wish to appropriate what he saw as my strength (or to take a valued part of me) in his act of taking the play knife. This dynamic is then repeated in the blue knife drama, wherein I, as younger brother, am instructed to try to steal the older brother's knife. Such maneuvers allowed Josh to locate smallness and loss on the other side, while he positioned himself on the side of victory and bigness. In so doing, he repeatedly strove to create a distinct border between a small and defeated "you" and a big and victorious "me." He also strove to conceal or defend against his longing for recognition. Yes, he was the admired victor, but one who dominated, and did not afford much beyond surface admiration.

The brittle dimension of his defenses can be noted in the ways in which borders need constant patrol. Anxieties that are to be averted have a way of sneaking back.[21] "Sneaking" is operative here; the manner in which the anxieties sneak back is in keeping with the way in which the act of identification is sneaky. Josh sneaks toward identification through various acts of appropriation and stealing. Identification is never fully claimed, is even denied. If he were to openly identify with a winner, he might risk being a loser (risk being small and in need), or risk the possibility that winning and losing could exist outside a dynamic of splitting.

Instead, Josh made repeated efforts to define the border and to sustain the split. He was a vigilant border guard, persistently fending off the anxiety of losing. Our roles as winner and loser were rigidly defined and controlled. The "play" in play was burdened by his rigid and paranoid vigilance. I often experienced the insistent thrust and grip of domination. At times my every move was controlled, and I was not allowed to voice anything other than that which was scripted by Josh. I am reminded here of another young boy, who in a similar play scenario, "tied" me to my chair and "taped" my mouth shut, for several sessions.[22]

To further aid and abet his border patrol, Josh repeatedly inflated his bigness and strength. Consider that he moved to "block tower baseball" following his loss at the board game. The goal of his performance in the baseball game was adoration. The psychoanalyst John Ross has linked such performances with machismo: "It is a dance whose aim it is to be applauded. The exhibitor reassures himself of the viability of his pretenses to virility while others reflect back to him and, in the process, magnify his machismo."[23] Josh enacted a macho victory in block-tower baseball through a kind of tumescent hammering.

Not only did he seek through such acts to bolster his bigness, but he also sought to disavow his experience of loss. He would not allow any expression of care or empathy in the face of defeat—in order to do so, he would have to cross the win-lose divide. He might also have to see himself as small and in need. Remember that he moved to block-tower baseball after I offered my thoughts about the difficulty he was experiencing relative to his quest to be big.

I want to reemphasize here that I am speaking at this point about the work of defense—often one's focus in the beginning of a treatment. As the treatment moved forward, it was, of course, important to grasp and address that which Josh was defending: his longing for recognition and love, his wish to belong to a family within which he could feel admired and desired. I reiterate this point about defenses because I think boys are too often simply taken for their defensive face value ("boys will be boys"). As I shall discuss, these defenses, when unmet, have the potential to shape particular power relations, such as misogyny and homophobia, that produce and promote a them-us traumatic split or divide—one that often haunts the psychic lives of men.

From Phallic Narcissism to the Third

A "boys will be boys" approach to male development reflects a pervasive reluctance to examine certain forms of male aggression. In particular, the "boys will be boys" approach serves to mask the masculine dilemma regarding the threat of losing, as well as, and in my view more important, boys' and men's conflicts with expressing their longings for love and recognition.

The exhibitionistic vigor and desire for adoration that fueled Josh's performance is not unusual for a boy his age. Nor is it unusual for a boy this age to engage in play that is colored by a kind of machismo or aggrandized exhibitionism; who among us has not been charmed by the phallic posturing of young boys? These exhibitions are, after all, often presented as acts of seduction: "Look at me, and admire me as the bigness that you desire." One would be positively churlish, and would be deprived of the pleasure of the admirer and desirer, to always resist. Moreover, as befits acts of seduction, however clumsy and lacking in finesse, these exhibitions are shot through with the vitality of yearning and a quest toward relating. If we do not reckon with the relational reach of this posturing, we lose the opportunity to understand how young boys may defend against their longings for love and recognition.

Josh's desire for admiration was, however, burdened by an unusual degree of vigor and vigilance. The seductive arc of his play was interrupted by his persistent anxiety regarding the possibility of loss. In this way, Josh affords us an enhanced or exaggerated view into a set of dynamics that have been said to characterize the psychic terrain of boyhood.

Traditionally, these dynamics have been theorized through the psychoanalytic vocabulary of castration and phallic narcissism. I find this persuasively critiqued vocabulary to be necessary but insufficient. While I utilize the concepts of phallic narcissism and castration, I am mindful of their limits. To reiterate and summarize the critique I offered through my rereading of Little Hans: these concepts (1) circulate in a discourse that promotes a narrowed focus on the penis as opposed to locating the boy's relationship to his penis (both in pleasure and conflict) within the broader bodily eroticism which more aptly characterizes boyhood, (2) promote phallic monism (there is only one sex organ, the penis), (3) encourage a view that elides gender and the sexed body, (4) highlight children's experiences of difference while virtually ignoring their experiences of similarity, (5) prize the developmental achievements of activity while overlooking the developmental possibilities of passivity, (6) overemphasize boys' conflicts with genital difference (penis-vagina) while underestimating the boy's conflicts with generational difference (big-small).

Pertaining to the issue of generational difference, my experience in working with young boys suggests that this conflict is often far more pronounced than conflicts they experience around genital difference, a point I made as well in my rereading of Little Hans. The dilemma is not so much who has a penis and who does not, but who has a big agentic penis and who does not. Along these lines, I have often found the notion of penis envy to be more useful in thinking about male development than female development.[24]

Yet I continue to find utility in thinking through the thrust of boys' battles to be big, not small, a winner, not a loser, as one variant of phallic narcissism (exhibitionistic, arrogant, sadistic, dominant). More to the point, I argue for the active clinical engagement of this aggression, including the anxiety and splitting that shadow this preoccupation. I argue for the active engagement and reflection upon the muscular aggression (the dogged mental muscularity of narcissism and the persistent physical pitch and push of boyhood) that often propels such preoccupation and anxiety. Following on the psychoanalysts Peter Fonagy and Mary Target, I propose engaging boys in the difficult process of thirdness (once again, reflecting from one point in a triangle toward the other two points, or stepping back from oneself and reflecting on one's mind versus action) as a psychic venue that offers a context of growth within which to actively grapple with boys' anxiety and aggression.[25] I have found this approach to be a very helpful way to speak to boys about their desires and how those desires, while carried forward through their bodies, are "thought" and "felt" in their minds and the minds of others.

This manner of engagement stands in contrast to the ways in which boys' narcissistic preoccupations and aggression are simultaneously prized and neglected through the "boys will be boys" approach to masculinity. Boys' aggression, which so often conceals their anxiety about losing, is neither adequately contained nor engaged. Their aggression and anxiety are not balanced through relationships with their parents, siblings, and peers. Boys are left to run amok, to relate through control and domination.

With these thoughts in mind, I consider how I employed the concepts of phallic narcissism and castration fear to understand what might be called the phallic quest that pervades the hour I report. An especially intriguing expression of this quest can be found in the symbolism and function of the knife. To begin, the knife is pocketed. It is literally and repeatedly put into a pocket. Calling to mind Mae West's famous quip ("Is that a pistol in your pocket, or are you just glad to see me?"), Josh simultaneously draws our attention to the penis and accentuates his own narcissistic interest in it.[26] This narcissistic interest is further expressed in the ways in which the knife is an object of desire. It is displayed as a taunting and desired object that is out of reach. One either has it or tries to get it. There is a sadistic edge to this taunting narcissistic display. But never, in the game, does the knife become a weapon, nor was it ever wielded in a threatening manner.

The desirability of the knife contrasts with the way in which the block-bat in the baseball game serves as an instrument of attack. This shift, which occurs following Josh's loss at the board game, might be understood as a move from phallic narcissistic interest or desire (the blue knife) to a sadistic phallic defense (the block bat) in the face of loss. The projectile force of *faggot* can be understood along similar lines: *faggot* functions, as does the block-bat, to strike at and fend off the threat of loss.

I want also to note that the knife was "pocketed" in another manner: it was stolen, once from my office, and then again in the many attempts at stealing that become the heart of the knife game. As such, the penis can be taken. Here we might question whether Josh was enacting his fear of castration or his feeling that in order to have the phallus he would have to steal it from another. The need to steal could be interpreted as generated by castration anxiety.

Along these lines, addressing his push toward appropriation proved most helpful in addressing Josh's anxiety. I worked to understand how his quest for phallic agency had been curtailed within his family: that he had not been afforded opportunities to consolidate the pleasures of the full-bodied muscular eroticism that characterizes phallic play. We spoke of this quandary as his "wish to be big" versus his "worry that he wouldn't have a chance to get big." For example, I pointed toward the way in which he so often dominated the play as indicative of his "worry that I might take over" or "that I won't let you be the one who gets to lead."

I set out to clarify that he had not been provided with equally important opportunities to metabolize his experiences of loss, and I began to comment on his efforts to avoid or disavow loss. We spoke mostly of these efforts as "cheating," but with time we were able to speak more directly about his attempts to "act big" when he lost at something like a game.

I sought to locate his phallic quest and his efforts to equilibrate pleasure and loss within certain family dynamics: his father's frequent absences, his mother's anger and anxiety, and his competition with his brother. A vantage point to this dilemma was offered through the recurrent play themes of stealing and spying. Recall that the older brother in the knife game was a spy, and that the younger brother was attempting to steal the older spy-brother's knife. I understood this play to be a portrayal of the older brother's ability to see into the "big" world, and through that act of seeing to garner power, authority, and autonomy. The powerless younger brother, on the other hand, could only attempt to steal the phallus, and fail.

Following on Britton and on Fonagy and Target, I approached this theme as an expression of Josh's experience of Oedipal triangulation.[27] As the fourth, Josh stood outside the triangle of his mother-father-brother—outside the triangle of the first family. He was having great difficulty creating his own usable Oedipal triangle. From the sidelines, he repeatedly enacted a dynamic of thwarted rivalry, which usually consisted of efforts to steal power through a kind of intrusive or illusory agency. He had limited experience with triangular opportunities, either as a participant in a relationship being observed by another or as an observer of a relationship between two others. Consequently, his world was made secure not through the creation of a benign space wherein one could be observed or thought about but through relations that were rigidly controlled and dominated. He attempted to engage others by way of physicality and aggression as opposed to the possibilities of mentalization and observation.[28] His aggression and quest toward phallic strength were not balanced through open desiring attachments or through the equilibrative experience of pleasure and loss that is characteristic of triangular opportunities. Instead, his aggression ran amok.

The Family as the Third

To a large extent, when he entered treatment, Josh felt his brother to be his only reliable family member. However, and understandably, the brother could neither promote nor tolerate this dependence. Josh's relationship with his brother, both as enacted in the play and as it was lived in daily life, provided me with something of a bridge to engage Josh's parents in a therapeutic dialogue about his experience of neglect. To a considerable extent, the therapeutic action that developed in working with Josh occurred in this parental dialogue.

In particular, I set out to understand the effect of his father's absence, as well as that of his mother's anxiety. In conjunction with work undertaken in the course of their couples treatment, the parents began to grasp that the father's absence made manifest a growing alienation within the couple. That insight led to the further understanding that as they turned away from each other they also turned away from their children. Left with two parents, each absent in his or her way, Josh was without parents whom he could actively engage.

Additionally, the mother began to question whether she was depressed. We were able to see that she had moved into an avoidant position from which she felt great injustice and limited capacity to change. She could feel especially "helpless" and "in the dark" with the children, and spoke of her guilt over leaving Josh to the care of his older brother. Both parents felt it likely that her depression predated the father's acceptance of his current job and traveling schedule, and that they had most likely concurred in his taking the job as a way to avoid facing her depression. The mother entered her own psychotherapy and sought psychopharmacological treatment as well.

The parents' increased understanding along these lines led the father to curtail his travel schedule in order to be at home more — a move that appeared motivated by his wish to recoup his marriage and be more available to his children. In addition, both parents arranged to spend more time with Josh on their own. I persisted, though, with both parents in order to draw them into an understanding of Josh's needs on the plane of psychic action.

Underscoring my efforts was my conviction that Josh needed parental minds he could actively engage. I explained that I thought it likely that his aggression and anxiety stemmed, at least in part, from neglect. I encouraged the parents to more directly contain and redress Josh's anxiety and aggression. We worked toward their being able to speak with Josh about his behavior and help him give voice to his fears, in order that he might be able to see himself as well. For example, as opposed to simply intervening in order to stop the boys from fighting, I worked with the parents to help them "scan" the situation: What was it about the circumstances? What was it about the arc of the day? What might have provoked or upset Josh? In particular, had something happened that might lead to his feeling diminished or humiliated? If so, might there be a way to recover?

Through my efforts to help the parents focus on Josh's experience, I sought to invite them into considering his mind: What did they think was on his mind? How did his mind look—was it crowded by anxiety, was it open? How might his generally aggressive outwardness cloud his capacity to look in? Through such questioning, I was attempting to illustrate that children come into their minds through processes of mutuality and intersubjective recognition. Guided here by Jessica Benjamin's documentation of the ways in which the breakdown of mother-son mutuality can lead to sadism and violence, I was especially keen to promote greater mutuality between Josh and his mother.[29] Key to our work in this regard were discussions about how the mother's fear of loss (the fear that she had lost hold of herself and her family) had interfered with her ability to "tune into" Josh's experience; instead of engaging his anxiety, talking about his fears, and helping him to "think" his mind, she had defensively drawn in and away from his mind.

Along similar lines, I posed Josh's need to observe others in order to be able to see his self. I suggested that in so seeing, he would come to appreciate the potential for relationships as well as the optimistic possibility of growth. We worked together to understand that his aggression often masked his anxiety about losing. I ventured that Josh needed help with being able to lose, and that thirdness offered such possibility. Through thirdness loss can simultaneously be experienced (observing others from outside, not inside; observing big others from the position of smallness) and recovered (being observed by others who are optimistic about one's growth). Josh was small in relation to his parents and brother, and there was real loss in such recognition. He did stand outside the exclusivity of his parents' relationship. Yet his smallness, which included the promise of growth, could be observed with optimism.

In the course of my work with Josh's parents, a theme evolved regarding their difficulty in sustaining such parent-child optimism. This theme had a familiar ring; I have encountered it with other parents of young boys. Both parents pointed to their difficulty in remaining open and optimistic to the possibilities of knowing Josh's mind in the face of his persistent activity and aggression. Parental fatigue is a commonplace. Yet my work with the parents of young boys suggests that there may be a particular brand of fatigue that Josh's mother summarized rather well: "Sometimes I want to either smack him or collapse. Given the choice, I collapse." In a similar vein, many parents of young boys speak about their difficulty maintaining their own psychic equilibrium and parental containing capacity in the face of their sons' aggression. Indeed, the phrase "boys will be boys" intones a degree of resignation in the face of boys' aggression.

Might this be one of the reasons that young boys are neglected or, alternatively, abused? Do we tire as a consequence of the diligence required to pursue and work through boys' aggression and activity? Does this dynamic of aggression and fatigue then reinforce boys' moves toward a less reflective and more physical mode of relating? Along these lines, consider Fonagy, Moran, and Target's hypothesis that if a child's expression is consistently experienced as aggression (provoking either an aggressive or deflective response), a psychological self cannot develop.[30] Aggression then becomes fused with self-expression, and mental contents (thoughts, desires) are expressed and managed physically, not psychically.

The parents' struggle with optimism notwithstanding, they did become more engaged with Josh's mind. This development allowed me greater flexibility in terms of what I could draw on in the therapy, especially as I could now enter into a therapeutic relationship beyond domination. For example, I was better able to speak about his anxiety regarding his own agency and opportunities to grow: Would there be room for him to get big? Could there be room for me to be big? Could he leave room for me to play? Could he be a winner sometimes and a loser at other times?

But perhaps most important of all, I could begin to take up his anxiety about losing and smallness and the ways in which he defended against it. First, it was important to understand Josh's experience of humiliation and loss at being small (the baby), and the ways in which he was so often forced to recognize that he would never be the biggest (the oldest). Daily occurrences brought this reality home: differing bedtimes, differing allowances, differing kinds of permission relative to activities outside the home (that his brother could ride the subway alone was an especially bitter pill). In this vein, we worked toward understanding that Josh could not change the reality of his family; he would always be the youngest. He could, however, have an independent mind and body of his own that could be recognized and prized. He could have a body and mind that could optimistically be seen to carry the promise of growth.

As Josh's dominating quest toward bigness and victory lessened, so did his defensive machismo. Fears of smallness and inadequacy emerged, as did anxiety about separation coupled with longings for dependence. Loss could be recognized and felt. Longing could be allowed and expressed. Less driven in his efforts to fortify his phallic narcissism and to subjugate his own passive longings, he could both allow for and extend empathy. A loss at a game might occasion a request for a "do over" or an inquiry that would lead to a better understanding of the directions. As the psychoanalyst Adam Phillips reminds us, Oedipus was ingenious enough to turn his losses into gains, while Narcissus was not.[31] Losses were also sometimes followed, at this point, by a shift in activity that would require that I be the one in the lead, such as reading a book. In this nonverbal way we were able to address his defense against the pleasures of smallness—the pleasure of surrender to the care and ministrations of a big other.[32]

Boys Will Be Boys

Josh's experience highlights that many boys default to the phallic narcissistic battle (however illusory or inflated), as opposed to the libidinal and relational opportunities offered within a less winner-take-all relationship with others. Such defensive battle is aided and abetted by the aggressive protest and bravado that is characteristic of machismo.

This picture of masculinity is given its inaugural and perhaps best expression through Freud's reflections on the "psychological strata" of masculinity:

> We often have the impression that with the . . . masculine protest
> [against passive desire toward another man] we have penetrated
> through all the psychological strata and have reached bedrock,
> and that thus our activities are at an end. This is probably true,
> since, for the psychical field, the biological field does in fact play
> the part of the underlying bedrock.[33]

Masculinity, as Freud distilled it, ends or concludes with protest. And while he took note of the defensive character of this protest, which he described as the repudiation of femininity and a manifestation of castration anxiety, he nevertheless concluded that efforts toward analyzing this protest were in vain. Such fear composes masculinity. It was bedrock.

Bedrock seems appropriate to machismo—a rigid solution that will brook no penetration, anxiety that cannot be questioned, cannot be soothed. But is it bedrock, or did Freud accede to the limits of a phallic narcissistic solution, and thereby mistake this illusory solution for the foundation of masculinity? As opposed to recognizing that this is *one* course that masculinity could take, Freud cast this as *the* masculine course.

Freud too quickly foreclosed the question of masculine strata. In a way, he gave up on men. He encased them in bedrock. Fossilized, men were cast as lacking the empathy, capacity for surrender, and nurturance that are needed in order to relate to others outside a dynamic of domination. According to this model, men's narcissistic attachment to their penises and their quest for phallic agency and strength trumps their relational needs.

The dependency and love between boys and boys is perhaps especially overlooked in this model that accedes to phallic posturing. In perhaps one more example of how cultural depiction outpaces psychology, these boy-to-boy relations are enjoying a rather robust representation through what might be called an off-kilter aesthetics of affect. In several different television series and films—*South Park, Jackass, Superbad,* to name a few—there is a move to examine the affective relations of boys with other boys. This move sinks from the high drama of theory, from the certainty of the parental, from the dire warnings of blind, stumbling Oedipus, toward the low, and often lowbrow topography of comedy, from Thebes to South Park.

The blockbuster films *Knocked Up* and *Superbad* offer particularly "choice" (as an adolescent patient of mine remarked) renderings of masculinity, with a particular emphasis on the homosocial bonds through which boys become boys. Masculinity is stripped, often quite literally, of its puffery, the phallus flags, the nerve unnerves. While heterosexuality and the authority vested in heterosexual masculinity may be presumptive, it is not presumptively climatic. The reproduction of matrimonial relations or the gateway to young heterosexual dating is held forward as a vexingly slippery position—hardly bedrock. Boys approach the "dark-continent" in the grip of one another.

The contradictory dynamics of phallic posturing, the phallic "cock-block," are given exquisite play in the 2007 teen sex comedy *Superbad*. At the center of this comedy is the friendship of two adolescent boys. We watch as they manifestly careen into a foulmouthed night of searching for liquor and sex, a night filled with a variety of bedrock boys and buffoon men dueling with one another. But just under the surface of this comedic romp we come to see that the two boys, something of a couple, are struggling to separate from each other, to loosen their homosocial and homoerotic tie as they move toward graduation, different colleges, and relationships with young women. The film deftly moves between their adolescent heterosexual phantasm and their overriding well-honed homosocial bonds. The narrative is threaded with questions about the boys' dependence upon each other, which they repeatedly deny. That is, until they end their odyssey in a sleeping bag

sleepover confessing their love for each other—naming the
boy-boy love bond that has for so long gone unnamed: "I love
you as long as I can remember," Curtis Mayfield joins in from
the soundtrack.

Men Will Hate Men

I rather like the optimism of *Superbad,* and happen to
share it. But I close this chapter, as I think we must, with some
speculative thoughts about the ways in which the disorganizing presence of losing and longing in boys' lives, when not addressed through the countering acts of reflection and contain-
ment, have the potential to morph into patterns of hate and
domination.

Thinking here, as I have been attempting to do throughout this chapter about boys' anxiety about loss, we might consider that loss likely begins at home. So, too, do most defenses.
As Josh illustrates, he borrowed the defensive employment of
faggot from his brother. These anxieties and defenses eventually move into the outside world and into peer relations. Consider again that Josh was referred for treatment because of his
anxiety and aggression as it emerged at school.

Turn then to consider how boys use *faggot* in a manner
that is diffuse, and naïve about its root meaning. In time, however, they learn the root meaning of *faggot* and more know-
ingly understand its power to threaten. The threat of *faggot*
becomes a way to extol and inflate their own masculinity as
they (dis)identify from those boys they believe to be losers, and
thereby also distance themselves from their own experience of
dependency with other boys and men.

We could further speculate that depending on the anxiety aroused by any given boy's own internal homosocial and/or homosexual desires, and/or the heterosexual desires that he associates with homosexuality (surrender, passivity), that boy may learn to respond to such anxiety through what Donald Moss has identified as a "phobic solution."[34] The offensive wish is projected into another. The marked other is then hated.

There is a particularly visceral (and less optimistic) scene in *Superbad* during which a menacing bully spits on Seth, one of the film's protagonists. The bully does so, at least manifestly, to reinforce (to mark) that Seth has not been invited to a graduation party (a party presumably intended for the socially superior). As the bully spits on Seth, he also reinforces and pronounces that Evan, Seth's "fucking faggot friend" is equally unwelcome.

These narcissistic and phobic solutions coalesce and aid in establishing patterns of splitting differences, and regulatory hierarchies, which serve to collapse the play in play. Such splitting and rigid regulation fuel homophobic and misogynist trends that often haunt the lives of men, serving to undo their attachments and leaving them all too often alone and psychically bereft.

These solutions are held in place by a number of cultural standard-bearers, including the insufficient psychoanalytic theorization of masculinity. Analysts have been content to let stand a theory of masculinity that rests largely on narcissistic and phobic defenses. I do not make this assertion unmindful of significant reassessments of the psychoanalytic theory of masculinity that have appeared in the past two decades. What I mean to point toward through my assertion is the fact that analysts have let stand an underproblematized theory of masculinity, and in so doing have been complicit in limiting the cultural reach of even our more modern revisionist efforts. This limit stands in marked contrast to the impact that the feminist retheorization of female subjectivity has had not only clinically but also culturally.

Perhaps it has served us (clinically and culturally) to fossilize men in a bedrock of protest and aggression. At the very least, it serves men, who after all have largely been the ones who theorize masculinity, to the extent that they do not have to take responsibility for their hate and anxiety. Boys will be boys. Men will hate men.

But perhaps such fatalism serves us all to the extent that we do not have to participate in the difficult task of engaging boys in a process of reflecting on their aggressive feelings and states, as well as the anxieties about loss. If we abandon boys to biological bedrock, we do not have to see ourselves simultaneously in interaction with them while entertaining their points of view. We can siphon aggression and hate into boys and men. We do not have to locate their hate and anxiety within ourselves in order to reflect on ourselves as we reflect on them. Instead, we make them brittle winners who are left to defend against inevitable loss. Left to thrust and parry through the aggressive protest of machismo. Left to make faggots of us all.

CHAPTER SIX

Fantastic Phallicism

Recognition, Relation, and Phallic Narcissism

IN THE TIME-HONORED TRADITION OF GENDER stereotypes, I begin this chapter with a man in a car, me in my car, to be precise. It is summer, and I am driving to the beach. The top is down. My seven-year-old nephew Alex is in the back seat, his blond hair wild in the wind. Eminem raps from the stereo speakers, and Alex is shouting, "Uncle Kenny, turn it up, turn it up!" I gladly comply.

The wind, the heat, the beat, Eminem raps about losing oneself in music, and in the moment of music. In his cocky syncopation he tells us that we want it. He tells to hold on to it. He blusters that we only get one chance to blow. He hastens us to go, and keep going. As we pull into a parking space, Eminem proclaims that the world is ours. He commands the role of king, and as I shift into park, we move along with him into what he calls a new order. I turn around and Alex is standing on the seat, raising one fist in the air, grabbing his crotch with his other hand, and doing his best Eminem. He shouts, "This is the life!"

This is *the* life, not this is *a* life, but this is *the* life. And in that moment I laugh and concur.

I begin with this moment of play in order to highlight the expansive operation of this terrain to which I often gladly travel with Alex. I move forward in this chapter to detail this terrain as phallic and narcissistic—aggressive, assertive, extending, thrusting—and to examine the relational potential of such bonds.

Modern analyses generally describe the thrust of narcissism into intimate unions in terms of a "doer" and "done to" dynamic. The oppressive narcissistic subject is the dominant figure, while the object is passive and oppressed; mutual recognition collapses due to the narcissist's lack of regard and desire for the other as other. I do not supplant this analysis. I believe there is ample evidence of such relations, and a clear need to address such oppression, both clinically and culturally.

I do, however, argue for another formation, as well as a variant formulation of certain expressions of narcissism. In something of a paradox, I am proposing that we look toward the nonnarcissistic possibilities of the narcissistic, and that we do not automatically split narcissism from mutual recognition. The formation I describe is derived from my clinical and cultural experiences with men and boys wherein phallic narcissism functions as a fantastic bid toward relation.

Fantastic spaces and relations are created that afford what I refer to as fantastic mutual recognition. In the particular play space I am describing, an imaginary big subject reckons with and often competes with another imaginary big subject. Infused with phallic narcissistic dynamics (as big subjects are wont to be), these bonds are often fueled by muscular erotic expansion and the erotic fervor of adoration.

This is *the* life. Sun, muscles, surf, and speed. Alex and I move with Eminem toward kingdom, and we hit the beach running. We bodysurf until I have to force Alex, his chilled and chattering body, out of the cold Atlantic toward the blanket and the sun. We scour the beach for treasure, and I play along with the pirate fantasies that unfurl; to sack and loot, to be a "Matey," or to be a "Captain" rescuing and resisting in the name of the law, these are the wishes, these are the anxieties, these are the roles that are traded.

Play lives between our bodies and our minds, as befits fantasy, and the fantastic manner in which bodies are materialized, called into being through reiterative processes of exchange and play. Bodies come alive through the force of the fantastic, and material reality is knit with psychic reality. If material reality is the yarn, psychic reality is the needles: Alex is not Alex; he is a pirate. I am not myself; I am a captain. The swords and the battle come alive through the material force of our bodies and minds. So, too, our bodies and minds come together through the fantastic force of the swords. Bodies are never wholly material; psyches are never wholly immaterial. We live perplexed, and we grow between our bodies, our minds, and the cultural practices that infuse such growth.

I am aware, for example, that at another time, I would have been quick to instruct Alex that this is *a* life, not *the* life. We are not kings, pirates, or captains; we are mere men and boys, succeeding and failing to materialize as men and boys, meeting and colliding with regulatory norms. We are pulled daily into untold moments of failure, disorder, and shame. Eminem is not a king, maybe more the jester, or a troubling troubadour at best.

I might have felt a twinge of guilt over not editing Eminem, pushing the skip button, to ensure that Alex was not exposed to something inappropriate. But isn't just a touch of lawlessness part of an uncle's mission? All the same, perhaps I am simply caught and caught out; the middle-aged middle-class fool in a sports car enacting and colluding in fantasies of narcissistic completeness, ecstatic externality, impermeable phallicism, and omnipotence fueled by a 420-horsepower engine and the imagination of a seven-year-old.

Did Alex and I come together in the custom of fathers and sons, men and boys, to form a phallic narcissistic bond to ward off fears of encroaching maternal omnipotence, castration, and other primitive fantastic terrors?[1] Did we move toward the fantastic command of captains and kings in an effort to undo the narcissistic injuries that are inevitably met in the gap between omnipotent fantasy and relative passive reality?

Undoubtedly. The repeated citation of cultural norms alone results in daily experiences of loss (as one fails to meet expectations) and defense (as one strives to succeed), not to mention the myriad fears and losses that construct the bonds of kinship. These losses are not always expressed as such, and these defenses are not direct but rather are enacted in play. Through play and the fantastic investment that is defense, our bodies are accumulated and materialized.

Here we might think of bodies as a loop. They are built, and genders are made through the thematic and dynamic repetition that informs play scenarios such as the one I describe with Alex. These play scenarios also express and cite prevailing cultural norms, as well as how motivated the players may be to adhere to such norms. Parent-child, social-child, and body-child exchanges, all of which are infused by the repeated enforcement of cultural practices, are projected back into these relationships and onto material reality, including the material reality of the body; hence the loop.

This intersubjective-body-mind-masculinity comes together (to the degree that a body and mind and gender ever come together) through the formation of fantastic phallic terrains that, as Walt Whitman might have it, "sing no songs . . . but those of manly attachment, projecting them along that substantial life."[2] But these attachments need not necessarily negate maternal subjectivity or effect a radical separation from the feminine.[3] While indeed phallic narcissistic fantasies can be employed in the service of defense, resulting in a defensive split from the feminine, they can also be employed toward recognition, masculine identification, and the promise of growth. Bodies and genders can be shaped through loss and defense; genders are often found in melancholic turns; they can also be materialized through pleasure, practice, and the creative possibilities of attachment and expansion.

Traditionally, boys and masculinity have been characterized by aggression, muscularity, exhibitionism, dominance, and phallic preoccupation. This view of boys is something of a normative mainstay. It is what we expect of them: "Boys will be boys." Psychoanalysts have sought to grasp this feature of boyhood and masculinity through the concept of phallic narcissism: the vigorous exhibitionism, the muscular eroticism, the arrogant domination, and the admixture of sadistic traits that manifest a boy's or man's psychically energetic attachment to his own body and mind, in particular his penis, over his attachments to others. Modern efforts, my own included, have mostly been directed at understanding phallic narcissism as a symptom, a defense, or a manifestation of character pathology.[4]

At this juncture, I consider how these narcissistic stances can be seen as fantastic bids toward relationship: invitations toward complementary bigness, invitations toward competitive bigness, the desire to push with force, the desire to be pushed forcefully, the quest for the self-confidence of mastery (to be distinguished from domination), the wish to grow, the longing to create and find a corresponding excitement and desire in an other, along with the practice of elastic play (roles are made, roles are traded) that affords fantastic recognition.

I make a bid for the mysterious power of fantastic ideals to resist disillusioning confrontations with reality. Yes, we tire of boys' quests toward the veneration of phallic glory. But might we also mourn those moments when a boy surrenders the thrust of phallic imagination, and settles for the tedium of phallic reality? In those moments might we grant the luxurious necessity of erotic imaginations as they build a world that if not better, is, at least, more alive?

Phallophobia?

Boys, or more properly, the attendant parenting dilemmas faced in raising boys, are now the subjects of a spate of recent popular psychology books.[5] Similar to their feminist psychoanalytic colleagues, the authors of these books locate the distress they identify in boys as stemming from the ways in which boys are prematurely separated from their mothers, and then led into a social structure that splits off boys' expressiveness and their capacities for self reflection; principle to this regulatory process is shame.

Recently, this analysis has been augmented as theorists contemplate what has come to be called "father hunger," a term introduced by the psychoanalyst James Herzog. As I read this theoretical turn, it addresses the role of father absence (either literal or psychic) in many boys' lives and makes a bid for reintroducing the idea of the involved father into children's lives. Without active parenting fathers, it is argued, boys are susceptible to unchecked aggression and violence, learning difficulties, and troubled relations with girls and women. Appeals are made for fathers to become more hands-on, more directly and daily involved in their sons' lives. In a related trend, a therapeutic move has been made toward a "fatherlike mentor"; analysts are encouraged to adopt a therapeutic stance akin to a guide-father who is phallic and relational, yet nurturing and strong.[6]

Whether in the form of popular self-help or the more rarified reach of feminist theory and psychoanalytic practice, we now find ourselves better prepared to address the multiple pathologies that haunt boys and men. These advances represent no small step; in particular, we are better prepared to redress the sadistic and narcissistic consequences of men's struggle to achieve power. The inarticulate despair that men face and instigate through their failed attachments *should* be in our therapeutic focus.

Yet our current discourse on boys and masculinity lacks something I think of as nearer a boy's experience of his body and mind. Our effort to think about boys consistently veers toward thinking about parents, and the work of good-enough parenting. It strikes me that this is understandable, and not a problem per se. Still, too often the boys presented in recent analyses come across as subjects cleansed of fantasmatic and regressive features. Too often a kind of dulled and false Eddie Haskell sociality is substituted for candor. No one talks about *South Park*. No one buys 50 Cent on the sly. No one dances on the goal line. No one is named McLovin. No one cuts a fart in chapel, as does Edgar Marsalla in *The Catcher in the Rye*. As Holden Caulfield says, "It was a very crude thing to do, in chapel and all, but it was also quite amusing."[7]

One finds no such amusement in our discourse on boys. No adult turns away to laugh, laughing perhaps in identification with the prank, the social rupture, the crude pleasures, the romantic ruthlessness we so often associate with boys. All is reverent; fathers are somber and earnest; mothers are even more so. Boys as they are often described, especially in recent popular analyses, seem more like aspiring Boy Scouts. When they fail to be obedient or readily reverent, their behavior is quickly read as a defense against states of need and longing, which are in turn linked with femininity. The masculinity that emerges remains tethered to a traditional domestic narrative, and the sexuality that emerges, when it does—and that is seldom—is cloaked in the domesticity of matrimonial relations and the reproduction of matrimony.

One could critically read these recent popular analyses, which are largely intended for parents, as lacking a more complex appreciation of boys' desires and subjectivities. Yet they do not differ that much from more scholarly or more in-depth clinical discourses. In the psychoanalytic domain to which we might look for analyses of desire and an appreciation for the contradictions of personhood, boys rarely appear. Indeed, children as speaking subjects rarely appear in modern psychoanalytic discourse. When analysts do turn to boys, we have principally concerned ourselves in the past four decades with the vulnerabilities boys experience in acts of separation from their mothers. This discourse has been primarily theoretical, not clinical; we work more often with ideas about boys than with boys themselves.

This turn toward boys in the context of mothering (and to some extent toward the nurturing father) has been in accord with our dominant concerns regarding the socializing force and authority we grant to early mother-son passion—the kind of bedrock authority psychoanalysts are often eager to grant to the past. But our theorizing about maternal subjectivity can too easily and mistakenly be read as guided by the moral principle of ready empathy, the moral virtue of passivity, and the guidepost of mutuality, and these valued states are in turn too easily read as feminine.

This common misreading (mother, girl, feminine equals attuned, mutual, good; father, boy, masculine equals aggressive, nonmutual, bad) situates so-called feminine empathy as the domesticating force that tames the beast in the nursery—the mother hen marshaling her chicks along the developmental pathway toward the authenticity and profundity of privatized mutual relational domestic sex. Something similar might be said in relation to the mentor-father, who is configured as good and wise, leading his son toward the mature reality and well-being of heterosexual matrimony. The burlap of desire too quickly becomes the pashmina of mutual recognition; no one's knees get scraped, and the intimate and unconscious dynamics that knit and unfurl desire and recognition are too quickly smoothed. Women's aggression and the productive possibilities of mother-child aggression are written over by the pressing demands of mutuality, which in turn is mistakenly read as empathy devoid of aggression.

Men's and boys' aggression, and phallic aggression in particular, is too easily read as defensive, violent, and sadistic. Fathers and paternal figures are configured as off the path, locked in relations with their sons that are seen to enact and promote domination, the subjugation of women, and the perpetuation of masculinities that are determined by the quest for idealized phallic authority. The overdetermination of this phallic quest is then configured as reinforcing maternal separations that are achieved through not-me splitting. Alternatively, the nurturing father is depicted as good beyond aggression. My colleague the psychoanalyst Eyal Rozmarin aptly and ironically refers to this father as "the father of circumcision — not the father of castration!"[8]

We have once again split gender as constructed through an originary relationship. This time we subscribe to the early mother-child dyad (shadowed by the nurturing father-child relationship), as opposed to the father-child dyad in the context of Oedipal triangulation emphasized in the first half of our psychoanalytic century. This early mother-child overdetermination turns us away from the fantastic construction and materialization of the body and mind beyond infancy and early childhood. It obscures desires for the disruption caused by aggression and narcissistic expansion as those desires evolve within and beyond their early determinants. Similarly obscured are desires that live either alongside or outside the reach of mutual recognition.

This move is understandably informed by our concerns for justice and diminished cruelty and violence. Given the slippery slope between aggression and violence, we have anxiously turned away from these aggressively tinged erotic and narcissistic states. But this move also draws upon a reflexive anti-aggression reaction, a recoiling or disavowal of the productive possibilities of aggression. A diminished understanding of the role of aggression in subject formation and erotic life keeps us ill informed about these erotic dimensions of masculinity.

Has a kind of phallophobia crept into our theorizing, perhaps mirroring the gynecophobia that ushered in our first psychoanalytic century? In this regard, it is intriguing to note a significant difference in the evolution of thought about femininity and masculinity. The need to rethink masculinity has followed in large measure on the assessment of men and boys as failed or failing social beings. Their behaviors and relations have become sites of anxiety and scrutiny. In contrast, the inaugural critique of femininity not only followed on the misperception of women as social-relational beings but also articulated the misrepresentation, indeed the disavowal, of women's bodies. Reconceptualizing feminine embodiment has been, and continues to be, a focal, often fiercely contested, feature of discussions about femininity. Not so for men. Male embodiment, boys' bodies, men's and boys' states of desire—what they seek, what they carry, what they bury—has, if anything, stalled with original Freudian formulations, or even regressed. It is almost as though the male body cannot be thought; it is as disavowed now as once women's bodies were.

Consider the ways in which boys' bodies are either erased or glossed: the word *penis*, for example, does not appear in any of the indexes of recent popular books written for parents about boys. The aggression and regression that are common features of boyhood play—to wit, *South Park*—are either muted or quickly interpreted as a cry for help; even the violence that so often informs boys' fantasies is too quickly read with alarm. As in a phobic reaction, might we funnel aggression and regression into boys so that we do not have to locate such aggression, regression, and pleasure within ourselves?

Paradoxically, might this phallophobia also issue from the conundrum of the phallic ideal and the fantasmatic character of the penis? Has the penis become unthinkable? Consider that Freud's position regarding the penis as originary, as an originating idealization, or maleness as the original ideal, has been repeatedly criticized and shown to be logically inconsistent with his propositions regarding the body as fantastically materialized. Yet we have not moved very far from either Freudian idealization or the critique thereof. We have not managed to create much in the way of potential space to imagine the fantastic phallic body, including the penis.

If, as I suggest, the penis is always a materialization that is dictated by fantastic readings and measurements, then what do we really know about the dynamics of phallic aggression and sexual arousal? What about the positive valance of phallic aggression? How might we consider the pleasures of phallic narcissism for subject and object alike, including the paradoxical manner in which as narcissism opens out it both expands and excludes the other? What about the hope and dread of the erection, phallic endurance, and the theater of ejaculation? How might we think about the expansion (the erection) of phallic activity and the penetration of another? Is such penetrating activity the temporary losing hold of the self as one folds into another, or is such activity a matter of losing hold of the other as one expands into and through the other (shatters in the other), or is such activity held in tension by mutual recognition, or is such activity a welcome retreat from mutuality, or is such activity an ever-shifting series of experiences and states, perhaps an ever-shifting series of dissociated flashes flickering through the heat of sexual passion?

Might we also consider the possibility of phallic states that encompass but also expand upon (and thereby deconstruct) phallic monism—states that might include the blind pride of aggression and possession, but also the empathy and recognition of surrender? What about the intricacies of phallic states as they morph through aggression, possession, surrender, regression, activity, and passivity?

In what could be read as an amusing answer to these questions, Seth, one of the boys in *Superbad*, a film David Edelstein labels "a pipeline to the adolescent id," repeatedly and manically draws penises: big, little, erect, deflated, smooth, hairy.[9] And in an exquisite illustration of phallic phantasm, he then animates them, making them into George Washington, a robot, a banana, the student protester in Tiananmen Square, a pilot, Pippi Longstocking, a dinosaur, Mr. T., passengers on the *Titanic*, Medusa, a train, a wizard, a surgeon, a cowboy, a marionette, a devil, an angel, and what appears to be Ronald Reagan.[10] Even the three protagonists of *Superbad*—Evan, skinny, shy, and a touch hysterical; Seth, foulmouthed, chubby, and manically cocksure; and Fogell (aka McLovin), the bespectacled last word in nerd—embody varying phallic states as they career along on their boozy sex-crazed odyssey.

Fantastic Phallicism

I move forward here by presenting two clinical moments, one with an eight-year-old boy, Robert, and the other with a twenty-seven-year-old man, Joseph. I discuss two moments of muscular and fantastic phallic exchange, how those moments were colored by both desire and destruction, and my efforts to understand the pleasure and anxiety of these moments.

As you will see, I reflect back on an hour with my adult patient, Joseph, while I am in session with my child patient, Robert. My thoughts about Joseph were stimulated through a countertransference association. These two patients were linked in my mind by way of their histories; each was raised by a single mother and had a limited relationship with his father, who left the home early in the boy's life. The vitality of a paternal transference and countertransference figured prominently in these treatments, as did the dynamism of maternal dis-identification and separation. I worked with both of these patients over many years, and the life of the transference and countertransference was varied and variously brought to life. But in the material I examine here, Robert and Joseph were more immediately linked in my mind through the ways in which the role of phallic narcissism and the thrust of phallic narcissistic expansion (up to and including the triumphant and aggressive edge of such expansion) was central to our work at the time to which I am referring.

Two days following a blizzard that had blanketed New York City with nearly two feet of snow, eight-year-old Robert arrived for his appointment dripping as the snow melted off his snow pants, his boots, and his hat. As he came into my office, he explained that he might "need some time to thaw." I noted his red face and hands, to which he responded, "Snowballs." He told me that his trip to the park before our appointment had been his first opportunity to play in the snow. His family had been in "stupid Florida" on the day of the storm. He then detailed his wish to have been in New York instead, saying, "Because I would pummel my brother with snow. And he would pummel me with snow. But it is more fun to pummel brothers than not." I laughed and found myself thinking about my walk home from my office the night before. I had observed three different pairings of young men as they threw each other into snowdrifts along the shoveled pathways. I remembered in particular one pair in which one member attempted not only to push his mate into the snow but also to pull off the other young man's coat, such that when he finally did fall, it was his skin that met the snow. As the tackled boy fell, skin to snow, he yelled, "Man, you are dead!" His friend ran down the street doubled-up in laughter.

As I was calling myself back from my own reverie, Robert had busied himself setting up a game he had begun at the end of our last hour, saying that he "couldn't wait to get back to it." The game was called Crash Car Derby and consisted of Robert and me positioned at opposite ends of a table, pushing match-box cars and trucks toward each other. I was assigned three cars, while he chose three trucks and explained, "It is only fair, you are bigger." The object of the game was to send your car across the table with enough force to knock the other car off the table. As the game gathered steam, we seemed to come to an unspoken agreement that we would guide the cars with our hands until the cars met head-on as opposed to sending them across the table on their own.

At one point I won and raised my hand to give Robert a high-five. As he raised his hand, I could see how red his hand had become from the pressure of pushing the cars. As our hands met in the high-five, I noticed that he winced. I said,

"It looks like your hand is hurt." He reluctantly allowed that in fact it did hurt a bit.

I immediately felt a wave of recrimination; what had I done, how had I gotten so carried away that I hurt an eight-year-old in the course of this game? My recrimination, though, was countered by a hovering feeling of pride: I had won! And yet I knew that it was not my job to win. Where was my analytic reflection in all of this? I reflexively apologized, and once again questioned my lack of analytic reflection. Robert said, "No biggie," and immediately wanted to reinstate the game. I took up my opposing position, but Robert could tell that I was not really in the game, and said, "Come on, you are not really playing." I said, "OK, but what about the fact that it might be a biggie? I am bigger than you. Doesn't that make this game unfair?" Robert grudgingly had to admit that in fact the game was tilted in my favor. I continued, "And what about the fact that I'm bigger, and that I can hurt you?" Once again, Robert reluctantly concurred, but added, "Not for long," as he raised his hand to show me that it was no longer red. To which I replied with the question, "It is better to pummel brothers than not?" Robert looked at me as if to say, "What?" I continued, "You know, like you said about you and your brother. Something about how it feels good to be in a struggle, even to be pummeled; maybe coming up against something, or someone bigger and stronger than you? Pushing back." Robert looked at me quizzically, and said, "Come on, let's play." We began the game again. But not far into this second round, Robert, sensing, I venture, my distraction (reflection/protection/guilt?), became frustrated, and said, "No, you have to do it harder!" as he rammed his car into mine.

Eventually Robert lost interest in the car game and moved on to a game that was a repetitive staple of his repertoire. This game varied somewhat but always involved a group of Lego men who were depicted in the midst of battle or sport. They were engaged in tests of prowess, endurance, loyalty, will, and cunning. Sometimes they made up opposing teams or nations, other times they engaged one another mano a mano. Each man possessed unique talents and was specifically armed. Weapons were named with enthusiasm and described in relation to their relative powers. Injury, wounds, bloody loss, dismemberment, and murder were intermingled with revival, repair, victory, and wholeness. I was not given a role in this play beyond that of the audience. Robert became the gaudy performer intermittently enacting transgressive and lurid spectacles of murder and mayhem, or the heroic rescue and repair of the law as it triumphed over enemies and evil.

As I watched these familiar scenes unfold, I was struck, as I had been on other occasions, by Robert's embrace of destruction and murder—an embrace that Leo Bersani and Ulysse Dutoit in a discussion of Genet refer to as the "erotic exaltation" and "erotic crescendo" of murder.[11] I then thought back to a recent hour with an adult patient, Joseph, a young man who was beginning to emerge from a history of depression and what I thought of as an underlying erotic repression. He recalled a moment from his childhood when he would meticulously build model airplanes and then use firecrackers to explode them. He said, "I would stick one in the front and stick one in the back, and boom!" He laughed, nervously I thought, and said, "I bet you didn't know that, did you?" I said that in fact I did not. Joseph then said, "I have the sudden urge to give you a high-five." Whereupon, he asked, "Now what do we make of all of that?" I ventured, "Contact? Though that seems perhaps too mild." There was a pause, and eventually Joseph said, "Well, I can't very well say I want to fuck you till you explode." There was another longer awkward pause, and Joseph then said, "I can't believe I just said that. Wow, what did I . . . ?" And in setting about or stumbling about to answer his own unfinished question, Joseph ventured that perhaps he had said what he said "just for the thrill of saying it, for the thrill of the pose."

He then began to speak for the first time about a series of recent anonymous sexual encounters. He indicated that he would meet men, "fuck them, and then leave them." Joseph took pains to clarify that he did not think of these sexual encounters as necessarily intimate. Rather, these trysts were marked by a kind of sensualist luxury and conquest; he could feel, he could act, he could exhibit himself with little to no knowledge of the other. He was not beholden to their needs, or to their desires. He was not labored by any intimate knowledge. He "gets off and gets on." He said, "I'm a dick, a total dick, and I love it."

He then indicated that he was worried about what I would think of him. Yet he also harbored the idea that I would be proud of him. I found myself pondering the ways in which Joseph seemed to be looking to me to join him through pride. Was I to be proud of his willful ignorance of the other, of the other's desires and personhood? Or was I to feel pride at his capacity to find men who wished to surrender to his desire, perhaps even express their own desire through the passion of veneration? No matter, I was to find my way to this pride consequent upon my joy in the face of his narcissistic expansion. I was to find my way through the push-and-pull he imagined. I was to explode.

I thought about the role of his anxiety as it may impede his capacity to bring such passion into more intimate relationships. I wondered whether that thought was a dodge; wasn't he bringing this passion into our relationship? Might I not like exploding? I thought about how easily one can get pulled toward policing patients' sexual lives, and the countertransference conundrum regarding the instantiation of regulatory norms into the moral authority that exercises control over erotic and aggressive impulses—both the patient's and one's own. I thought about the transference implications of how he might wish to fuck me and leave me, and how he might not wish to be burdened with his growing awareness (both perceptive and fantastic) of my subjectivity, awareness inherent in analyses as they gather time and depth. In this way, was I becoming like his mother, about whom he was acutely aware, and from whom he struggled to separate? Was his joyful ignorance of these men whom he could leave an enacted not-me wish, a longing for objects with whom he would not become "trapped," as he often said of his mother? Or were his hasty retreats a way to defend against troubling wishes to be venerated?

I thought as well about the ways in which his temporary attachments to the men he described might enact the ambivalence inherent in a melancholic paternal internalization, a simultaneous quest for, attachment to, identification with, and rejection of these men. Might we see here the shadow of his father? I began to think of his penis as a paternal ghost. I thought about how few usable paternal-parental figures there had been in his life, how little opportunity he had had to elaborate, enact, and perform fantastic phallic states, and to learn what is gained and what is lost through these dynamics.

I did not, however, bring these thoughts forward. It seemed

premature. It seemed best to trust that such thoughts would find their way into our work with time (as in fact they did). I thought it best at this point to sit with his performance, however clumsy, however confusing, however narcissistic, and however his nervousness may have in fact countered the aggression, the heat of the pose.

And in the way in which one can hold multiple patients in mind, I turned back to Robert. I began to think about the ways in which his destructive celebrations were marked by a kind of salubrious perversity whereby the very display countered the destructiveness of his erotic energy. Like Joseph, Robert was reaching toward me through his play spectacle, looking for me to take in and appreciate his lawless triumphal ecstasy as bombs fell and bodies exploded. He was not looking to me at this point to engage in a complementary pattern of domination. He was looking to me to witness his efforts to sort out those dynamics within himself. He was not looking toward me to be the law. Robert, in fact, enacted the discipline of the law in the form of the hero who inevitably prevailed (albeit with less flair than the bad guy). He was looking to me to grasp and contain the satisfaction and the intolerable logic of triumph and murder, or perhaps more precisely the pose of triumph and murder. He was looking to me to witness the destruction of objects in the wake of muscular eroticism, and his efforts to calibrate his desires for destruction and repair.

Perhaps this is what I had failed to do in the car crash game. In this game, Robert *was* looking for me to assume a complementary competitive position. And I backed away from my own pleasure and active expansion as the victor. I backed away from the ways in which I temporarily lost hold of the other in the grip of competitive passion. I backed away from my identification with the young men on the street in the snow; I backed away from "Man, you are dead!" I backed away from the pleasures of destruction. After all, the game was called *Crash* Car Derby.

I am not suggesting that what I did was less than responsible. In fact, Robert does look to me, as do all children toward adults, to embody the discipline and protection of the law. His need for me to contain and survive his murderous and aggressive impulses, as well as to reflect them back to him in our mutual effort toward thinking about his emotional states, is indeed one function of the law, as it has been a significant feature of our transference-countertransference relationship. It is, of course, our responsibility as adults to monitor and modulate our own competitive and passionate responses to children. It is, of course, our responsibility as adults to recognize a child's pain, even if he might not wish us to. It is one of the ways in which we love them. As Emily Dickinson might have said it, "If you saw a bullet hit a Bird—and he told you he wasn't shot—you might weep at his courtesy, but you would certainly doubt his word."[12]

But another way in which we love children is as aggressive, exhibitionistic, fantastic, resilient, competitive, and murderous, and in order to find those dimensions of our love we have to identify them in ourselves. We have to feel them within ourselves, even feel it in our relations with them. In this regard, I think many boys present a particular dilemma for parents and other parenting adults (such as teachers and therapists) through their persistent activity and aggression, through the pitch, push, punch, and pull of their muscular eroticism and expansive narcissism, an eroticism that is often shadowed by aggressive and sadomasochistic dimensions, an eroticism that is often fueled by the endurance of pain, an eroticism that is often laced with violence or the near violent.

Along with the ways in which we could, and we must, look at this aggressive and violent play as defensive, there is also a countervailing dynamic, wherein the profit and pleasure of fierce competition, up to and including the endurance of pain, can be a productive terrain that not only holds forth the promise of growth but also opens onto reflections about growth and narcissistic expansion. Consider in this respect that one of the pleasures of childhood is growth, the accumulation of body mass, height, strength, and finesse. Consider further that growth happens between the body, the mind, and the bodies and minds of others. Children are constantly engaging adults in fantasies of bigness as they position themselves between their bodies and minds and the bodies and minds of adults. Time and again I have found, at the heart of our clinical work, a boy's reach to be bigger.

Surely this reach is often in the service of a not-me defense: "I am not small. You are not big." But just as surely, I find boys reaching for the yes-me experience of identification and the assurance of growth by creating play that affords recognition: look at me pretending to be big, look at me practicing to be big, look at me as the big one you desire, look at me competing as big with big you (hence we are both big, hence we are subject to subject, master to master), look at me invade you, look at me shatter you, look at me murder you, look at me repair you, look at me resurrect you, look at me look at you looking at me grow.

Parents daily come face to face, body to body with these dynamics as they struggle to help their boys move with and through the pleasures of phallic narcissism toward more contained and delimited mutual erotic pleasures. But as the psychoanalyst Jody Davies has recently pointed out, parents speak not only through the "no" of delimiting sexual pleasures but also through the "yes" of their romantic and sexual attachments to their children.[13] In league with Davies, I would add that parents also speak through the identificatory "yes" of the push and pull of aggressive play, play that may venture outside the bounds of mutuality, that may even depend on momentary destruction and nonmutuality. Such play often surfaces in competitive games and play scenarios that draw the players into a trading of complementary roles.

In our current theorization and clinical interest in the utility of reflection gained by stepping back and looking at a relationship and the dynamics that inform the bond, I venture that such games have become rather suspect—although children frequently remind me, "It is only a game." To which I, in the spirit of reflection, generally reply, "Yes, but that doesn't mean we can't think about it; right?" But honestly, I think they often have a point: within the game itself there is mutual recognition. The game itself serves as something of a silent third; the game holds us, as we move between complementary roles.

The challenge for the adult is to stay in the game, to not reflexively recoil from the aggression and competition. To rise to the challenge, and at the same time offer a bounded and safe holding environment. This challenge becomes even greater as competitive games often involve physical contact. Here I believe we return to an aspect of child therapy that is rarely discussed—the subtle ways in which a child therapist is often in the position of having to negotiate the muscular eroticism of children. I would like here to specifically draw our attention to the ways in which the erotic and materializing realm of touch between men and men and between men and boys is largely absent from our psychoanalytic literature.

It could be argued that psychoanalysis was hatched in the fertile terrain of the erotic lives of the male analyst and female patient. Fortunately, our modern discourse has traveled some distance from the "dark continent" that was occasioned by that birth. Of particular note here is the manner in which our modern understandings of femininity have re-imagined the vitalizing necessity of the maternal body and the erotic magnificence of the maternal embrace, as they inform both our diagnostic understanding and our clinical techniques.[14]

The erotic lives of the male patient and male analyst have not enjoyed the same liberatory reconsiderations. Complex discussion (either clinical or theoretical) of the paternal erotic body or embrace do not appear in our literature. Moreover, I venture that, constricted as we are by our anxiety with regard to the erotic male body, it struggles to appear in our consulting rooms, at least to the degree that it is consciously interpreted and analyzed. While there is scant modern consideration of the erotic lives of male analysts and female patients, there is even less discussion of the erotic lives of the male patient and male analyst, and often this discussion goes undistinguished from homosexual panic. One does not linger, one does not tarry, one moves quickly along. And if these aspects of the treatment are not literally called a "phase," they are implied to be so.

The luxury of the paternal embrace, the potentialities of the paternal "yes," the paternal body as a site of sustaining growth are virtually absent from our literature. The paternal remains a site of "no": the guard against incest, the usher of separation. Male-to-male eros is materializing only as it sets in play the identificatory antecedents of separation. Even the "new" nurturing mentor father—the one less given to "no"—is largely devoid of father-son erotic exchange, other than to stand as an example of mature heterosexual desire.

The paternal body remains shadowed by the predatory, pederastic, and panicked masculinity that haunts our psychoanalytic and widely held cultural conceptions of male sexuality. Consider in this regard that a prominent film critic described Jack Twist, the more sexually active and desirous on-again-off-again lover of Ennis Del Mar in *Brokeback Mountain*, as a "sexual predator."[15] Jack's open desire is read as predaceous and despoiling as opposed to offering an opening for Ennis, an intimate union wherein their desires might meet, where mutual recognition might flourish. More important, such a reading misses, indeed closets, the way in which Ennis comes undone in the space of his and Jack's desire, and for the first time in his life comes to know himself as a person of depth, a person of deep feeling.

While we might be smug about this film critic's representation of Jack, we have done little ourselves toward opening a space for recognition and desire between men. Our discussions of men and boys largely hinge on ideas about identification, a kind of psychology of inheritance between father and son. Multiplicity, for all of its ubiquity, has not found its way into the erotic lives of fathers and sons, or the complex network of fantasies that bind fathers and sons, men and boys.

For example, what of the fantastic work of the gaze? What of young boys' eager wishes to see their father's bodies, and the bodies of other men? What of the pleasure in seeing, and the swell of the voyeur? What of the energized embodiment one feels in the act of comparison, or the act of exhibitionism?

What of the body-to-body, embrace-to-embrace, strong-arm-to-strong-arm push and pull of muscular eroticism? These bodily communications are crisscrossed with a range of fantasies, a range of entries, entreaties, and foreclosures.

To see big. To seem big. To feel big. To be big in relation. To expand toward another and within another through phallic narcissism, and the fantastic mutuality found therein. To fantastically construct a body in relation to another. To live large. As Biggie Smalls, the rapping ironic oxymoronic prince of fantastic phallicism, syncopates, "When I give it to ya, throw it right back."

Perhaps we can hear an echo of Biggie in Robert's "No biggie," pointing toward my failure to hold onto my own wishes for the expansion of victory. Or my failure to reckon with my own wish to hold onto the big position, and in turn to fully embody my wish for triumph, and then find a way to speak with him about it. In falling out of the game, I fell away from his effort to locate his body and mind in relation to mine, even up against mine. We lost the opportunity to examine both the productive and the destructive possibilities of competition. We lost the opportunity to examine how in the grip of narcissistic expansion we sometimes lose sight of the other, or in the quest for narcissistic expansion we lose sight of our selves.

The challenge for us as theorists is to stay in the game as well, to not reflexively recoil from aggression, to not leave life at the infantile mother-child border, to not disavow the aggressive excess of sexual life. To lose sight of these dynamics is to lose sight of many men and boys, the variety of fantastic phallic states, the complex potentialities of masculinity, and the perplexing excess of sexual excitement.

We risk losing sight of the promise of growth, and of our

responsibility to children not only to provide them with opportunities to grow but also to share their pleasure in the wish
to grow—to share their longings to transcend boyhood as they
move toward the differently complicated congress of adult
masculinity.

As I was finishing this book, I enjoyed many hours of play
with a three-year-old boy who lives next door to me. He was
interested in all things big, ranging from my bike to my shoes
to my swimming goggles. One day we were swimming, and
as I was coming out of the water with sun in my eyes, I felt
him touch me through my bathing suit, "Kenny, you got a peanuts!" (I must confess I was a touch taken aback. At three he
was not held back by body boundary rules; his unfettered curiosity led the way.) I laughed and said, "Yes, I do." He then pre-
dictably asked, "How come you got a big peanuts?" I laughed
again, and said, "Big boys grow. You will too." He smiled and
exclaimed, "I love a peanuts!"

Notes

Introduction

1. Whitman, *Leaves of Grass*, 163.

2. Freud, *Analysis of a Phobia, Notes upon a Case*, "Some Psychical Consequences," *New Introductory Lectures.*

3. Freud, *Three Essays*, "Some Psychical Consequences"; "Female Sexuality."

4. Horney, "Genesis of the Castration Complex" and "Flight from Womanhood"; Jones, "The Phallic Phase."

5. Brunswick, "Preoedipal Phase."

6. Bonaparte, "Passivity, Masochism, and Femininity"; Deutsch, *The Psychology of Women*; Lampl-de Groot, "Problems of Femininity."

7. Boehm, "The Femininity Complex in Men"; Horney, "Genesis of the Castration Complex" and "Flight from Womanhood"; Klein, "Early Stages of the Oedipus Conflict."

8. For summaries and illuminating critiques of this history see Birksted-Breen, *The Gender Conundrum*; Chodorow, "Gender in the Modern-Postmodern and Classical-Relational Divide"; Dimen and Goldner, "Gender and Sexuality"; Harris, "Gender in Linear and Nonlinear History."

9. Aron, "Reevaluating the Distinction"; Goldner, "Feminism (Still) Rules."

10. Stoller, "Contribution to the Study," *Sex and Gender.*

11. Benjamin, *Bonds of Love*; Chodorow, *Reproduction of Mothering*. John Ross similarly emphasized the role of maternal dis-identification and separation in his effort to retheorize male Oedipal development in *What Men Want*.

---

12. Diamond, *My Father Before Me*; Herzog, *Father Hunger*; Ross, *What Men Want*; Samuels, *Political Psyche*; Trowell and Etchegoyen, *Importance of Fathers*.

13. See in particular Diamond, "Masculinity Unraveled," *My Father Before Me*.

14. Chodorow, "Enemy Outside"; Diamond, *My Father Before Me*; Herzog, *Father Hunger*; Kindlon and Thompson, *Raising Cain*; Pollack, *Real Boys*; Ross, "Beyond the Phallic Illusion."

15. See in particular the work of the sociologists Michael Kimmel and R. W. Connell.

16. This modern "congress" of gender theorists is large and expansive, and consists of psychoanalysts, psychologists, sociologists, historians, cultural theorists, queer theorists, feminists, philosophers, and literary theorists. Refer to the bibliographic entries for the following—those whom I gratefully acknowledge as having been most influential in the development of my thinking: Jessica Benjamin, Leo Bersani, Judith Butler, Nancy Chodorow, Muriel Dimen, Dianne Elise, Jane Flax, Diana Fuss, Virginia Goldner, Adrienne Harris, Michael Kimmel, Lynne Layton, Eve Sedgwick, Kaja Silverman, Michael Warner. It is important to note here as well the contribution of the ongoing critique of the psychoanalytic theory of homosexuality—a significant body of work that has produced a number of vital re-readings that are advanced, at least in part, via criticism of normative regulation. See the bibliography entries for works by Ken Corbett, Tom Domenici and Ronnie Lesser, Jack Drescher, Richard Isay, Kenneth Lewes, and Ralph Roughton.

17. Foucault, *Order of Things*, *Use of Pleasure*, *History of Sexuality*, and *Politics of Truth*.

18. Freud, *Interpretation of Dreams*, 533n1.

19. Loewald, *Papers on Psychoanalysis*; Widlocher, *Infantile Sexuality and Attachment*; Winnicott, *Through Pediatrics* and *The Maturational Processes*; Benjamin, *Bonds of Love* and *Shadow of the Other*; Fonagy et al., *Affect Regulation*; Laplanche, *New Foundations* and *Essays on Otherness*.

20. Butler, *Bodies That Matter* and *Undoing Gender*.

21. See, for example, Cheng, *Melancholy of Race*; Collins, *Black Sexual Politics*; Eng, *Racial Castration*; Halberstam, *In a Queer Time and Place*; Muñoz, *Dis-identifications*.

CHAPTER ONE. Little Hans

1. These returns to Little Hans and the developmental rethinking that results therefrom include: (1) the widening of Oedipal theory to include pre-Oedipal mother-child bonds, as well as increased emphasis on Oedipal father-son desires (Frankiel, "Analyzed and Unanalyzed Themes"; Ross, *What Men Want*; Ross, "Trauma and Abuse"); (2) the waning of Oedipal theory and psychosexual stage

premises in favor of developmental considerations that attend to parent-child attachment patterns (Benjamin, *Bonds of Love;* Wakefield, "Max Graf 'Reminiscences'"); (3) the move beyond the determining forces of infantile sexuality and neuroses toward a greater appreciation of the developmental struggles of childhood and adolescence (Young-Bruehl, "Little Hans"); (4) the increased attention given to the means by which parents parent, and the psychic-familial terrains created thereby; (5) the role of siblings in a child's early life (Blum, "Little Hans"; Fromm and Narváez, "Oedipus Complex"; Hinshelwood, "Little Hans's Transference"; Ross, "Trauma and Abuse"); (6) the role of a mother's pregnancy, and the importance of a child's birthing fantasies (Balsam, "The Vanished Pregnant Body"; Lax, *Becoming and Being a Woman;* Ross, *What Men Want* and "Trauma and Abuse"); (7) the dynamics of children's quests to grow (Chused, "Little Hans 'Analyzed'"; Fromm and Narváez, "Oedipus Complex").

2. Freud, *Analysis of a Phobia.*

3. Ibid., 22.

4. It is intriguing to note that these contrasting strands continue to inform psychoanalytic considerations regarding child development; what are the respective contributions of infantile sexuality (desire) as opposed to attachment (primary love)? See, for example, Green, "Has Sexuality Anything to Do with Psychoanalysis?"; Fonagy, *Attachment Theory and Psychoanalysis;* Holmes, *Search for the Secure Base;* Laplanche, *Life and Death in Psychoanalysis, Problématiques,* and *Essays on Otherness);* Widlocher, *Infantile Sexuality and Attachment.*

5. Freud, *Analysis of a Phobia,* 24–25. Near the end of his discussion of the case, Freud writes, "The boy had found his way to object-love in the usual manner from the care he had received when he was an infant; and a new pleasure had now become the most important to him—that of sleeping beside his mother" (111).

6. Ibid., 25.

7. Ibid., 26.

8. "[Hans's] anxiety, then, corresponded to repressed longing. But it was not the same thing as the longing: the repression must be taken into account too." Ibid., 26.

9. Ibid., 28.

10. Ibid., 110*n*2.

11. Ibid., 17.

12. For example, in his reflection near the end of the discussion, he suggests that if it were up to him, he would have "confirmed [Hans's] *instinctive premonitions* by telling him of the existence of the vagina and of copulation" (emphasis added). Ibid., 145.

13. Ibid., 34.

14. Ibid., 28; it is worthy of note that Hans's father actually says of little girls,

in correcting his statement that they do not have genitalia: "They don't have widd-lers like yours" (31). He does not give a name to the vagina, but he does allow for female genitalia. At another juncture as well, and in answer to a question from Hans as to whether Hannah's widdler will grow, his father says, "Yes, of course. But when it grows it won't look like yours" (62).

15. Ibid., 34.

16. Ibid., 35.

17. Ibid.

18. Ibid., 50.

19. Ibid., 37.

20. Ibid., 39.

21. Ibid., 41.

22. Ibid., 42–43; emphasis added.

23. Ibid., 65.

24. Ibid., 81, 83.

25. Ibid., 92.

26. Ibid., 98, 97.

27. Graf interviews. Hans's given name was Herbert Graf. His father was Max Graf, and his mother was Olga Brychta Graf. I continue to refer to Herbert as Hans in keeping with the fictive name bestowed upon him by Freud. I refer to him as Hans/Herbert when I quote from his interview with Eissler. I do so with the hope that it will prove less confusing for the reader, but also because Hans, like Dora or the Rat Man, has become an iconic figure within the psychoanalytic canon, and it seems best to retain the fictive name of each in our critical dis-course.

28. Freud, *Analysis of a Phobia*, 6, 141.

29. See Halpert, "The Grafs," for an in-depth historical contextualization.

30. The duration and the dates of this treatment are not reported, and the historical record is unclear. While Freud reports the treatment as having oc-curred during Olga's adolescence, there is supposition that the treatment was simultaneous with Hans's treatment. See Katan, "Dr. Anny Remembers Child Analysis."

31. Max was interested as a music critic in how psychoanalytic theory might be employed toward an understanding of musical processes. Eventually (around 1900), Freud invited Max to join what would later become the Vienna Society, in-cluding among the participants Adler, Stekel, Ferenczi, and Jung. Max regularly attended these weekly meetings for about three years. It seems that Freud was also a frequent dinner guest at the Graf home during this time, and that the Graf

and Freud families were sufficiently close to occasion an invitation to the wedding party for Freud's oldest son.

32. Blum, "Little Hans."

33. Freud, *Analysis of a Phobia,* 122.

34. Sprengnether, *Spectral Mother.*

35. Consider in this regard the following exchange between Eissler and Hans/Herbert:

> H/H: She is physically wonderful, and, she is a very nervous, and always was a very nervous person, and I am quite sure that in these surroundings where we all lived without that process could have resulted in some damage.
> E: You think it [analysis] helped her?
> H/H: No! It didn't help my mother at all!

It seems Hans/Herbert may have meant to say "lived with" the process of psychoanalysis, as opposed to "lived without." Perhaps this slip registers something of Hans/Herbert's wish to live without the process, or outside the process of psychoanalysis. At another juncture he speaks of consulting an analyst as an adult: "But I didn't like it at all!"
Another aspect of the interviews that speaks to Olga's apparent disinclination toward Freud are details about her and Max's friendships with Adler, whom Max describes as one of their closest friends. As Max indicates (and as has been documented by others), Adler and Freud fell out over differing ideas, and Max, it seems, tried to no avail to forge some manner of rapprochement. The interviews suggest that Olga, in particular, may have felt some allegiance to Adler in his differences with and alienation from Freud.

36. See Benjamin, *Bonds of Love* and *Like Subjects Love Objects;* Chodorow, *Reproduction of Mothering;* Stoller, "Contribution to the Study."

37. See Benjamin, *Bonds of Love;* Chodorow, *Reproduction of Mothering;* Fonagy, *Attachment Theory and Psychoanalysis;* Fromm and Narváez, "Oedipus Complex"; Horney, "Genesis of the Castration Complex" and "Flight from Womanhood"; Fonagy and Target, "Playing with Reality"; Fonagy et al., *Affect Regulation.*

38. Juarrero, *Dynamics in Action.*

39. Freud, *Obsessional Neurosis,* "Leonardo da Vinci," "Special Type of Choice of Object," *History of an Infantile Neurosis,* "Some Psychical Consequences," *New Introductory Lectures, Moses and Monotheism.*

40. Lewes, *Psychoanalytic Theory.*

41. Ibid., 82.

42. Riviere, "Womanliness as a Masquerade."

43. Freud, *Analysis of a Phobia*, 145.

44. Consider in this light that Freud declares at the end of the essay, "Strictly speaking, I learnt nothing new from this analysis, nothing that I had not already been able to discover (though often less distinctly and more indirectly) from other patients analysed at a more advanced age." Ibid., 42.

45. Ibid., 147.

46. Ibid., 111.

47. Aron, "Internalized Primal Scene"; Benjamin, *Bonds of Love* and *Like Subjects*; Britton, "Missing Link"; Fonagy and Target, "Playing with Reality."

48. Freud, *Analysis of a Phobia*, 27.

49. Ibid., 148 (1922 postscript).

50. Ibid., 110.

51. In response to Hans's maternity fantasies, Freud remarks, "It was with his mother that Hans had had his most blissful experience as a child, and he was now repeating them, and himself playing the active part, which was thus necessarily that of mother" (93n2).

52. See Coates, "Is It Time to Jettison the Concept of Developmental Lines?"; Fajardo, "New View"; Fonagy et al., *Affect Regulation*; Harris, *Gender as Soft Assembly*; Thelen and Smith, *Dynamic Systems Approach*.

53. Ross, "Trauma and Abuse."

54. Freud, *Analysis of a Phobia*, 5.

55. The multiple triangles and potential multiple primal scenes created in the course of this case could lead one to unthink the family as we presume it to be. Principal among these triangles is the one created by Freud, Hans, and Max, leading in turn to an unexamined homosexual primal scene. But also of interest is the triangle created by Freud, Max, and Olga, or the triangle that was perhaps created by Freud, Adler, and Olga.

56. Freud, *Analysis of a Phobia*, 90 (Freud's emphasis).

57. Might this breakdown in mutual recognition also be indicated in the shift in tense? His father is in the present ("You know"), while Hans is left in the past ("I didn't know").

58. For a similar analysis see Chused, "Little Hans 'Analyzed.'"

59. Freud, *Analysis of a Phobia*, 18.

60. For a similar analysis see Person, "Omni-Available Woman."

61. Freud, *Analysis of a Phobia*, 34, 107.

CHAPTER TWO. Nontraditional Family Reverie

1. U.S. Census Bureau, "Majority of Children."

2. Laing, *Politics of the Family.*

3. See Butler, "Response to 'The Doer and the Deed'"; Corbett, "More Life"; Flax, *Disputed Subjects;* Layton, "The Doer and the Deed."

4. Flax, *Disputed Subjects.*

5. I follow here upon Bion, "Attacks on Linking," as well as Bion, *Learning from Experience.* I am also following in the clinical tradition of D. W. Winnicott; see in particular *Through Pediatrics to Psycho-analysis.* Key here as well are the clinical revisions of Peter Fonagy and Mary Target; see "Playing with Reality."

6. Ehrensaft, "Alternatives to the Stork."

7. Once again I am following on D. W. Winnicott; see in particular *Through Pediatrics to Psycho-Analysis.*

8. Fonagy and Target, "Playing with Reality," 1: 231.

9. Freud, *History of an Infantile Neurosis.*

10. Aron, "Internalized Primal Scene"; Britton, "Missing Link." See also Britton, *Belief and Imagination.*

11. Britton, "Missing Link."

12. Aron, "Internalized Primal Scene," 214.

13. Ibid., 213.

14. Green, "Has Sexuality Anything to Do with Psychoanalysis?" 880.

15. See Coates, "Is It Time to Jettison the Concept of Developmental Lines?"; Fajardo, "New View of Developmental Research"; Fonagy, Gergely, Jurist, and Target, *Affect Regulation;* Harris, *Gender as Soft Assembly;* Thelen and Smith, *Dynamic Systems Approach.*

16. Chodorow, "Reflections on the Authority of the Past."

17. For a comprehensive annotated bibliography of these data, refer to American Psychological Association, *Lesbian and Gay Parenting.*

18. Harris, *Gender as Soft Assembly.*

CHAPTER THREE. Boyhood Femininity

1. For descriptions offered within the traditional discourse of developmental psychiatry see Coates, "Ontogenesis of Boyhood Gender Identity Disorder," "Etiology of Boyhood Gender Identity Disorder," and "Psychotherapeutic Intervention"; Coates, Friedman, and Wolfe, "Etiology of Boyhood Gender Identity Disorder"; Coates and Wolfe, "Gender Identity Disorder in Boys"; Friedman,

Male Homosexuality; Friedman and Downey, "Psychoanalysis, Psychobiology, and Homosexuality"; Green, *"Sissy Boy Syndrome"* and "Childhood Cross-Gender Behavior"; Stoller, *Sex and Gender,* vol. 1, and *Presentations of Gender*; Zucker, "Gender Identity Disorders in Children" and "Reflections on the Relation"; Zucker and Bradley, *Gender Identity Disorder*; Zucker and Green, "Gender Identity Disorder."

For theological/clinical perspectives see Nicolosi, *Healing Homosexuality*; Nicolosi and Nicolosi, *Parent's Guide*; Rekers, *Handbook*.

2. Zucker and Bradley, *Gender Identity Disorder,* 55.

3. See Ehrensaft, "Raising Girlyboys"; Rottnek, *Sissies and Tomboys.*

4. Brown, "Supporting Boys or Girls."

5. Stoller, *Presentations of Gender,* 183.

6. See Harris, "Conceptual Power of Multiplicity" and *Gender as Soft Assembly*; Thelen and Smith, *Dynamic Systems Approach.*

7. Friedman, *Male Homosexuality,* 199; Zucker and Bradley, *Gender Identity Disorder,* 25.

8. Dimen, "Deconstructing Difference."

9. See Friedman, *Male Homosexuality*; Green, *"Sissy Boy Syndrome"*; Stoller, *Sex and Gender.*

10. Green, *"Sissy Boy Syndrome,"* 275.

11. See Lothstein, "Selfobject Failure and Gender Identity"; Stoller, *Sex and Gender* and *Presentations of Gender*; Greenson, "Dis-Identifying from Mother"; Nicolosi and Nicolosi, *Parent's Guide*; Rekers, *Handbook*; Coates, Friedman, and Wolfe, "Etiology of Boyhood Gender Identity Disorder"; Coates and Wolfe, "Gender Identity Disorder"; Zucker and Bradley, *Gender Identity Disorder.*

12. Butler, *Undoing Gender,* 3–4.

13. Zucker and Bradley, *Gender Identity Disorder,* 222–24.

14. Riviere, "Womanliness as a Masquerade."

15. Rekers, *Handbook,* 257.

16. See Manninen, "Ultimate Masculine Striving."

17. Zucker and Bradley, *Gender Identity Disorder,* 19.

18. See Manninen, "Ultimate Masculine Striving"; Pollack, *Real Boys.*

19. Nicolosi and Nicolosi, *Parent's Guide,* 34.

20. Isay, *Being Homosexual.*

21. Freud, *Mourning and Melancholia,* 257.

22. Sontag, "Notes on Camp."

23. Davidson, *Emergence of Sexuality,* 444.

24. Shamir and Travis, *Boys Don't Cry?* 2.

25. Zizek, *Looking Awry,* 8.

26. Grosz, *Volatile Bodies,* 198.

CHAPTER FOUR. Trans States

1. Ginsberg, *Howl,* 34.

2. Ibid., 9.

3. Sontag, "Notes on Camp."

4. Cvetkovich, *Archive of Feelings.*

5. Gould, *Bully for Brontosaurus,* 29–30.

6. Butler, *Bodies That Matter,* 9.

7. Greenson, "Dis-Identifying from Mother."

8. Nicolosi, *Healing Homosexuality*; Rekers, *Handbook.*

9. Some years ago I set about to track down Nicolosi's so-called scholarly references, only to find my way into Christian bookstores, and pamphlets or religious tracts that advocated, among other things, the laying on of hands.

10. For analyses of the clinical insufficiency of reparative therapies see Drescher, "I'm Your Handyman"; Shidlo and Schroeder "Changing Sexual Orientation."

11. Butler, *Undoing Gender,* 98.

12. Fairbairn, "Revised Psychopathology."

13. For a related first-person account of her efforts to seek guidance in understanding her feminine boy, see Southgate, "My Girlish Boy."

14. Coates, Friedman, and Wolfe, "Etiology of Boyhood Gender Identity Disorder," 482.

15. See Green, "*Sissy Boy Syndrome*"; Nicolosi, *Healing Homosexuality*; Rekers, *Handbook*; Stoller, *Sex and Gender,* vol. 1.

16. See Friedman, *Male Homosexuality*; Zucker and Bradley, *Gender Identity Disorder.*

17. Cheng, *Melancholy of Race,* 46.

18. Rekers, *Handbook,* 277–79.

19. Coates, Friedman, and Wolfe, "Etiology of Boyhood Gender Identity Disorder," 483.

20. Frost, *Robert Frost Reader,* 391.

21. Freud, *Mourning and Melancholia,* 253.

22. Ibid., 248.

23. I thank Virginia Goldner, whose conversation regarding these ideas has moved my thinking in ways too intricate to detail, but not so obscure as to cloud my gratitude.

24. Green, *"Sissy Boy Syndrome,"* 122.

25. Ibid.; Stoller, *Sex and Gender,* 127.

26. I found myself thinking about the gravity of the original Hans Christian Andersen story, of the weight of fateful decisions and how the pain of transformation is revealed. In order to gain her legs, the little mermaid agrees to endure great pain. Andersen describes her dancing, "though each time her foot touched the floor it seemed as if she trod on sharp knives."

CHAPTER FIVE. Faggot = Loser

1. Wolf, "Another American Asking and Telling," 568.

2. Pascoe, "'Dude, You're a Fag,'" 337.

3. Eminem, "Interview with Eminem."

4. Stoller, "Contribution to the Study" and *Sex and Gender,* vol 1.

5. Benjamin, *Bonds of Love;* Chodorow, *Reproduction of Mothering* and "Enemy Outside."

6. See Elise, "Unlawful Entry"; Garbarino, *Lost Boys;* Kindlon and Thompson, *Raising Cain;* Kimmel, *Manhood in America;* Person, "Omni-Available Woman"; Pollack, *Real Boys.*

7. Diamond, "Masculinity Unraveled," 1101.

8. Person, "Omni-Available Woman," 72.

9. Chodorow, "Enemy Outside," 35.

10. Daniel Shaw, in an online discussion of the case I present here, captures this high-stakes quest with remarkable humor and insight: "My son's interest in penises, mine, his, his sister's lack thereof, has been about at the same level as his interest in his body in general—a high level of interest. However, his interest in winning, as opposed to losing, seems keenest of all, and there are moments when I have to stop myself from wondering if I've got a sociopath because of the extraordinary lengths he'll go to cheat, in whatever game we play, in order not to lose." Personal communication within an online colloquium organized by the International Association of Relational Psychotherapy and Psychoanalysis (IARPP), 2005.

11. Straker, "Anti-Analytic Third," 731.

12. Butler, *Excitable Speech*, 159.

13. Donald Moss, personal communication within IARPP colloquium.

14. Ibid.; Stephen Frosh, personal communication within IARPP colloquium; Steven Cooper, personal communication within IARPP colloquium.

15. Straker, "Anti-Analytic Third," 731.

16. Bromberg, *Standing in the Spaces*.

17. Straker, "Anti-Analytic Third," 729.

18. For contemporary discussions of thirdness see Aron, "Clinical Choices" and "Analytic Impasse and the Third"; Benjamin, *Like Subjects, Love Objects* and *Shadow of the Other*; Bromberg, *Standing in the Spaces*; Gerson, "Relational Unconscious"; Ogden, *Subjects of Analysis*.

19. Benjamin, *Bonds of Love*; Chodorow, *Reproduction of Mothering* and *Femininities, Masculinities, Sexualities*; Gilligan, *In a Different Voice*; Pipher, *Reviving Ophelia*.

20. See Diamond, "Masculinity Unraveled"; Kindlon and Thompson, *Raising Cain*; Pollack, *Real Boys*.

21. Moss, "Introductory Thoughts," 286.

22. Boys are on red alert for the "icky" or the ponderous. The therapist is rather constrained in the realm of child therapy as to what he or she can actually say. As one boy in my practice frequently reminds me, "Now Corbett, don't go all psychological on me."

23. Ross, "Beyond the Phallic Illusion," 65.

24. My manuscript editor Dan Heaton has pointed out that Woody Allen has repeatedly returned to this theme for comic effect. In *Annie Hall* (1977) Allen recycled a punch line from his standup routine of the sixties: when Annie says that her therapist has mentioned penis envy, Allen's Alvy Singer replies, "I'm one of the few males who suffers from that." Six years later in *Zelig*, he reprised the joke again, as the chameleon-like title character observes, "I worked with Freud in Vienna. We broke over the concept of penis envy. He thought it should be limited to women."

25. Fonagy and Target, "Playing with Reality."

26. Twice uttered onscreen by Miss West, first in her 1933 film *She Done Him Wrong*, with Cary Grant, and then again in 1978, in her last film, *Sextette*, with George Hamilton.

27. Britton, "Missing Link"; Fonagy and Target, "Playing with Reality."

28. Fonagy, Moran, and Target, "Aggression and the Psychological Self."

29. Benjamin, *Bonds of Love*.

30. Fonagy, Moran, and Target, "Aggression and the Psychological Self."

31. Phillips, *Terror and Experts*, 79.

32. Ghent, "Masochism, Submission, Surrender."

33. Freud, "Analysis Terminable and Interminable."

34. Moss, "Introductory Thoughts," 286.

CHAPTER SIX. Fantastic Phallicism

1. For a synthesis of this proposition, drawn, as it is, from long-standing feminist concerns, see Elise, "Unlawful Entry."

2. Whitman, *Leaves of Grass*, 92.

3. Be this as it may, while we have recently been inching toward more nuanced understandings of men's homosocial relations (perhaps a generative consequence of queer theory), I don't think we have come nearly as far in seeing and understanding heterosexual men in relation to women. We don't know enough at this point about how feminism is lived between a mother and son, even though we know that a modern man raised by a feminist is not the same man who showed up in Stoller's 1960s office. We don't know enough about how modern feminist-inflected relations are lived between husband and wife. We do not even have the concept of heterosociality. We do not know enough about the complicated (probably even contradictory) love and/or desire of the other, as the very word *heterosexual* speaks. The fantastic feminine other in the eyes of men is remarkably underanimated and shallow in its representations. And we continue to conflate matrimonial and heterosexual.

4. See, for example, Chodorow, "Enemy Outside"; Elise, "Unlawful Entry"; Manninen "Ultimate Masculine Striving"; Ross, *What Men Want*; Person, "Omni-Available Woman."

In addition, it is intriguing to note the early feminist critique that presaged this modern rereading. See Horney, "Genesis of the Castration Complex" and "Flight from Womanhood"; Lampl-de Groot, "Problems of Femininity"; Jones, "Phallic Phase"; Brunswick, "Preoedipal Phase."

5. See, for example, Pollack, *Real Boys*; Kindlon and Thompson, *Raising Cain*; Garbarino, *Lost Boys*.

6. See in particular Diamond, "Masculinity Unraveled" and *My Father Before Me*; Herzog, *Father Hunger*.

7. Salinger, *Catcher in the Rye*, 17.

8. Eyal Rozmarin, personal communication.

9. Edelstein, "Boys of Summer."

10. See Goldberg, *Superbad: The Drawings*.

11. Berasni and Dutoit, "Forms of Violence."

12. Dickinson, *Master Letters,* 32.

13. Davies, "Falling in Love with Love."

14. Wrye and Welles, "Maternal Erotic Transference" and "Maternal Erotic Countertransference."

15. Shalit, review of *Brokeback Mountain.*

References

American Psychological Association. *Lesbian and Gay Parenting.* 2005, http://www.apa.org/pi/lgbc/publications/lgparenting.pdf.

Andersen, Hans. *Hans Andersen's Fairy Tales.* Boston: DeWolfe, Fiske, 1898.

Aron, Lewis. "The Internalized Primal Scene." *Psychoanalytic Dialogues* 5 (1995): 195–238.

———. "Reply to Schwartz." *Psychoanalytic Dialogues* 5 (1995): 249–55.

———. "Clinical Choices and the Relational Matrix." *Psychoanalytic Dialogues,* 9 (1999): 1–29.

———. "Analytic Impasse and the Third: Clinical Implications of Intersubjectivity Theory." *International Journal of Psychoanalysis* 87 (2006): 349–68.

———. "Reevaluating the Distinction Between Psychotherapy and Psychoanalysis: What Does Feminism Have to Do with It?" Paper presented at the annual meeting of Division 39 of the American Psychological Association, New York, April 2008.

Balsam, Rosemary H. "The Vanished Pregnant Body in Psychoanalytic Female Developmental Theory." *Journal of the American Psychological Association* 51 (2003): 1153–79.

Benjamin, Jessica. *The Bonds of Love*. New York: Pantheon, 1988.

———. *Like Subjects, Love Objects*. New Haven: Yale University Press, 1995.

———. *The Shadow of the Other*. New York: Routledge, 1997.

Bersani, Leo. *The Freudian Body*. New York: Columbia University Press, 1986.

———. "Is the Rectum a Grave?" Pages 197–222 in *AIDS: Cultural Analysis/Cultural Activism*, ed. Douglas Crimp. Cambridge: MIT Press, 1989.

———. *Homos*. Cambridge: Harvard University Press, 1995.

Bersani, Leo, and Ulysse Dutoit. "The Forms of Violence." *October* 8 (1979): 17–29.

Bion, W. R. "Attacks on Linking." *International Journal of Psycho-analysis* 40 (1959): 308–15.

———. *Learning from Experience*. London: Tavistock, 1962.

Birksted-Breen, Dana. *The Gender Conundrum*. New York: Routledge, 1993.

Blum, Harold. "Little Hans: A Centennial Reconsideration." *Journal of the American Psychoanalytic Association* 55 (2007): 749–66.

Boehm, Felix. "The Femininity Complex in Men." *International Journal of Psychoanalysis* 11 (1930): 444–56.

Bonaparte, Marie. "Passivity, Masochism, and Femininity." *International Journal of Psychoanalysis* 16 (1935): 325–33.

Britton, Ronald. "The Missing Link." Pages 83–102 in *The Oedipus Complex Today*, ed. Ronald Britton, Michael Feldman, and Edna O'Shaughnessy. London: Karnac, 1989.

———. *Belief and Imagination*. New York: Routledge, 1998.

Bromberg, Philip M. *Standing in the Spaces: Essays on Clinical Process, Trauma, and Dissociation*. Hillsdale, N.J.: Analytic Press, 2001.

Brown, Patricia Leigh. "Supporting Boys or Girls when the Line Isn't Clear." *New York Times*, 2 December 2006.

Brunswick, Ruth Mack. "The Preoedipal Phase of the Libido Development." *Psychoanalytic Quarterly* 9 (1940): 293–319.

Butler, Judith. *Gender Trouble: Feminism and the Subversion of Identity*. New York: Routledge, 1990.

———. *Bodies That Matter*. New York: Routledge, 1993.

———. *Excitable Speech: A Politics of the Performative*. New York: Routledge, 1997.

———. "Response to Lynne Layton's 'The Doer and the Deed: Tensions and Intersections Between Butler's Vision of Performativity and Relational Psychoanalysis.'" *Gender and Psychoanalysis* 2 (1997): 515–20.

———. *Undoing Gender*. New York: Routledge, 2004.

Cheng, Anne Anlin. *The Melancholy of Race: Psychoanalysis, Assimilation, and Hidden Grief*. New York: Oxford University Press, 2001.

Chodorow, Nancy. *The Reproduction of Mothering*. Berkeley: University of California Press, 1978.

———. *Feminism and Psychoanalytic Theory*. New Haven: Yale University Press, 1989.

———. *Femininities, Masculinities, Sexualities: Freud and Beyond*. Lexington: University Press of Kentucky, 1994.

———. "Reflections on the Authority of the Past in Psychoanalytic Thinking." *Psychoanalytic Quarterly* 65 (1996): 48–49.

———. "The Enemy Outside: Thoughts on the Psychodynamics of Extreme Violence with Special Attention to Men and Masculinity." *Journal for the Psychoanalysis of Culture and Society* 3 (1998): 25–38.

———. *The Power of Feelings*. New Haven: Yale University Press, 1999.

———. "Gender in the Modern-Postmodern and Classical-Relational Divide: Untangling History and Epistemology." *Journal of the American Psychoanalytic Association* 53 (2005): 1097–1118.

Chused, Judith. "Little Hans 'Analyzed' in the 21st Century." *Journal of the American Psychoanalytic Association* 55 (2007): 767–78.

Coates, Susan. "Ontogenesis of Boyhood Gender Identity Disorder." *Journal of the American Academy of Psychoanalysis* 18 (1990): 414–38.

———. "The Etiology of Boyhood Gender Identity Disorder: An Integrative Model." Pages 245–65 in *Interface of Psychoanalysis and Psychology*, ed. James Barron, Morris Eagle, and David Wolitzky. Washington, D.C.: American Psychological Association, 1992.

———. "Psychotherapeutic Intervention for Boys with Gender Identity Disorder and Their Families." Paper presented at the 41st annual meeting of the American Academy of Child and Adolescent Psychiatry, 1994.

———. "Is It Time to Jettison the Concept of Developmental Lines? Commentary on DeMarfneffe's Paper 'Bodies and Words.'" *Gender and Psychoanalysis* 2 (1997): 35–54.

Coates, Susan, Richard Friedman, and Sabrina Wolfe. "The Etiology of Boyhood Gender Identity Disorder: A Model for the Integration of Temperament, Development, and Psychodynamics." *Psychoanalytic Dialogues* 1 (1991): 481–521.

Coates, Susan, and Sabrina Wolfe. "Gender Identity Disorder in Boys: The Interface of Constitution and Early Experience." *Psychoanalytic Inquiry* 15 (1995): 6–38.

Collins, Patricia Hill. *Black Sexual Politics: African Americans, Gender, and the New Racism.* New York: Routledge, 2004.

Connell, R. W. *The Men and the Boys.* Berkeley: University of California Press, 2001.

Corbett, Ken. "The Mystery of Homosexuality." *Psychoanalytic Psychology* 10 (1993): 345–57.

———. "Homosexual Boyhood: Notes on Girlyboys." *Gender and Psychoanalysis* 1 (1996): 429–61.

———. "Speaking Queer: A Reply to Richard C. Friedman." *Gender and Psychoanalysis* 2 (1997): 495–514.

———. "More Life." *Psychoanalytic Dialogues* 11 (2001): 313–36.

———. "Nontraditional Family Romance." *Psychoanalytic Quarterly* 70 (2001): 599–624.

Cvetkovich, Ann. *An Archive of Feelings.* Durham, N.C.: Duke University Press, 2003.

Davidson, Arnold. *The Emergence of Sexuality.* Cambridge: Harvard University Press, 2001.

Davies, Jody. "Falling in Love with Love: Oedipal and Postoedipal Manifestations of Idealization, Mourning, and Erotic Masochism." *Psychoanalytic Dialogues* 13 (2003): 1–27.

Deutsch, Helene. *The Psychology of Women: Psychoanalytic Interpretation.* Vol. 1, *Girlhood;* vol. 2, *Motherhood.* London: Research Books, 1946.

Diamond, Michael J. "Masculinity Unraveled: The Roots of Male Gender Identity and the Shifting of Male Ego Ideals Throughout Life." *Journal of the American Psychoanalytic Association* 54 (2006): 1099–1130.

———. *My Father Before Me: How Fathers and Sons Influence Each Other Throughout Their Lives.* New York: Norton, 2007.

Dickinson, Emily. *The Master Letters of Emily Dickinson.* Amherst: University of Massachusetts Press, 1998.

Dimen, Muriel. "Deconstructing Difference: Gender, Splitting, and Transitional Space." *Psychoanalytic Dialogues* 1 (1991): 335–52.

———. "The Third Step: Freud, the Feminists, and Postmodernism." *American Journal of Psychoanalysis* 55 (1995): 303–19.

Dimen, Muriel, and Virginia Goldner. "Gender and Sexuality." Pages 93–114 in *Textbook of Psychoanalysis,* ed. Arnold Cooper, Glen Gabbard, Ethel Person. Arlington, Va.: APPI Press, 2005.

Domenici, Tom, and Ronnie Lesser, eds. *Disorienting Sexuality: Psychoanalytic Reappraisals of Sexual Identities.* New York: Routledge, 1995.

Drescher, Jack. *Psychoanalytic Therapy and the Gay Man.* Hillsdale, N.J.: Analytic Press, 1998.

———. "I'm Your Handyman: A History of Reparative Therapies." *Journal of Homosexuality* 36 (1998): 19–42.

Edelstein, David. "The Boys of Summer." *New York,* 16 August 2007, 156.

Ehrensaft, Diane. "Alternatives to the Stork." *Studies in Gender and Sexuality* 1 (2000): 371–98.

———. "Raising Girlyboys: A Parent's Perspective." *Studies in Gender and Sexuality* 8 (2007): 269–302.

Elise, Dianne. "Unlawful Entry: Male Fears of Psychic Penetration." *Psychoanalytic Dialogues* 11 (2001): 499–531.

Eminem. "Interview with Eminem: It's Lonely at the Top." NY Rock, February 2001, http://www.nyrock.com/interviews/2001/eminem_int.asp.

Eng, David. *Racial Castration: Managing Masculinity in Asian America.* Durham, N.C.: Duke University Press, 2001.

Fairbairn, Ronald. "A Revised Psychopathology of the Psychoses and Psychoneuroses." *International Journal of Psychoanalysis* 22 (1941): 250–79.

Fajardo, Barbara. "A New View of Developmental Research for Psychoanalysts." *Journal of the American Psychoanalysis Association* 46 (1998): 185–207.

Flax, Jane. *Disputed Subjects.* New York: Routledge, 1993.

Fonagy, Peter. *Attachment Theory and Psychoanalysis.* New York: Other, 2001.

Fonagy, Peter, Gyorgy Gergely, Elliot Jurist, and Mary Target, eds. *Affect Regulation, Mentalization, and the Development of Self.* New York: Other, 2002.

Fonagy, Peter, George Moran, and Mary Target. "Aggression and the Psychological Self." *International Journal of Psychoanalysis* 74 (1993): 471–85.

Fonagy, Peter, and Mary Target, "Playing with Reality." 2 parts. *International Journal of Psychoanalysis* 77 (1996): 217–34, 459–80.

Foucault, Michel. *The Order of Things.* New York: Vintage, 1973.

———. *The Use of Pleasure.* New York: Pantheon, 1985.

———. *The History of Sexuality,* vol. 1. New York: Vintage, 1990.

———. *The Politics of Truth.* Los Angeles: Semiotext(e), 1997.

Frankiel, Rita. "Analyzed and Unanalyzed Themes in the Treatment of Little Hans." *International Review of Psychoanalysis* 19 (1992): 323–33.

Freud, Sigmund. *The Interpretation of Dreams.* Pages ix–627 in *The Complete Works of Sigmund Freud,* vol. 3. 1900; London: Hogarth, 1955.

————. *Three Essays on the Theory of Sexuality.* Pages 123–46 in *Complete Works*, vol. 7. 1905; London: Hogarth, 1955.

————. *Analysis of a Phobia in a Five-Year-Old Boy.* Pages 1–150 in *Complete Works*, vol. 10. 1909; London: Hogarth, 1955.

————. *Notes upon a Case of Obsessional Neurosis.* Pages 153–251 in *Complete Works*, vol. 10. 1909.

————. "Leonardo da Vinci and a Memory of His Childhood." Pages 57–138 in *Complete Works*, vol. 11. 1910; London: Hogarth, 1955.

————. "A Special Type of Choice of Object Made by Men." Pages 163–76 in *Complete Works*, vol. 11. 1910.

————. "Mourning and Melancholia." Pages 237–58 in *Complete Works*, vol. 14. 1917; London: Hogarth Press, 1955.

————. *From the History of an Infantile Neurosis.* Pages 1–124 in *Complete Works*, vol. 17. 1918; London: Hogarth, 1955.

————. "Some Psychical Consequences of the Anatomical Distinction Between the Sexes." Pages 243–58 in *Complete Works*, vol. 19. 1925; London: Hogarth, 1955.

————. "Female Sexuality." Pages 221–44 in *Complete Works*, vol. 21. 1931; London: Hogarth, 1955.

————. *New Introductory Lectures in Psychoanalysis.* Pages 3–182 in *Complete Works*, vol. 22. 1933; London: Hogarth, 1955.

————. "Analysis Terminable and Interminable." Pages 59–137 in *Complete Works*, vol. 18. 1937; London: Hogarth, 1955.

————. *Moses and Monotheism.* Pages 3–137 in *Complete Works*, vol. 23. 1939; London: Hogarth Press, 1955.

Friedman, Richard C. *Male Homosexuality.* New Haven: Yale University Press, 1988.

Friedman, Richard C., and Jennifer Downey. "Psychoanalysis, Psychobiology, and Homosexuality." *Journal of the American Psychoanalytical Association* 41 (1993): 1159–98.

Fromm, Erich, and Narváez, Fernando. "The Oedipus Complex: Comments on 'The Case of Little Hans.'" *Contemporary Psychoanalysis* 4 (1968): 178–87.

Frost, Robert. *The Robert Frost Reader: Poetry and Prose.* Ed. Edward

Connery Lathem and Lawrance Thompson. New York: Henry Holt, 2002.

Fuss, Diana. *Identification Papers.* New York: Routledge, 1995.

Garbarino, James. *Lost Boys.* New York: Anchor, 1999.

Gerson, Samuel. "The Relational Unconscious: A Core Element of Intersubjectivity, Thirdness, and Clinical Process." *Psychoanalytic Quarterly* 73 (2004): 63–98.

Ghent, Emmanuel. "Masochism, Submission, Surrender." *Contemporary Psychoanalysis* 26 (1990): 108–36.

Gilligan, Carol. *In a Different Voice: Psychological Theory and Women's Development.* Cambridge: Harvard University Press, 1982.

Ginsberg, Allen. *Howl.* San Francisco: City Lights Books, 1956.

Goldberg, David. *Superbad: The Drawings.* New York: Newmarket, 2008.

Goldner, Virginia. "Toward a Critical Relational Theory of Gender." *Psychoanalytic Dialogues* 1 (1991): 249–72.

———. "Ironic Gender/Authentic Sex." *Studies in Gender and Sexuality* 4 (2003): 113–39.

———. "Feminism (Still) Rules: Commentary on Papers on Gender and Embodiment." Paper presented at the annual meeting of Division 39 of the American Psychological Association, New York, April 2008.

Gould, Stephen Jay. *Bully for Brontosaurus: Reflections in Natural History.* New York: Random House, 1991.

Graf, Herbert. Interview with Kurt Eissler. Box R1, Sigmund Freud Papers, Sigmund Freud Collection, Manuscript Division. Washington, D.C.: Library of Congress, 1955.

Graf, Max. Interview with Kurt Eissler. Box 112, Sigmund Freud Papers, Sigmund Freud Collection, Manuscript Division. Washington, D.C.: Library of Congress, 1952.

Green, André. "Has Sexuality Anything to Do with Psychoanalysis?" *International Journal of Psychoanalysis* 76 (1995): 871–84.

Green, Richard. *The "Sissy Boy Syndrome" and the Development of Homosexuality.* New Haven: Yale University Press, 1987.

———. "Childhood Cross-Gender Behavior and Adult Homosexuality: Why the Link." *Journal of Gay and Lesbian Mental Health* 12 (2008): 17–28.

Greenson, Ralph. "Dis-Identifying from Mother: Its Special Importance for the Boy." *International Journal of Psychoanalysis* 49 (1968): 370–74.

Grosz, Elizabeth. *Volatile Bodies.* Bloomington: Indiana University Press, 1993.

Halberstam, Judith. *In a Queer Time and Place: Transgender Bodies, Subcultural Lives.* New York: New York University Press, 2005.

Halpert, Eugene. "The Grafs: Father (Max) and Son (Herbert a.k.a. Little Hans)." *Psychoanalytic Study of the Child* 62 (2007): 111–42.

Harris, Adrienne. "Gender as Contradiction." *Psychoanalytic Dialogues* 1 (1991) 107–244.

———. "The Conceptual Power of Multiplicity." *Contemporary Psychoanalysis* 32 (1996): 537–52.

———. *Gender as Soft Assembly.* Hillsdale, N.J.: Analytic Press, 2005.

———. "Gender in Linear and Nonlinear History." *Journal of the American Psychoanalytic Association* 53 (2005): 1079–95.

Herzog, James. *Father Hunger.* Hillsdale, N.J.: Analytic Press, 2001.

Hinshelwood, R. D. "Little Hans's Transference." *Journal of Child Psychotherapy* 15 (1989): 63–78.

Holmes, Jeremy. *The Search for the Secure Base: Attachment Theory and Psychotherapy.* New York: Brunner-Routledge, 1996.

Horney, Karen. "On the Genesis of the Castration Complex in Women." *International Journal of Psychoanalysis* 5 (1924): 50–65.

———. "The Flight from Womanhood: The Masculinity-Complex in Women, as Viewed by Men and by Women." *International Journal of Psychoanalysis* 7 (1926): 324–39.

Isay, Richard. *Being Homosexual.* New York: Farrar, Straus, and Giroux, 1989.

———. *Becoming Gay: The Journey to Self-Acceptance.* New York: Holt Paperbacks, 1997.

———. *Commitment and Healing: Gay Men and the Need for Romantic Love.* Hoboken, N.J.: Wiley, 2006.

Jackass. Created by Aron Watman, Paul Greenberg, Spike Jonze, Johnny Knoxville, Jeff Tremaine, and Vito Viscomi. MTV, 2000–2002.

Jones, Ernest. "The Phallic Phase." *International Journal of Psychoanalysis* 14 (1933): 1–33.

Juarrero, Alicia. *Dynamics in Action: Intentional Behavior as a Complex System.* Cambridge: MIT Press, 1999.

Kaftal, Emmanuel. "On Intimacy Between Men." *Psychoanalytic Dialogues* 1 (1991): 305–28.

Katan, Anny. "Dr. Anny Remembers Child Analysis." *Clinical, Theoretical, and Applied Psychoanalysis* 1 (1990): 12–25.

Kimmel, Michael. *Manhood in America: A Cultural History.* New York: Free Press, 1996.

Kindlon, Dan, and Michael Thompson. *Raising Cain.* New York: Ballantine, 1999.

Klein, Melanie. "Early Stages of the Oedipus Conflict." *International Journal of Psychoanalysis* 9 (1928): 167–80.

Knocked Up. Directed by Judd Apatow. Universal Pictures, 2007.

Laing, R. D. *The Politics of the Family.* New York: Vintage, 1968.

Lampl-de Groot, Jeanne. "Problems of Femininity." *Psychoanalytic Quarterly* 2 (1933): 489–518.

Laplanche, Jean. *Life and Death in Psychoanalysis.* Baltimore: Johns Hopkins University Press, 1976.

———. *Problématiques.* Paris: Presses Universitaires de France, 1987.

———. *New Foundations for Psychoanalysis.* Trans. David Macey. Oxford: Blackwell, 1989.

———. *Essays on Otherness.* New York: Routledge, 1999.

Lax, Ruth. *Becoming and Being a Woman.* New York: Aronson, 1997.

Layton, Lynne. "The Doer and the Deed: Tensions and Intersections Between Butler's Vision of Performativity and Relational Psychoanalysis." *Gender and Psychoanalysis* 2 (1997): 515–20.

———. *Who's That Girl? Who's That Boy?* 1998; Hillsdale, N.J.: Analytic Press, 2004.

———. "Gendered Subject, Gendered Agents: Toward an Integration of Postmodern Theory and Relational Analytic Practice." Pages 285–313 in *Gender in Psychoanalytic Space*, ed. Muriel Dimen and Virginia Goldner. New York: Other, 2002.

Lewes, Kenneth. *The Psychoanalytic Theory of Male Homosexuality*. New York: Simon and Schuster, 1988.

Loewald, Hans. *Papers on Psychoanalysis*. New Haven: Yale University Press, 1989.

Lothstein, Leslie. "Selfobject Failure and Gender Identity." *Progress in Self Psychology* 3 (1988): 213–35.

Manninen, Vesa. "The Ultimate Masculine Striving." *Scandinavian Psychoanalytic Review* 15 (1992): 1–26.

Moss, Donald. "Introductory Thoughts: Hating in the First Person Plural, the Example of Homophobia." *American Imago* 49 (1992): 279–91.

Muñoz, José Esteban. *Disidentifications: Queers of Color and the Performance of Politics*. Minneapolis: University of Minnesota Press, 1999.

Nicolosi, Joseph. *Healing Homosexuality: Case Histories of Reparative Therapy*. New York: Aronson, 1993.

Nicolosi, Joseph, and L. A. Nicolosi. *A Parent's Guide to Preventing Homosexuality*. Downer's Grove, Ill.: Intervarsity, 2002.

Ogden, Thomas. *Subjects of Analysis*. Northvale, N.J.: Aronson, 1994.

Pascoe, C. J. "'Dude, You're a Fag': Adolescent Masculinity and the Fag Discourse." *Sexualities* 8 (2005): 329–46.

Person, Ethel. "The Omni-Available Woman and Lesbian Sex: Two Fantasy Themes and Their Relationship to the Male Developmental Experience." Pages 71–94 in *The Psychology of Men*, ed. Gerald Fogel, Fredrick Lane, and Robert Liebert. New York: Basic, 1986.

Phillips, Adam. *Terror and Experts*. Cambridge: Harvard University Press, 1995.

Pipher, Mary. *Reviving Ophelia*. New York: Random House, 1994.

Pollack, William. *Real Boys*. New York: Henry Holt, 1998.

Rekers, George. *Handbook of Child and Adolescent Sexual Problems.* New York: Lexington/Jossey-Bass/Simon and Schuster, 1995.

Riviere, Joan. "Womanliness as a Masquerade." *International Journal of Psychoanalysis* 9 (1929): 303–13.

Ross, John Munder. "Beyond the Phallic Illusion: Notes on Man's Heterosexuality." Pages 49–70 in *The Psychology of Men,* ed. Gerald Fogel, Frederick M. Lane, and Robert S. Liebert. New York: Basic, 1986.

———. *What Men Want: Mothers, Fathers, and Manhood.* Cambridge: Harvard University Press, 1994.

———. "Trauma and Abuse in the Case of Little Hans." *Journal of the American Psychoanalytic Association* 55 (2006): 779–98.

Rottnek, Matthew, ed. *Sissies and Tomboys: Gender Nonconformity and Homosexual Childhood.* New York: New York University Press, 1999.

Roughton, Ralph. "Response to Bergeret's 'Homosexuality of Homoeroticism: "Narcissism Eroticism."'" *International Journal of Psychoanalysis* 83 (2002): 949–52.

———. "The Two Analyses of a Gay Man: The Interplay of Social Change and Psychoanalysis." *Annual of Psychoanalysis* 30 (2002): 83–99.

Rubin, Gayle. "The Traffic in Women: Notes on the 'Political Economy' of Sex." Pages 157–211 in *Toward an Anthropology of Women,* ed. Rayna R. Reiter. New York: Monthly Review Press, 1975.

Salinger, J. D. *The Catcher in the Rye.* 1951; New York: Bantam, 1966.

Samuels, Andrew. *The Political Psyche.* London: Routledge, 1993.

Sedgwick, Eve. *The Epistemology of the Closet.* Berkeley: University of California Press, 1990.

Sextette. Directed by Ken Howard. Briggs and Sullivan, 1978.

Shalit, Gene. Review of *Brokeback Mountain. Today Show,* January 5, 2006. New York, NBC television.

Shamir, Milette, and Jennifer Travis. *Boys Don't Cry? Rethinking Narratives of Masculinity and Emotion in the U.S.* New York: Columbia University Press, 2002.

She Done Him Wrong. Directed by Lowell Sherman. Paramount Pictures, 1933.

Shidlo, Ariel, and Michael Schroeder. "Changing Sexual Orientation: A Consumer's Report." *Professional Psychology: Research and Practice* 33 (2002): 249–59.

Silverman, Kaja. *Male Subjectivity at the Margins.* New York: Routledge, 1992.

Slap, Joseph. "Little Hans's Tonsillectomy." *Psychoanalytic Quarterly* 30 (1961): 259–61.

Sontag, Susan. "Notes on Camp." Pages 154–66 in *A Susan Sontag Reader.* New York: Farrar, Straus, and Giroux, 1964.

Southgate, Martha. "My Girlish Boy." Pages 17–24 in *What Makes a Man: Writers Imagine the Future,* ed. Rebecca Walker. New York: Penguin, 2004.

South Park. Created by Trey Parker and Matt Stone. Comedy Central, 1997–.

Sprengnether, Madelon. *The Spectral Mother: Freud, Feminism, and Psychoanalysis.* Ithaca: Cornell University Press, 1990.

Stoller, Robert. "A Contribution to the Study of Gender Identity." *International Journal of Psychoanalysis* 45 (1965): 220–26.

———. *Sex and Gender.* 2 vols. London: Karnac, 1968, 1975.

———. *Presentations of Gender.* New Haven: Yale University Press, 1985.

Straker, Gillian. "The Anti-Analytic Third." *Psychoanalytic Review* 93 (2006): 729–53.

Superbad. Directed by Greg Mottola. Columbia Pictures, 2007.

Thelen, Esther, and Linda Smith. *A Dynamic Systems Approach to the Development of Cognition and Action.* Cambridge: MIT Press, 1994.

Trowell, Judith, and Alicia Etchegoyen, eds. *The Importance of Fathers: A Psychoanalytic Re-evaluation.* London: Brunner-Routledge, 2002.

U.S. Census Bureau. "Majority of Children Live with Two Biological Parents." February 20, 2008, www.census.gov/Press-Release/www/releases/archives/children/011507.html.

Wakefield, Jerome. "Attachment and Sibling Rivalry in Little Hans." *Journal of the American Psychoanalytic Association* 55 (2006): 821–50.

———. "Max Graf's 'Reminiscences of Professor Sigmund Freud' Revisited: New Evidence from the Freud Archives." *Psychoanalytic Quarterly* 76 (2006): 149–92.

Wallin, David. *Attachment in Psychotherapy.* New York: Guilford, 2008.

Warner, Michael. *The Trouble with Normal: Sex, Politics, and the Ethics of Queer Life.* Cambridge: Harvard University Press, 2000.

Whitman, Walt. *Leaves of Grass: The 1892 Edition.* New York: Bantam, 1993.

Widlocher, Daniel. Ed. *Infantile Sexuality and Attachment.* New York: Other, 2001.

Winnicott, D. W. *Through Pediatrics to Psycho-analysis.* New York: Basic, 1958.

———. *The Maturational Processes, and the Facilitating Environment: Studies in the Theory of Emotional Development.* London: Hogarth, 1965.

Wolf, Marc. "Another American Asking and Telling." Pages 539–618 in *Political Stages: Plays That Shaped a Century,* ed. Emily Mann and David Roessel. New York: Applause Theatre and Cinema Books, 1999.

Wrye, Harriett Kimble, and Judith K. Welles. "The Maternal Erotic Transference." *International Journal of Psychoanalysis* 70 (1989): 673–84.

———. "The Maternal Erotic Countertransference." *International Journal of Psychoanalysis* 72 (1991): 93–106.

Young-Bruehl, Elisabeth. "Little Hans in the History of Child Analysis." *Psychoanalytic Study of the Child* 62 (2007): 28–43.

Zizek, Slavoj. *Looking Awry: An Introduction to Jacques Lacan Through Popular Culture.* Cambridge: MIT Press, 1992.

Zucker, Kenneth. "Gender Identity Disorders in Children: Clinical Descriptions and Natural History." Pages 1–23 in *Clinical Management of Gender Identity Disorders in Children and Adults,* ed. Ray Blanchard and Betty W. Steiner. Washington, D.C.: American Psychiatric Press, 1990.

———. "Reflections on the Relation Between Sex-Typed Behavior in Childhood and Sexual Orientation in Adulthood." *Journal of Gay and Lesbian Mental Health* 12 (2008): 29–59.

Zucker, Kenneth, and Susan Bradley. *Gender Identity Disorder and Psychosexual Problems in Children and Adolescents.* New York: Guilford, 1995.

Zucker, Kenneth, and Richard Green. "Gender Identity Disorder of Childhood." Pages 661–70 in *Treatments of Psychiatric Disorders,* vol. 1, ed. T. Byram Karasu. Washington, D.C.: American Psychiatric Association, 1989.

Index

Adler, Alfred, 239*n*35

Adoption, 53

Affect states: and experience of self, 140; of feminine boys, 92–93, 105, 112, 153–54, 156, 158, 163–66; and gender, 112, 123–24; "not-me" affect states, 7, 175, 217, 226, 229

Aggression: as acting out of depression and alienation, 175; and anxiety about losing, 194, 199; in boys' play generally, 4, 218–19, 228–30; "boys will be boys" approach to, 184, 191, 194, 200, 207, 212; clinical engagement of, 14, 193–94; and exhibitionism, 175; and *faggot* as term, 173–74, 184; and father hunger, 214; and father-son relationship, 7, 106–7; feminine boys' conflicts with, 105–6; and "Josh," 177, 178, 196–200, 205; and "Lincoln," 156, 161; and parental fatigue, 200; parents' response to, 200, 228–30; and phallophobia, 213–20; reflexive antiaggression reaction, 218; and sexuality, 233; unmetabolized ag-

gression, 156; and violence, 217–19; of women, 216–17

Aggressive protest bravado, 184

Aim, 22–25, 47–49, 51

Alienation, 7, 175

Allen, Woody, 245*n*24

American Psychological Association, 89

Analysis of a Phobia in a Five-Year-Old Boy (Freud), 19–51

Andersen, Hans Christian, 244*n*26

"Andy": anger and anxiety of, 57–62; and anxieties about growth, 66–68; and butch-gendered surface of one of his mothers, 57–59, 65; and countertransference by therapist, 68–69; fantasies of generally, 78; fantasy of, about father-donor, 62–66, 70–71, 82; and father-donor, 52, 62–67, 70–72, 76, 82; interests of, 79–80; and learning to ride bicycle, 82; and masculinity, 79–80; normative logic and lesbian mothers of, 56–62; play by, 66–68, 78; and primal scene, 76–78; on sex, 76–78;